MOSS GARDENING

MOSS GARDENING

Including Lichens, Liverworts,
and Other Miniatures

GEORGE SCHENK

TIMBER PRESS
Portland • London

Twelfth printing 2010

Timber Press, Inc.
The Haseltine Building
133 S.W. Second Avenue, Suite 450
Portland, Oregon 97204-3527
www.timberpress.com

2 The Quadrant
135 Salusbury Road
London NW6 6RJ
www.timberpress.co.uk

Printed in Hong Kong

Library of Congress Cataloging-in-Publication Data

Schenk, George.
Moss gardening: including lichens, liverworts, and other miniatures/George Schenk.
p.   cm.
Includes bibliographical references (p.   ) and index.
ISBN-13: 978-0-88192-370-4
1. Moss gardening. 2. Mosses. I. Title
SB433.55.S3 1997
635.9'36—dc20

96-9357
CIP

Dedicated to the person who pauses to study small things in Nature

Contents

Preface

A preface is needed, please supply. It is your introduction to the
book, briefly describing its origin, scope, and interest. Who would
be interested in this book? Why would it be of interest to him or
her? How did it come about? Toot your own horn a little. Why
should the reader look to what you say as a dependable source of
information and observations on the topic?

THE ABOVE exhortation arrived as a note from the publisher of this
book. My reply to Timber Press and to you is this: In the first chapter, As One Moss Gardener to Another, I have probably answered those
queries, although not so directly as they have been asked, and I have certainly answered others that I myself have posed.

Chapter 1 has much to say that is of vital assistance toward a fuller understanding of almost everything that follows. And I will own up that in
writing the chapter I also had in mind soft and sneaky salesmanship. Since
I have been asked for something more direct, and can see the need, here
goes: What qualifies this book as being worth your time and money? Well,
it is a thoroughgoing treatise on its subject. It tells almost as much about
the mechanics of moss gardening as the *Kama Sutra* does about dancing.
Like that book, this work of mine may offer more variations on the theme
than you really care to know. But I discuss the many aspects of moss gar-

dening under separate chapters, so you can select those that you want to read about and follow.

Yet the book serves as far more than a manual on planting and maintaining moss. *Moss Gardening* is also a landscaper's book, the first in English, and perhaps in any language, to outline landscape gardening with mosses and others among the tiniest of ornamentals, toward effects that may not be tiny, that may be grand, even scenic. In this book a planting of moss is never presented as an isolated garden feature but always as an integral part of a garden community that may include trees, shrubs, shrublets, and perennial flowers. There is more. The book even describes how to garden delightfully with mosses by not putting a hand in the enterprise at all: one does it with eyes only. If you decide on such ocular gardening, the book can be enjoyed as the ultimate word on no-work gardening. Or if you are a seeker of light exercise while gardening, this book will show you ways to garden lightly. Or again, *Moss Gardening* can guide you in vigorous activity. Those alternatives are all within the book. And there is still more. This book treats not only landscape gardening with inchling plants; it provides, in its chapter called Portraits, introductions, person-to-plant, to scores of the world's most engaging species of mosses and moss allies. You can meet them here and add them to your life as a naturalist.

Now, to toot my own horn a bit here, as I have been invited to do. I am a gardener little grounded in botany and much more of a groundling. In *that* distinguished capacity, however, I wear no fewer than ten badges of merit, an almost constant decoration of humus under my fingernails. Good dirt it is, and I've probably worn a pound or two of it just in my moss gardening these many years.

Acknowledgments

Most of the people who have helped me out during the 11 years I have worked on this book (and have stepped away from it for long intervals while working with the subject plants to gain experience) have been named in the text. But several others remain to be introduced:

Phyllis Anderson, a colleague in garden writing and garden design, supplied a report on the Hagopian moss carpet in Stockton, California.
Richard Brown, who manages the Bloedel Reserve, Bainbridge Island, Washington, provided the extraordinary recipe of the making of the moss

garden there, in which one of the steps on the way to success was an induced failure.

George and Norma Francisa of North Vancouver, British Columbia, have kindly put up with my moss gardening on their property for a good many years.

Ikiru, a writer of haiku, has generously allowed the use of a pertinent example—in the poet's own English translation of a poem originally Japanese.

Don Normark, a career photographer with whom I've worked since 1960, and once again have found to be a friend indeed in time of need, has donated a mug shot of me for use on the book's dust jacket.

Sue Olsen, a fern nurserywoman, gave information about the filmy fern house in the Royal Botanic Gardens, Kew, England.

Constance Raphael is the proper name of the "Banty" of my affection and irritation, in the chapter, Bonsai Mosses.

Mo Yee, a friend located in Auckland, New Zealand, has contributed immensely to this book, in many ways, not least in caring for the garden we share, with its mossy and lichenous container landscapes.

To all who have helped, a hearty handshake or kisses on both cheeks, depending on gender. And gratitude always.

About the Photography

Photographer Pamela Harper provided Plates 4, 15, and 27; Aaron Johanson, Plates 12 and 13; Marc Treib, Plate 11; Mo Yee, Plate 86. The rest of the photographs were taken by me. I used 35 mm film, ASA 50 mostly; an $f/22$ aperture, and natural light for every picture. A tripod proved essential in taking close-up plant portraits, as did a lens booster that the manufacturer calls a "2× macro focusing teleconverter"; it was used together with the general purpose lens that came with the camera.

Photographer Aaron Johanson, who took pictures for me in Japan, has written a letter containing information that will be helpful to anyone else who would photograph there in the temple gardens:

The temples have become quite fussy about photographers. It seems essentially a matter of money, and then of the strange rules that accompany permission. None allowed me to use my tripod, nor any camera larger than 35 mm format. Saihoji, however, does not permit photographers to enter without making prior written appeal. A meeting is held to decide if the objective warrants permission. Aside from the time that would take, there is a charge of around $40. The purpose is to limit the number of applicants, and it seems to be effective. Sanpo-in initially denied me permission, but I came back again the next day and was persistent enough to get the picture. Permission came in the form of turning a blind eye. I have a feeling that I would have saved a lot of trouble by not asking in the first place. Gioji was very sympathetic, and they have reason to be: $20 for letting me in before the herd of people (plus nearly another $40 for taxi fare, as the first bus arrives after opening, naturally). The other places did not permit anyone in before hours, so I had to contest with the masses of people whom you can see (unfortunately) in the back of some of the pictures.

I haven't used any of the herd pictures. The fact of nearly overpowering numbers of visitors in Japan's as well as in most of the planet's smaller and would-be more personal public gardens is a nagging problem in the horticultural world these days. What comes in the coming century, with its soon to be doubled population? The taking of reservations to get into the more famous gardens is almost certainly in the offing. And will there be ticket scalpers skulking outside garden gates as there are now in front of theaters? Time—and procreation—will tell.

CHAPTER ONE

As One Moss Gardener to Another

THE MOSS plant earns our respect, even our sense of awe, as one of the world's lengthier successes in the business of living. Fossil traces confirm an age of moss that goes back about 400 million years, give or take an eon. Moss is older and more lowly than a fern, but higher and more august on life's ladder than an alga, and decidedly more filled with evident joy than the lichen, that slow sharer of many places where moss lives. On sheer face value, the bun or mat of moss is an impressive creation despite lack of height. Images of the plant probably stand out as clearly in a person's mind as those of a pine tree, a dandelion, or a head of lettuce. We pause to study moss, especially after a rain, and carry away a lasting impression of a plant velvety green and vibrant and yet soothing. Moss is a human experience well noted.

The idea of growing mosses (they become plural when we begin noticing the many kinds) most often comes to gardeners, I would think, as it came to me, on meeting these plants rain-fresh in woods and fields. What charmers to bring home to the garden, the susceptible gardener supposes. But how practical is the notion? Much depends on the willingness of the kind of moss one would grow. The particular moss the gardener falls in love with in the wilderness may be cultivated easily or it may prove intractable. (Mosses of easy nature are described in Chapter 14, Portraits).

The most practical garden mosses may, however, not be in the wilderness. They may already be in the garden waiting to be recognized, and they include even the "weed" mosses invasively present in a weakening grass lawn. In many a place these mosses are misunderstood friends, better garden prospects than a sulky crop of grass. Do I hear hoots of protest from devoted greenswarders? Well, I too am a mower and edger of grass, and I know the feeling of accomplishment that comes with having done a good job of neatening the home turf. At the same time I find a perfectly satisfying excuse for lawn moss in those places where grass wants out and moss wants in. The moss is there because it is probably better suited to the location than is any other ground-covering plant, and will ask only a little help from the gardener—possibly less than anything that you might plant—in order to make of itself a permanent, luxuriant, grass-free carpet. This certainly works in some places, as I will show.

Here and now I had better broaden my reply to the question of the practicality of moss gardening. The whole truth is, there is no saving of garden work in the growing of mosses that do not occur naturally in the garden. If you *plant* mosses, their maintenance will provide about as much exercise in the sun or shade as will the care of any other kind of plant. Even so, there are solid reasons, on a level above practicality, for being a moss gardener. All the pleasures, sensuous and intellectual, of pleasure gardening apply here, and the harvest of these qualities is practically as unlimited as the species of moss themselves—15,000 spread over the globe from the Arctic to the Antarctic, 1200 in North America alone.

Moss gardening, then, is the first business of this book: the use of mosses in garden compositions of large size down to a tininess. Closely secondary is the cultivation of other small cryptogams (spore-bearing plants) that are moss-like in their creeping, clinging habit of growth and, in some cases, in their appearance: These visual allies are lichens, liverworts, lycopodiums, and certain of the selaginellas. Despite their smallness, these are plants that, like the true mosses, can be highly effective in garden use. Like mosses, they are garden mood-makers, as mystical as any tree.

It happens that I garden each year in several countries, a fact I believe I must bring in, in order to clear up what might otherwise be a mystery in these pages, where I speak of moss and lichen gardens of mine as being located in various places about the world, in all of which I am apparently present as designer, gardener, and reporter. Actually, that is just the way it is. I visit old friends who live in the vicinities of Seattle and Vancouver, Auckland and Manila, and on the properties of these amiable people I garden for entertainment and education, and for the enjoyment of everyone concerned. I stop at one place for a few months and then go on to the next in an itinerary that I have repeated year after year since the late 1970s, when I retired from my landscaping and nursery business and sold my Seattle-area property.

My gardening with mosses, lichens, and all, in far-flung places, has led me to the discovery of a geographical ease in the hobby: Wherever you live, the plants that you have at hand, native to the property or nearby, are among the best of kinds for your garden. So if you do not have the species I write about, there is no problem. You will almost certainly find others just as valuable. Chances are, however, that you will turn up close at hand, say, within 25 feet or 25 miles, a number of the primitive plants included in this book. Many of the species or genera that are of proven usefulness in gardening range throughout much of the world. These are the ones that have earned mention for their availability as well as their value.

Of the array of cryptogams gathered in these pages, only the liverworts are related to the mosses. The other plants, while they are not related, have garden needs and uses similar to those of mosses. The mosses and their garden allies are plants that bring to surfaces—of the soil, garden walls, roofs, statuary, and stone—a mellowing tone metaphorically like that of the browning coats of varnish that the old masters gave their paintings. But with these plants the tinting comes in a great range of greens, grays, gilt, and rose, a cosmetic application of age rather than of youth.

Mosses and lichens, especially, form an effective part of a garden's patina of time. Even in a garden laid out only 5 years before, an early presence of these plants supplies an appearance of age. There is a precise term for the venerable quality in a landscape that mosses and lichens help instill, the word *shibusa*, invented by the Japanese to save dithering with descriptive language. I wonder if there has ever been another people on earth with a collective mind so admiring of the richness that time brings to the garden that they have needed such a mot juste to go straight to the thought? Not likely. After all, these were the people with enough early finesse to have given us the original moss gardens. Ages ago, during Japan's feudal era, that country's landscape gardeners began to incorporate mosses in their compositions. Certain of their gardens survive to this day, beloved for their immemorial carpets of moss.

Outside of Japan, ground-covering mosses more extensive than a few square yards remain rare in gardens, sufficiently unusual to gain the possessor of a garden moss carpet a certain amount of admiration from a world of grass lawn attendants. Far more common than carpet gardening with mosses is the cultivation of these plants in containers, a place they share with lichens and the several other kinds of cryptogamic small fry. There must be thousands of gardeners, myself included, happily absorbed in creating miniature landscapes with these plants in containers or merely growing them in pots and enjoying them close up. Chapter 10, In Containers, gives this delight due emphasis.

Every chapter in this book has been written with a concern mainly for the garden beauty that can be made with the subject plants, and minimally with the science that makes quite another order and sense out of them. The writing, in its attunement with aesthetics, avoids the intricacies of the botany of these plants, a lexical briar patch bristling with such terms as appendiculate, synoicous, annulus, calyptra, percurrent, archegonium, papillose, trigones, elaters, opercula, antheridia, tracheids, and a great many other thorny words. The smaller the plant, it seems, the more thickety the terminology. Fortunately, it *is* for the most part avoidable by a gardener whose real interest is garden art rather than science.

Now, I don't disparage a more scientific approach to these plants. The better one knows the structure, the taxonomy, and the natural range of a plant, the more resonant one's sense of reward as its successful grower. In the case of mosses and such, this knowledge is hard won, I find, for the reference works on these plants are only marginally penetrable by amateurs such as myself. Just now I have in front of me a book on mosses and liverworts written by bryologists (specialists in bryophytes, a branch of the cryptogams) for others of their discipline. The authors' classification of species is based in considerable part on comparisons of the shapes of cells in fragments of tissues excised from the plants, studied microscopically, and shown in line drawings.

While I have yet to pursue my garden art by vivisection and microscope, I use—and recommend—a kind of lens known as a loupe. This tool is purchasable at stores that outfit college botany students and should be of at least 10 power (better, 12), which will give magnification sufficient to identify the easier species of mosses and other miniatures. Science aside, a loupe makes a great toy, always providing a tingle of amazement in bringing these little plants up to a comradely closeness. For myself, in a gardening life devoted in part to the miniature cryptogams, I am constantly astonished, whenever I stop to examine one of them, to find once again how much companionship there is in so small an entity.

There remains the matter of knowing the plants by name. Here a modicum of science, in the form of nomenclature, comes in handy. Consider the practically innumerable mosses: English-speaking people have always called these plants simply "moss" (or in Old English, *mōs*) with hardly any finer differentiation. There are exceedingly few folk names in English for the mosses. The only such names known to me, of genuine origin in the voice of the people and in general use, are feather moss or fern moss for plants of the genus *Thuidium* and for other pinnately leafed mosses, peat moss for *Sphagnum*, rose moss for *Rhodobryum* of rosy tint, cushion moss or white moss for *Leucobryum*, umbrella moss or tree moss or ground pine for *Climacium* and others that are like tiny trees, extinguisher moss for *Encalypta*, with its hooded spore case that suggests a candle snuffer; and hairy cap moss for the various species of *Pogonatum* and *Polytrichum*.

Some who write about mosses for plain gardeners (my style, exactly, with both pen and trowel) consider it a kindness to their readers to christen all the plants with "common" names, mostly of their own invention or that of other writers. I have decided not to follow. So, I deal out the Linnaean binomials for these little plants insofar as I know them. Where I do not give the name, frankly I don't know what it is, and I think I am not alone among moss gardeners in my paucity of science. I am reassured and relaxed on this score whenever I talk or write to other hobbyists: On the whole we are a collection of babes in the woods when it comes to botany. No matter. We function nicely with few or no binomials for our plants. Our gardening seems decidedly less than technical and more attuned to the sensuous values of the mosses and the other primitive miniatures. "Primitive miniatures": time and again I will be referring to the mosses, lichens, liverworts, lycopodiums, and selaginellas by that term, to save having to trot out all their names. "Miniature cryptogams," "the least of ornamentals," "the moss allies" are other terms I'll be using for the sake of brevity.

Nomenclature comes in handy—but it may be that you have not the least interest in learning scientific binomials that are usually longer than the tiny plants to which they pertain are tall. In that case the word "moss" may be adequate by itself in referring to all mosses if you decide that it is so. You don't need the binomials, or even the sparse common names, in reading and understanding this book and in gardening with its plants. A moss is a moss is a moss, as Gertrude of the single rose might have said if she had been a moss gardener. In like mind, the bare name "lichen" will do nicely for all plants of that classification, "selaginella" for all of that tribe, and so on. Or, if you prefer, you might call the plants after their habitats, for example, tree moss, rock moss, lawn moss, woodland moss. Such were the names that I gave to various mosses when I was a small child, names that I still use at times.

Whatever their identity, wherever they are found, the mosses and liverworts, the lycopodiums, the lichens, and the moss-like selaginellas are usually plants with garden capabilities. Which is to say, the world's thousands of species in these groups of plants have garden values and uses that are often unknown. Any gardening you do with these miniature cryptogams will be, in some measure, experimental. Success in that case brings more than the usual satisfactions in gardening. One earns plaudits, if only in one's mind, for inventiveness and derring-do as a gardening pioneer.

CHAPTER TWO

Definitions

WHEN IS a plant called moss truly that, and when is it not? What makes a lichen a lichen and no other life form? And so on for the other primitive plants that fall within the scope of this book: How do we tell them apart and know them for what they are?

Mosses. Mosses, as the world knows, are little green plants. In some species, however, the green is masked by silver, rose, yellow, or any of several other colors in many tints. Still, the principal color of mosses is green—green in multifarious hues. There is really no such thing as "moss green," unless a person includes in the term every shade of verdancy ever seen.

Below ground the moss plant puts out root-like extensions of its stem. Not true roots, they are more like down, wispy and brief. Even so, these less-than-roots (technically, rhizoids) hold the plant in place. The aboveground parts of the moss plant include a slim stem dressed with tiny leaves in the form of needles, or of scales tight against the stem, or of egg shape or boat shape, or elaborated into miniature fronds. The leafy stem multiplies in the process of growth; the one becomes a colony. The colony, depending on the particular species' power to expand, may round itself off as a small pat, or sweep onward, even to cover yards of ground.

Mosses have no vascular system—no pipes that send up water and soil nutriments, or send down food from the leaves. In these plants the transportation of vital elements is accomplished osmotically, from cell to cell.

There are no flowers, either: Mosses are far too early and lowly in life's hierarchy to come into flower. The glory of bloom would begin ages later in evolution. Mosses, together with the other plants of this book's concern, reproduce by spores, microscopic motes of life that sail forth, sometimes across oceans and continents, on currents of air or water.

Plate 1 shows in close-up a typical moss growing as a colony. Here, both male and female plants are present. In this particular kind, *Polytrichum*, sexual differences are easily discernible during the season of spore bearing. Many of the plants in the photograph are topped with a capsule filled with spores. In those, the leafy stem is part of the female plant (technically, the female gametophyte). Alongside the females are male plants (male gametophytes) with shorter stems that terminate in flower-like cups within which sperm cells are produced. But not many moss genera display the male anatomy as noticeably as does *Polytrichum*. The identifying feature is more often minute or is hidden among the leaves. The bare-stem portion with its capsule lofted above the leaves of the female plant is a third kind of plant, the offspring of the male and the female, called the sporophyte. It is produced following fertilization of the egg cells (borne by the female) by the male plant's sperm. The spores from its capsule will disperse and grow into male or female plants, completing the cycle called "alternation of generations." In many other kinds of moss one plant may bear both the female and male reproductive structures. Sporophytes are still produced following fertilization, however.

Non-Mosses. Nearly everyone knows, in addition to the true mosses of one's acquaintance, a number of non-mosses that go by the name. "Moss" is a handy term applied to many finely textured, vaguely moss-like plants that have no kinship whatsoever to mosses, or none any closer than that of being disparate members of the vegetable kingdom. Non-mosses include Irish moss (*Arenaria verna*, a flower-bearing ground cover), another Irish moss (this one an oceanic alga, source of carrageenin, a thickener used in processed foods), Spanish moss (*Tillandsia*, a pineapple relative, but nothing like in form—a long dangle of stringy gray branches, famed for its habit of hanging from oaks in the South), reindeer moss (several lichens of the genus *Cladonia*, an exigency diet of reindeer in the depth of winter), and moss pink (*Phlox subulata*, a bright spring flower sequined upon a moss-fine mat well known to rock gardeners).

Specialists in rock gardening grow many other kinds of flowering plants,

Plate 1. Male plants (bearing cups) and females (bearing sporophytes with capsules) of the moss *Polytrichum juniperinum*.

such as *Scleranthus*, mossy saxifrages, *Bolax*, *Cotula*, heathers and thymes of extremly dwarf form that resemble moss closely enough to be taken for it by the uncritical or uninformed. *Scleranthus*, a moderately rapid growing ground cover, has even been used as a moss substitute in supposed-to-be Japanese gardening; so has *Arenaria*.

Liverworts. Liverworts are relatives of the true mosses. Both kinds of plants belong to the phylum Bryophyta, in which mosses make up the class Musci, and liverworts, the class Hepaticae (which term comes, as you will no doubt figure if you did not know already, from the Latin word for liver). Liverworts are either leafy or pad-form (thallose). Plants of the latter kind are undifferentiated into leaves and stems—they exist as a mainly flat, irregular patch of green tissue. They lie pressed against soil, stone, or dead wood, which the plants depend on being moist at least at times.

The liverwort *Marchantia* (Plate 2), well hated in horticulture as that enemy that forms smothering little green blankets over small plants in

Plate 2. *Marchantia polymorpha*, the classic pad-form liverwort. It is a beauty with its glossy lobular pads and starfish thalli (spore-carrying structures). And it is a beast, for reasons explained in the text.

pots, is the type plant of the pad-form Hepaticae, the original holder of the title liverwort, which in modern times has been applied to both leafy and thallose members of the clan. In medieval medicine *Marchantia* was one of the plants included in the Doctrine of Signatures, by which vegetation whose shape resembled that of one or another part of the human body was thought to be potent in treating illnesses of the particular organ.

Marchantia is somewhat liver-like in its blobby outline; hence "liverwort," a wort—a plant—supposedly good for liver ailments.

The leafy liverworts, in contrast, have nothing of liver in their appearance. These finely leaved little mat plants (Plate 3) seem quite like mosses until one looks at them close up, or better yet under magnification. Then they are seen to resemble seaweeds as much as mosses. There is an ances-

Plate 3. *Porella* (bottom half of the picture), a typical leafy liverwort, growing on a tree stump with two other leafy liverworts. For scale, find at lower left an inch- (2.5-cm-) long hemlock (*Tsuga*) needle.

tral harkening in that seaweedy resemblance, mosses and liverworts supposedly having evolved from algal seaweeds, when those plants climbed
out of the sea and modified themselves for a life on land.

Lycopodium **and** *Selaginella.* Club mosses (in Latin, *Lycopodium*) and selaginellas, unlike mosses, have specialized water-transporting vascular tissue and are thus more closely related to ferns. The spores of *Lycopodium*
and *Selaginella* are usually carried on club-like structures. The spores of
Selaginella are of two kinds; those of *Lycopodium*, of one: Therein lies the
most salient technical difference between these plants, as far as I can make
out. *Lycopodium* and *Selaginella*, however, can be told apart as readily as
great apes and human beings by general appearances. Some lycopodiums
form tufting plants with scale leaves on stringy branches that divide into
stringy-fingered hands; others sprawl over the ground for some feet on
ropy branches dressed with coarse needles. While the selaginellas—those
moss-like kinds included in this book—may be either scale-leaved or
needle-leaved, they never stretch out on ropy branches. Rather, they are
slow creepers, huddled, short-branched—in certain of the scale-leaved species, kinky and intricate of branch, and seemingly furry.

Plate 4. *Lycopodium complanatum*, a scale-leaved club moss, at woodside.
(photographer, Pamela Harper)

Small confession: If I were reading the intricately branched descriptions above in somebody else's book, I think that I would be lost at this point. When one comes down to it, differences in the anatomy and habits of apes and people, or of club mosses and selaginellas, are mostly of degree rather than of kind. Happily, I have pictures to show of the various types of the two plants in question (Plates 4–6, 88, 94, and the picture of *Selaginella sibirica* on the book's jacket).

Plate 5. *Lycopodium clavatum*, with cones. This club moss is ropy of branch and needle-leaved. In the foreground, the true mosses *Racomitrium lanuginosum* (yellow-green) and *R. heterostichum* (dark green).

Plate 6. At front and center, *Selaginella sanguinolenta* 'Compressa', 10 inches (25 cm) in diameter, 10 years old. Taller and located at the back, ferny-leaved *S. caulescens*. *Selaginella remotifolia* 'Compacta', *Cassiope*-like in branch and leaf, fills the container at the left. These grow at Grand Ridge Nursery, Issaquah, Washington, in response to the artistry and care of alpine gardener Steve Doonan.

Still other selaginellas—popular in greenhouse gardening—stand up on stout, slender, or wiry-thin stems with a plumy fan of leaves at top. This latter type of *Selaginella* is of a shape halfway between that of the more ferny mosses and of ferns themselves.

Lichens. Lichens are partnership plants, made up of an alga and a fungus—two unrelated kinds of vegetation—united in an extraordinary symbiotic relationship. Or, in the view of some lichenologists, the two plants are involved as master and slave with the fungus in control. I prefer the happier interpretation, with the two as equal partners. In any case, the two live together in fixed arrangement, in many thousands of fixed arrangements, each one a different species of lichen, and each lichen species a practical life form of ancient origin.

The arrangement of the two different plants that make up the lichen is rather like that of a pie, in which the fungus forms the crust at top, bottom, and sides, while the alga forms the filling. One does not see the alga at all unless a cross section of the lichen is made and examined under a microscope. Sealed inside the shell of fungus, the alga is protected from excessive sun and drying wind: this, at least, in the more pleasant reading of the relationship. To go on in the same vein, the alga probably absorbs some mineral food drawn in from the tissue of the fungus; while the fungus in turn receives a share of the organic compounds manufactured by the alga. It would seem that the unity of the plants allows them, as a lichen, to inhabit places too harsh for habitation by either an alga or a fungus living on its own: on the surfaces of rocks, for example, located 4 miles (6.5 km) high in the Himalayas, or underneath the surfaces of rocks in Antarctica. But in the grim, alternative view of this putative partnership, the fungus takes from the alga and gives little or nothing in return.

Various lichens are classified as one or another of three general types: crusty (crustose, in formal botany), papery or leaf-like (foliose), or shrubby (fruticose). Crusty lichens cling to rock or bark as tightly and as flat against the surface as a coat of paint. Map lichen (*Rhizocarpon geographicum*, Plate 7) is typical of the group. The crusty lichens seem twice like paint, first from afar and second when a person closely examines their surfaces: allover beady, or fractured and fissured into a network of irregular flakes. Either way, they are like very old paint on canvas or cabinetry. Old indeed, some of the crusties go on living for millennia, a life span determined by measuring growth in diameter over a period of decades. Individuals of the species *R. alpicola* (a close relative of *R. geographicum*) 19 inches (48 cm) in diameter, growing on rocks in northern Sweden, are estimated to be 9000 years old. Such plants move onward more slowly than earth's continents, their infinitesimal progress dictated by the brutal harshness of the places they inhabit, deserty or icy most of the year. A crustose lichen, *Acarospora chlorophana*, that I photographed on desert rock (Plate 66) and then returned to photograph a decade later, showed expansion so minute as to be almost unmeasurable.

Papery lichens inhabit rock, bark, and soil, and rise up a little from their foothold material in the form of ruffly patches, crudely floral in form, or rounded and ear-like. The upper and the lower "leaf" surfaces of papery lichens are of differing appearance, a feature that distinguishes the group. Boulder lichen (*Parmelia conspersa*, Plate 8) is a typical papery lichen. Mainly flat, this plant forms a rosette that pushes on from its perimeter at a yearly fraction of an inch. The advancing edge of the plant is made up of

Plate 7. Map lichen (*Rhizocarpon geographicum*), a "crusty" species, borrowed from an outdoor display of container plants for a few weeks' stay indoors—no harm to it.

many irregular lobes, remindful of bluntly rayed snowflakes in photomicrograph portraits.

Shrubby lichens, unlike the other two types, arise well above the surface of the soil, bark, or stone on which they grow. They stand up as little shillelagh stalks stout and plain; or in many species the stalk divides and redivides into an intricate lace of branches. In either case the epidermis is the same on all sides of the plant. Easter lichen (*Stereocaulon paschale*, Plate 9) exemplifies the more lacy of the shrub-form lichens. Goblet lichens (*Cladonia*, Plate 10) are shrubbies that remain simply stalked.

Plate 8. *Parmelia conspersa*, a "papery" lichen of worldwide range.

Plate 9. Easter lichen (*Stereocaulon paschale*), an intricately branched "shrubby" lichen species, planted on a shard of pahoehoe lava.

Plate 10. Detail of a trough garden with goblet lichens (*Cladonia*), "shrubby" but not branchy, brought here on their native rock and now stepping off the stone to form new colonies amid alpine phloxes. At Grand Ridge Nursery, Issaquah, Washington.

CHAPTER THREE

In the Gardens of Japan

MOSSES INVITED themselves into the gardens of Japan and thereby invented moss gardening. It happened the same way that so much of garden art has happened throughout the world. Worthy plants appear in a garden unexpectedly from seed. They prosper. They improve the composition. They instruct gardeners, who have only to accept Nature's constructive criticism of their work.

The writings of Zen Buddhist monks who lived as far back as a thousand years ago record an appreciation of the mosses that grew in their temple gardens. At the beginning, before any deliberate use of these plants in garden designs, there must have been a kind of communication between monks and mosses during the ritual reveries that are fundamental to the Zen faith. The holy men may well have perceived that the mosses and they both stood for the serenity to be found in a reductive simplicity in life. Early on, the monks extended sanctuary to the mosses that showed up in their temple environs. Later, the monks began to plant mosses or encourage their natural arrival in most of their garden designs.

Where is the evidence supporting my claim of this serendipitous beginning of moss gardening? In subterranean indication: In such moss-muffled temple gardens as Saihoji in Kyoto (Plate 11), ancient groupings of stones can still be made out as tumulary shapes rounded beneath a depth of moss. Saihoji, now the most famous of moss gardens, was originally one more stark agglomeration of stones in a garden style of the mid-fourteenth cen-

Plate 11. The garden of Saihoji in Kyoto, Japan, laid out in the fourteenth century, nowadays famed as the world's foremost moss garden. (photographer, Marc Treib)

tury when it was set out. The life of the garden—if you will, its *heartbeat* as a living organism all these centuries later—pulses within its mosses. These came with time.

At 4½ acres (1.8 hectares), Saihoji is Japan's, and the world's, most extensive example of a naturalistic moss garden: natural, but not Nature's own, and by Nature's measure, not large. In purely natural environments such as among coastal rocks, in forests, on moors and tundras, mosses cover miles of ground. Saihoji is natural in that its mosses planted themselves, and in that its trees and shrubs are left unpruned to form their own growth patterns and to provide shade for the mosses. Saihoji probably fails to qualify for that Holy Grail of modern gardening, however, the low-maintenance landscape. Gardeners are constantly at work here, sweeping away debris, weeding the mosses, patch-planting threadbare places in the carpets. Even such a naturalistic garden requires diligent effort to keep it from reverting too much to a nature raw and erasive.

In the latter decades of the twentieth century an additional problem in maintenance showed up at Saihoji and at the other mossy gardens of Kyoto, in the form of tour buses, too many buses exhaling toxic fumes. The mosses suffered, and now at Saihoji and elsewhere a limited number of buses are allowed in the parking lot in any one day. Still, a plethora of people, hordes of tourists native and foreign, presents a serious problem in aesthetics. Unless the viewer is skilled at shutting out disturbances from a train of thought, it is nowadays impossible to experience the calming and imagination-awakening qualities of Japan's mossy gardens, the very benefits for which the gardens were designed by Zen monks so long ago. But let that be. The mosses and other floor plants of the gardens are still wonders for seeing and musing upon, once the mind focuses on them.

Saihoji's approximately 100 kinds of mosses, liverworts, and lichens are given free play over soil and stones. They sweep over earth and any impediment, forming a tapis vert of many hues, ranging from deepest plush green to brighter peapod colors and varying toward goldish green, bronze, milky jade-greens and gray-greens. The deeply piled carpet, mainly of moss, absorbs sound, exhales moisture that tempers the air, and works a tranquillity equal, in its way, to a down quilt, a lullaby, and easeful sleep. The orchestration of this soothing garden composition is, contrarily, a ceaseless, centuries' old struggle among the plants. Each kind must discover its own territory on soil or stone and hold its place or lose it. Degree of shade or sun, constant moistness of soil or periodic drought, richness or sparseness of humus designate each location as better suited to one species than to any other. Yet soil conditions and lighting slowly change in the garden, and as a result, decade by decade the tapestry of plants transforms.

Two of the major contenders among the mosses are *Leucobryum* (provider of the garden's pale jade tints), and *Polytrichum* (dark green). Both of these mosses are abundant natives of North America, Europe, and elsewhere in the Western world, and wherever they are found they are among the most valuable of mosses for gardens. We can see in the example of Saihoji the need to be observant of the habitat requirements of these or any other kind of moss we would plant. But there is that other way to a moss garden, the serendipitous method of the monks who were the originals at this and who sat contemplatively while various mosses appointed themselves to particular garden sites. More on this relaxed alternative appears in Chapter 7, Moss Carpets.

Certain Japanese gardens contain only small areas of moss, yet to profound effect. Here (Plate 12) moss (of the genus *Polytrichum*) conveys a different sense, nothing of the downy ease of Saihoji but of the sublimeness of our natural planet, unmarred by humankind. To the willing imagination, the countless separate plants in a moss colony only inches tall stand as a forest seen from afar. In this view, a mere handspan of moss may project the hopeful vision of a forested world, greenly wholesome.

Ryoanji Garden in Kyoto is a prime example of this illusory size and extent seen in small patches of *Polytrichum*. Centuries old, the garden is a flat oblong framed by a stucco wall. The ground area is not large—about the size of a tennis court, as I recall in mind's eye—but is famous for its infiniteness. The floor of the garden is covered with coarse sand from which arise several groupings of stones. The sand is kept meticulously raked into patterns formed by the rake tines: into rings around the stones; and elsewhere, into plow lines as straight and seemingly unending as those of a cornfield in Iowa. The only green in the garden is in small areas of *Polytrichum* within, and closely around, the groupings of stones, which provide protection to the moss in disallowing the reach of the rake. I have no doubt (but no proof) that the moss was never planted but came in long ago as a weed and was allowed to stay once the monks made up their minds that while the moss compromised the daringly abstract and austere concept of the garden, it added an irresistible pictorial quality. With the com-

Plate 12. Islands of *Polytrichum* moss kept meticulously edged year after year. At Sanpo-in, Kyoto, Japan. (photographer, Aaron Johanson)

ing of the moss, stone groupings were transfigured into mountains arising from green islands surrounded by a sand sea. A little moss can go a long way.

Polytrichum commune (Plates 12, 13) is the moss species most widely planted in the gardens of Japan. The country's contemporary landscape gardeners also plant other mosses much like *P. commune* in appearance, among them *Pogonatum contortum*. Any of these mosses may be set out solo or may be combined in a freeform or a formal pattern, perhaps with the moss *Stereodon plumaeformis*, low in growth and feathery-branched. This species contrasts effectively with the sturdy little treelets of *Polytrichum* or *Pogonatum* (which the Japanese liken to the forest tree, *Cryptomeria*). Still other primitive miniatures, such as *Selaginella japonica* and *Lycopodium clavatum*, are used as small-area ground covers.

But *Polytrichum commune* outweighs all these others put together. Several of Japan's moss gardens of early twentieth century or of more recent origin contain planted designs of *Polytrichum*, geometric or organic in shape, set off by a surrounding soil topping of white sand. One of the earlier of these compositions—a dazzler for its hard edges separating mossy green from mineral white, visually magnetic for its balance of artifice and nature—is the moss garden at Sanpo-in Temple in Kyoto (Plate 12). Here the moss forms broad, flat pads of a planned irregularity, carefully edged to maintain their shapes. Transitory patterns of sun and shadow, cast in part by surrounding shrubbery, change the garden hourly during the day. Monet, had he been Japanese, might have set up his easel here and had no need of haystacks or waterlilies.

Polytrichum is to be found in the gardens of most of Japan's Zen temples; and if we could get around superhumanly we would no doubt find it in thousands of tiny private gardens, covering ground between stepping stones, or forming an edging plant at the base of shrubbery, or planted without obvious purpose, just for the viewing. By now, the garden values of this and other mosses, first observed and employed by creative monks a millennium ago, have been handed down, in their exemplary gardens, to a whole nation of householders.

In its second thousand years, moss gardening would seem destined to serve even greater purpose in Japan, as in the rest of a world increasingly dense with people and their structures, and diminished in land available for gardening. People such as ourselves will surely still inhabit this constantly more curtailed planet, gardeners stubbornly uncitified, and in search of a bit of soil and plants to fit, in order to make a more perfect world in little that they may call their own: in a word, a garden. Mosses will fit most handily in this brave new garden of the future, and will work their age-old garden spell, the summarizing of our green planet even in the smallest of spaces.

Plate 13. Carpet of *Polytrichum* at Gioji Temple, Kyoto, Japan. (photographer, Aaron Johanson)

CHAPTER FOUR

In Public Gardens of the West

BEYOND Japan, a search in public gardens for useful examples of moss gardening might seem to come down to slim pickings. Most of the planet contains exceedingly few moss gardens that we the public can get in to see. But look again more closely. Europe and North America are home to many public gardens (and private ones, as well) in which mosses and those other omnipresent primitives, the lichens and liverworts, have been allowed to grow spontaneously in patches on the ground, pavements, walks, roofs, and elsewhere. The extent of the plants may not be large, but still they deepen the soul of the garden and provide instructive pictures—previews of the potential artistry of these plants in our home gardens when we are not too neat and unnatural in our maintenance.

As for that rarity in the Western world, the moss garden fully deserving of the name and at the same time open to visitors, the original North American example, is in the Bayard Cutting Arboretum on Long Island, New York. Located on marshy ground, the arboretum's moss garden dates from the 1920s and, I presume, carries on in health and beauty. I have not visited in some years, but if I am correct in my presumption of continuing heartiness, there is no surprise in that, since marsh mosses are well-nigh immortal if gardeners will only keep other plants from overgrowing and smothering them.

On the West Coast of North America during the mid-twentieth century and more recently, ground-covering mosses were planted or appeared (more the latter) in Japanese-style public gardens located in Portland, Oregon's Washington Park; in Seattle, Washington's Washington Park Arboretum; and at the University of British Columbia in Vancouver. Something of the spirit that inhabits the temple gardens of Japan has actually been captured in these immigrant landscapes, a soulful ghost that utterly eludes most of our would-be Japanese gardens, public or private. It is an aura that emanates not least from the mosses in the West Coast gardens: *Calliergonella cuspidata* and *Rhytidiadelphus loreus* at the Washington Park Arboretum, *Pseudotaxiphyllum elegans* (synonyms, *Isopterygium elegans*, *Plagiothecium elegans*) at the University of British Columbia, and *Polytrichum* mosses (the only kinds that have been planted) at all three locations.

I know of two moss gardens, American in location and in character, that employ mosses in ways quite as distinctive as anything one might see in Kyoto. These are the gardens at Doe Run, a private estate open to garden groups by appointment, and at the Bloedel Reserve, formerly a private garden but now open to both groups and individuals. Doe Run, in Unionville, Pennsylvania, is the address of the world's first moss house. The Bloedel Reserve, on Bainbridge Island in Washington state, embraces a woods carpeted with moss and decorated with mossy logs and stumps.

The Bloedel mosses are volunteers, encouraged by artful method. Ground was prepared for them—weeded and raked to a smoothness—in sunny and shady places but was then planted immediately with the flowering carpeter known as Irish moss (*Arenaria verna*), with the idea that if this faux moss grew, fine, let it, but wherever it died out, as would seem likely to happen here and there due to excessive shade or moisture or dryness, that would be all right, too, since true moss would come and fill in the blanks. In any case there would be a mossy cover on the ground from the very start.

Flats of sacrificial Irish moss were purchased for the job in measure totaling thousands of square feet. Planted, it began to give way within a year to arriving true mosses. Within several years much of the Irish moss had been supplanted by bona fide bryophytes. First came *Eurhynchium praelongum* (synonym, *Stokesiella praelonga*), which took hold in dryish ground, and *Brachythecium frigidum*, in ground damp or quite wet much of the year. Later, both these mosses were elbowed out in many places by a more determined ground-covering moss, *Rhytidiadelphus loreus*. The entire succession of plants, from the *Arenaria* to this latter and probably ultimate moss, took place swiftly. The earliest plantings of Irish moss were made in 1980, with later plantings in the mid-1980s. By about 1990 the *Rhytidi-*

adelphus had become predominant in all areas. This softly yellow-green moss is perfectly satisfying as a peaceful cover. But happily, as a staving off of monotony, the earlier comers, *Eurhynchium* and *Brachythecium*, hold their own in certain spots better suited to them than to the pleasant interloper. Another successful minor player in this competition among the Reserve's mosses is *Atrichum undulatum*, which holds on in darker places than the others can endure.

Occasional plants of the original Irish moss remain amid the tide of *Rhytidiadelphus*. Upon the soft chartreuse of this true moss the earlier plants form welcome islands of fine, dark green foliage and tiny, white star flowers. And one other dark green, tiny-leaved, tiny-flowered (in light violet) mat plant, *Mentha requienii*, has come on its own and established itself as a nestler amid the moss. This species, which was set out years before as a ground cover in a nearby area, is in any garden an incorrigible dier-out, mover-on, and shower-up from seed feet or yards from where it was planted. It is always a tiny cheer at any garden party of plants, never a sloppy inebriate nor an aggressive boor in its growth habit (except perhaps, tidy though it is, it might overwhelm the most minute plants in an alpine garden).

Mentha equals mint, and *M. requienii* is the minikin of this aromatic genus yet huge in its aroma. The plant usually announces itself by scent before you see it. Then one looks down to find the source: little dots of leaves, lentil-sized, ivy-dark, closely set in a ground-hugging mat. Trod upon unwittingly (no real harm to it) where it grows in one's path, or brushed with one's fingertips, this least of mints releases a blast of minty volatiles fully as alerting to the nose and palate as a pony glass of crème de menthe.

In the Bloedel Reserve's moss garden, the *Mentha*, like the *Arenaria*, is an enrichment wherever it appears (sparingly) within the sweep of *Rhytidiadelphus*. The mint prefers moist, sunny ground but tolerates some dryness and half shade. It makes one of the most recommendable companions for any vigorously carpeting moss in a not too dark place. Plant it in the spring, or scatter seed after scratching an opening for it if the ground has been taken over already by moss.

Here and there along the paths in the Reserve, grass lawn is a neighbor to the mosses. Where neatness counts (as beside a dwarf maple carpeted beneath with moss) the grass is kept sharply edged. In more casual areas, such as the meeting place of lawn and moss along the edge of a grove of full-size maples, the moss and the lawn have been allowed to establish a natural zone of transition several feet wide. Here, on ground where the sun becomes progressively dimmer inwardly beneath the trees, the grass grows thinner and thinner to nothingness, while the moss grows thicker and thicker to a quilty fullness. Both treatments, edging or transitional, are equally good-looking in their appropriate places.

The handling of volunteer mosses in the Reserve provides examples of moss gardening technique that are applicable anywhere. At the same time the garden displays features special to the Pacific Northwest environment, probably not to be found elsewhere, and possibly not to be duplicated outside the cat's cradle of this particular ecosystem. The Reserve's mosses grow at the edge of, or well beneath, Pacific Northwest conifers, natural second-growth woods, now half a century or more in age. Within this living long house, decaying stumps and logs have been left in place by garden planners and have become thickly upholstered with mosses, turning dead wood into furry sculptures. The presence of these curious, blurry objects gives the Bloedel moss garden a difference. What we have here is hardly a Japanese moss garden. Thanks for that. A moss garden must be a piece of, at peace with, its particular surroundings.

Doe Run, with its moss house, is the garden of Sir John R. H. Thouron, who allows that he has "always liked some of the mosses," enough so that in 1961 he had a special building constructed to provide a secure place for them on his grounds. The 15- by 15-foot (4.5- by 4.5-meter) structure is a handsome specimen of up-from-the-fundament architecture, with a solid roof of slates, solid east and west walls of fieldstone, an open-air north face, and a gridwork doorway in its south-side stone wall. The apertures allow a free flow of air through the little house and admit bright daylight without hot sun, conditions to the liking of the mosses. Watering is by a mist system, twice a day, 5 minutes each session, the year around except during severe frost when the water must be shut off to prevent the bursting of pipes. Water, as needed, is then sprinkled on by hand.

The community of mosses in the house is a collection of trophies gathered by Sir John on trips to England, Scotland, and Belgium. Additional species have come from woodlands in the United States. Terrestrial mosses grow at floor level side by side with other petrophytic mosses on their native rocks.

This pioneer structure, a kind of unheated orangery for mosses, will likely be joined by other moss houses in other gardens in decades to come as interest in growing these plants increases. That such a future is likely was touched on in the previous chapter, as a result of the decade-by-decade diminution of land available for gardening, accompanied by a suitable downsizing of garden plants. Adding to that is the insatiably exploratory nature of gardening itself, always searching for new worlds of plants and just now discovering that of the mosses.

A successfully designed moss house must solve the basic problem—insufficient humidity—that makes so many of the world's more spectacular bryophytes practically ungrowable in the open garden. Several botanical gardens, such as Kew in London, have worked on this problem and applied to it the latest technology of humidification, *not* however in the interest of cultivating mosses but filmy ferns (of the family Hymenophyllaceae). The invention of special houses for these ferns occurred as a consequence of fern-fancying in Britain during Victoria's reign, a time of intense popular interest in collecting and growing ferns, and in minutely differentiating clones of several native species given to variation. The hobby and the trade heated up to a fever pitch summarized by the word pteridomania. The collecting of pressed herbarium specimens of mosses was another Victorian passion in Britain, one that continued until the Second World War. Strangely, the cultivation of living mosses never caught on at the time. If it had, the Victorians would have hit quickly upon the superb idea of growing mosses together with filmy ferns in the same houses. As it is, the idea awaits development in horticulture.

It happens that the humidification requirements of filmy ferns coincide with those of the more baroque of forest mosses, which in fact the filmies rather resemble. What a natural thing, then, to combine the two kinds of plants and so multiply the beauty, curio factor, and scientific scope of the display. Filmy ferns might actually become a minor component, there being so far fewer of these in Nature than of elegant mosses.

Kew's Filmy Fern House, in answer to the needs of both the filmies and the more recalcitrant of bryophytes, faces north, with a high wall to the south that blocks much of the sun. Light enters only from overhead. In sunny summer weather Venetian blinds made of aluminum close off any direct penetration by the sun's rays. Humidity of rain forest lavishness is provided by a misting system driven by compressed air (a better method than the spray-line and spinning-disk systems formerly used at Kew, which tended to corrode and clog).

The house was built in the mid-1960s as an enlargement of Kew's previous Filmy Fern House ("a walk-in Wardian case" in the phrase of old-time staffers who remember the structure). Kew's collections of filmies and of its other delicate ferns that require coolness and constantly moist air were immediately planted in the new house on fresh, unweathered tufa rock-work. At first the ferns sulked and grew sluggishly on this raw medium. But within several years a natural growth of moss appeared on the tufa, benefiting the filmies and the other ferns by helping to make the mineral mellow and fertile. Tree ferns, terrestrial ferns, and ferny selaginellas have been planted in community with the now-vigorous filmy ferns, augmenting the foresty character of the glassed-in garden. For the moss enthusiast all that is lacking is a generous addition of our plants.

If there is no room for them now, then mosses may find homes in the filmy fern houses of the future, or in houses exclusively their own, the moss houses of a more refined horticultural world to come. Let the imagination run. Outside the house, near its entrance, there could be mosses of sunnier persuasion, some on massive stones, others as carpets. These outdoor mosses would appear especially refreshing after a rain in winter, when mosses are at a peak of activity while all the higher greenery in the winter landscape stands in suspense.

Back to the present. While the moss house at Doe Run earns the distinction of being the world's first, even now there is another house that we the public may see, a house that is home to several volunteer mosses and liverworts that grow there splendiferously, no lesser word will do. The place is the Fern House—a house for tree ferns and other sizable species—at the Royal Botanic Garden, Edinburgh. *Conocephalum conicum* (Plate 14), a liverwort native to Scotland and to much of the world, is foremost in vigor among the primitive miniatures within the house. The moss *Hypopterygium atrotheca* (Plate 21) is a close second in its determination. The Garden's bryologist, David G. Long, tells me that the latter species was probably introduced with living plants from the southern hemisphere (but not originally to this glass house) and was first described as an inhabitant of Scotland in 1928. It has done well for itself (and for viewers) in the Fern House, blanketing stones and soil with its miniaturized ferny foliage. Meanwhile, the *Conocephalum* has become a peculiar beauty in the building, peculiar in that any such pad-form liverwort is apt to be condemned out of hand by those of us who know these plants as takeover thugs in our container gardens. But here at Edinburgh we see one of the known supects

Plate 14. The liverwort *Conocephalum conicum* cloaks a tree fern trunk in the Royal Botanic Garden, Edinburgh.

in different guise, as a kind of harmless (probably helpful) garment covering the trunks of tree ferns with a splendid shag, palely green and uniform. Even so, it gives one's sense of right and wrong a twist: It seems a thing as wrongfully beautiful as, say, one of those Hawaiian feather cloaks in a glass museum case. The plant reserves an additional communication for those of us who may give the *Conocephalum* garment a stroke with the hand (an illicit action, against the rules of the House). Touched, it breathes out a scent like that of guavas or apples or some other fruit one cannot quite place.

Our tour of mosses in public gardens has shuttled forth and back, from the future to the present. Now I embark into the past in describing a famous moss garden in England, destroyed by gales of unprecedented force that occurred in 1987 and 1990. The winds knocked over the more than 200-year-old planted beech wood that had shaded and protected the moss nearly throughout the twentieth century. The woods are gone, the mosses too, but the composition remains fresh for those of us who knew it when it was there.

The location was Savill Garden in Windsor Great Park near London. There the moss *Leucobryum glaucum* grew as a greenish gray carpet (Plate 15) that extended from bole to bole at the base of massive old beeches. In a perfect copy of the habit of the *Leucobryum* of Japan, the English plant covered the ground with a multitude of low, rounded waves remindful of a blanket of the cloud species *altocumulus undulatus* as seen from an airplane far above. Just as in Japan, the moss came into the garden on its own and made a plain woods into something visionary.

Savill Garden's moss carpet beneath mature beeches formed perhaps the most serene of all garden compositions in Britain, a country famed for serenity in landscape design. In his book, *The Well-Chosen Garden*, Christopher Lloyd describes this British moss patch in a few words that catch the ambiance of moss gardening so aptly that I can do no better than quote them:

> One of the most satisfying features in the Savill Gardens at Windsor in spring is the undulating carpet of white fork moss, *Leucobryum glaucum,* underneath the beeches as you enter. A wealth of colour and business awaits the visitor, but those mosses under those smooth grey trunks have a simplicity and dignity which are, in their own way, matchless.

Plate 15. Detail of Savill Garden's celebrated cloud carpet of *Leucobryum* moss, later destroyed by storms in 1987 and 1990. (photographer, Pamela Harper)

Very well, the message of the *Leucobryum* was—is—*simplicity* and *dignity*, the same news as that delivered by garden mosses everywhere. And I will add to Lloyd's two keynote nouns, qualitative of mosses, the word *gratuitousness*. Nearly all the mosses of notability in gardens around the world are a gift, a natural occurrence, a nice surprise. The only human factor in the equation is a sensibility on the part of gardeners: This looks good, let it be.

In many another of Britain's historic gardens, mosses and lichens are a memorable, if minor, presence dependent on just such passive good sense. Sightings include mosses in company with alpine flowers in peat terrace gardens at Branklyn (Plate 48) and elsewhere; lichens and waterlilies side by side at Wisley, the more primitive of the two plants on paving beside a pool (Plate 71); a sizable spread of the moss *Mnium hornum* surrounding the base of a great beech at Chatsworth; and small carpets of the same moss beneath shrubbery at Bodnant (Plate 35), where the rhododendron 'Matador' in partnership with the *Mnium* puts on perhaps the most luminous event in world moss gardening, during the month of June, when the crystalline red corollas of the shrub drop upon the rich moss and linger there for days, reluctantly giving up their life glow. Chatsworth offers the questing moss gardener two additional pictures: a broad lawn delightfully busy with mosses and many flowering weeds (as described in Chapter 7, Moss Carpets) and fantastic stacks of stones now mossy with garden age, a composition envisioned and erected by the gardener Joseph Paxton early in the reign of Victoria. Paxton's stones are the apotheosis of the nineteenth century idea of the rockery as a design of rocks foremost, plants rather incidentally.

Paxton's rockery is far from an arrangement in any of the usual styles of the time, however, neither the ruined pyramid of tumble-down stones and hanging plants, nor the mound of earth stuck with upright shards of shale so like almond slivers in Victorian pastries, nor even the naturalistic outcropping (still in vogue with many of us who garden with rocks). Paxton was no such stylish stone plunker. His work earns him remembrance as an original, a sculptor whose stone art seems dateless, at once primordial, contemporary, and futuristic, also weird. His garden rocks stand as mineral kebabs of colossal size: Four-ton hunks of sandstone, each eroded and mossy stone an individual in shape, were carted here from ancient sediments. Paxton had them stacked singly, one atop another, in towers more or less 12 feet (3.5 meters) high and without mortar except in a few hidden places. Scary constructions they are, a thump to one's sense of bodily security, exhilarating as well, stones about to fly.

The planting around the stone towers is a curiously agreeable gathering of seeming incompatibles chosen for ample size. Among the plants are mature shrubs of *Rosa rugosa*, floral spires of *Delphinium*, and the enormous biennial *Heracleum mantegazzianum*, which seeds about and sends up its rhubarb-like leafage and platter-size corymbs of white flowers. This giant is here at its best in the gardens of the world, perfectly in scale and in wild character with an otherworldly landscape. The plant has endured undeservedly bad press in North America since being discovered by newspaper reporters seeking sensation. They have made out the *Heracleum* to be a weed newly arrived and dangerously on the march. Actually, it has been around throughout the twentieth century as a none-too-aggressive ornament of waysides. The supposed danger connected with the *Heracleum* is the rash that contact with the plant can cause in a few people—a nettle sting, nothing more (a physician friend of mine has reported this to me

49

after having read medical records). At Chatsworth hundreds of thousands of visitors pass closely by the *Heracleum*. There is no cautionary sign, but neither have there been any complaints.

The *Heracleum* and the rest of the planting beside Paxton's stones nearly make a garden. Moss (*Hypnum cupressiforme*) puts the topper on the ensemble, civilizing the wild stonework, saving it from seeming intolerably brutal, allowing the visitor to embrace it visually as a part of the garden world's likable bizarrerie, a thing on a par with the garden grotesques of the Italian Renaissance.

Next stop is the garden at the Villa d'Este in the hills north of Rome (Plates 16–18), a redoubt of mosses and liverworts. Far better known for water than for bryophytes, the Villa's landscape is a hillside waterworks display comparable to a sky full of fireworks competing for attention. This orgy of aquatechnics dates from some year soon after 1550. To modern visitors the place can be thoroughly disorienting. We come not only to hectic waters but to a time seemingly more artesian than our own. The garden is a poltergeist of its era, engulfing us in a wash of the bullish self-assurance, ingenuity, filthy lucre, crudity, jokiness, and joy of the age. Face to face, we meet the garden's cinquecento greeters, a witches' retinue of gargoyles in a long row forever disgorging water from stony mouths.

Water, water everywhere. Water explodes in fountains, arcs from statuary breasts, drops in curtain falls and chutes, and finally fans into quiet ponds at the bottom of the garden. The way down is accompanied by sounds as boisterous as the sights, a roaring, gurgling, splashing, and always the percussive plunk of water dripping.

Mossy greens cover little ground in the garden. The domain of the bryophytes is the surface of wet stonework walls and statuary, on which mosses (*Brachythecium* is one, *Cratoneuron* is one more if I do not mistake) and other diminutive plants cling in a green thickness built up through centuries. Gardeners control the soft coat of greenery only in a few small areas such as on the faces of the gushing gargoyles, from which plants are periodically scraped, leaving each phiz bare but furred around with a ruff of foliage. Examined closely, the greenery will be seen to consist, in places, preponderantly of pad-form liverworts (*Lunularia* and others) along with maidenhair ferns, but the broader impression is that of moss, and of a mossy garden. The liverworts, unallowable weeds in most gardens, here

Plate 16. The Hundred Fountains in the garden at Villa d'Este, an Italian Renaissance bulimia of spewing statuary, more lately the lushest mossy garden in Europe.

attain (as they have in the Fern House at Edinburgh) the nobility of being in exactly the right location. What is that maxim, "There are no weeds, only plants out of place"? Of course.

All in all, the garden at the Villa d'Este is, for some of us, even more evocative of the Renaissance than are the frescoes, oil paintings, or other artifacts of the period. That is not to say the Villa's trumpery water devices and spewing statuary are masterpieces of Renaissance sculpture. The carving is hardly more than journeywork. But the fact that it is visible only in those few spots not covered by the mercy of greenery conceals obtuse artisanry just enough to make art of it in making it mysterious. As at Chatsworth, the garden at the Villa grandly exemplifies one of the more intriguing talents of the bryophytes, the way they have of turning cold stone into a warmly hospitable resting place for our eyes and all our faculties.

Plate 17. The faces of gargoyles, along with carvings of the heraldic d'Este eagle, are scrubbed clean. But all the rest of the journeyman artwork is allowed a dignifying coat of moss.

Plate 18. Lions, griffins, dogs, or dragons? Mosses have turned crude carving into a fine mystery at Villa d'Este.

CHAPTER FIVE

Mossy Rocks

"Over here, boys, it's a beauty!"

I AM GIVING voice here to old memories of collecting huge boulders from rock slides in the mountains during my days as a landscape designer, one who worked frequently with natural stones. Mossy rocks were the gems of the trade. Customers loved them. In order to get such prize goods, my crew and I would drive for hours until we reached a mountainside talus of granite or serpentine. We were three: a truck driver, his helper, and myself. The driver had a permit to remove rocks from certain locations in national forests, and a truck with a winch for the hauling. Often the stony slope of the day's journey would be located in dry pineland on the eastern side of the Pacific Northwest's Cascade Range. If the day was warm we would climb the rocks with more than usual caution, concerned not only that the next stone step upward might be precariously balanced, but that a diamondback might be coiled there. Rattlesnakes abound in rock slides in the dry country.

I would search for stones of irregular shape—dynamic sculpture—lying on the surface of the slide, where open air had fostered a few centuries' worth of moss growth on the rock's aged epidermis, and perhaps lichen as a bonus. I would select stones as big as a refrigerator, and others in sizes ranging down to that of a radiator, always working toward a variety that would allow lively, rhythmic rock composition (Plate 19). We would then

Plate 19. Mossy boulders in a woods. From the standpoint of design, this grouping has a balance of mossiness and stoniness that is usually ideal: about half and half. Stones much more than half covered by moss are seemingly soft blobs that lose their symbolic quality as pieces of the planet, solid and secure.

loop cable around each rock and winch it aboard but would first place flattened corrugated paper cartons between the steel and the stone as protection for the moss. (In Japan, dealers in garden stones take even greater care of mossy rocks by using ropes instead of cables.)

Years in number amounting to a good third of a long lifetime have passed since those days of trucking out rocks, and afterward maneuvering them into place as garden sculpture. Recently, I reexamined one of those rocks, at 4 tons as large a mossy specimen as we ever hauled. The mineral is serpentine; the mosses, *Polytrichum piliferum*, a *Dicranum*, and *Racomitrium heterostichum*, in community on the slightly concave top of the stone. The *Polytrichum* is still dominant there as it was decades ago, sustained, as are the other mosses, by a mere inch-depth of dust and humus that have accumulated in the stone's concavity during the passing of centuries.

The rock came from a sunny slide in the mountains, a location searingly hot and dry in summer and early autumn. The garden site in which I placed the rock is also open to full sun and all weather, without which the mosses could not have acclimated to the garden and would have died long ago. Moss gardening's lesson number one is evident in that rock with its longevous mosses: Provide garden sun in an amount matching the wilderness sun to which the mosses are accustomed, or shade with comparable shade. These are factors of first importance in gardening with mossy rocks, just as they are in gardening with every other kind of cryptogam in this book.

On the whole, I had better luck transplanting mossy rocks from sun to sun than from shade to shade. There would be no problem with the shade-to-shade transfer if garden humidity equaled that of the woods, but often it does not. The lingering dew and dampness of the forest seems as important as shade to the health of certain woodland mosses, especially those that grow on rocks. Of course if one has a shade garden large enough and leafy enough to capture real woodland humidity, the accommodation there of almost every kind of moss that grows in woods for miles around becomes entirely possible. That would make quite an adventure in gardening.

As for myself, I have never had the luck of such moist garden shade to work with and have pretty much given up trying to grow rock-inhabiting mosses from the deep woods (terrestrial mosses from the same environment are, however, more tractable). But mossy rocks found in sunny places remain for me a temptation and a garden satisfaction. And even more: I just love a mossy rock, reverence it, visually explore its surface with something of the exaltation of a John Muir hiking in wild places.

So I think does most of the world, of gardeners and nongardeners alike, love a mossy rock. Our affection is of a special kind given to nothing else in earth's landscape known to me, for nothing else seems to hold so much worldly example and welcoming comfort in so small a piece of the planet. In the rock itself we perceive the world raw and uninhabitable. In the moss on the rock, we see the world breathing greenly and preparing for our habitation. Moss on stone is as a comforting hand on a human shoulder (Plates 20, 21).

The dialectic of moss on stone—an interface of immensity and minuteness, of past and present, softness and hardness, stillness and vibrancy, yin and yang—is to be found not only in the mossy behemoth that might be trucked into the garden, but also in a mossy rock small enough to hold in the palm of the hand (Plate 22).

Plate 20. Too much moss obscures boulders here at the corner of a garden terrace. The rocks are good-looking weathered specimens that deserve more exposure. If, on the other hand, they were sharp-edged cubes blasted out of a quarry and more suited to a mortared wall, a full coat of greenery would be an improvement. The flower is Welsh poppy (*Meconopsis cambrica*), a great naturalizer from self-sown seed, especially valuable in wildish gardens.

Plate 21. Sometimes (not often) moss growing splendidly on equally splendid stone is more to be admired in a garden than an exposed mineral surface. To fine effect the moss *Hypopterygium atrotheca* has here been allowed to cover first-rate weather-sculpted sandstones. At the Royal Botanic Garden, Edinburgh.

Plate 22. "Dinosaur egg" colonized by *Racomitrium* mosses, *R. heterostichum* and *R. fasciculare.* All the spiritual values of mossy rocks come down even to a cobble such as this, small enough to hold in the hand.

A mossy rock will fit, with improving effect, almost anywhere in a naturalistic garden: as part of a wall or an alpine garden, at pathside or waterside, in combination with shrubbery or ornamental grasses, or placed apart and featured as sculpture (Plate 61). Small-size mossy rocks are picturesque in container gardening (see Chapter 10, In Containers). Certain mossy or lichen-encrusted rocks form container gardens in themselves, container and plants united in an artistic entirety that wants nothing more than prominent display (Plate 23).

There are, however, not enough available mossy rocks to go around in the gardening world (see also Plate 24), which insufficiency leads some gardeners to attempt growing their own. On bare garden rocks these determined souls pour various libations to stimulate the germination and growth of mosses from spores the breezes bring. A slurry of farmyard manure is one such stimulant. Other fertilizers long in use might be called folk potions. Of these, egg white lightly beaten together with water is perhaps the most popular, and innocuous; plain milk and unsalted buttermilk have their subscribers. Beer, and its end product, are other known tonics for the growing of moss on bald rocks. Another gardener has achieved a measure of fame by gathering up slugs and snails and squishing them over her garden rocks. The fame or notoriety comes, I suppose, as an inevitable part of letting people see such a thing being done. Who could forget, and would not tell? The gardener swears by the slug–snail poultice, in her experience a potent elixir for the mossing of stone.

Any such fertilizing will probably hasten the growth of moss on rocks, hasten but not assure. The rock has to be of the right texture and in the right place. It matters much, in a sunny location, whether the rock is smooth or rough. Smooth rocks in a sunny setting, though soused repeatedly, will probably never support mosses, even if the gardener waits a thousand years. (I have an example in mind that will bear out this lengthy claim.) On the other hand, a rough, bare rock placed in a sunny garden may begin to grow self-sown mosses of such genera as *Tortula* and *Ceratodon* within 5 years and become satisfyingly furry within 10. Conclusion: If the rock surface and the site are right for mosses, even a rock as raw as a peeled potato will rather soon grow mosses without human assistance.

Consider the strange, unalike twinship of two boulders of mammoth size that I have studied in their station on a stream margin in Canadian mountains, approximately where deposited by a glacier thousands of years

Plate 23. *Grimmia* moss on lava rock, *Tortella* moss at its base, in a frostproof stoneware pot. Old lava flows are fruitful places for finding mosses growing on especially interesting stones.

ago. The rocks rest side by side, as they have through the millennia, in the same sunlight, with the same amount of moisture affecting both monoliths. The two rocks are granitic and thus acidic (pH is all-important with mosses, few of which tolerate alkalinity). But one of the rocks is of a hard granite worn smooth by glacial abrasion, and to a lesser extent by rains and floods since the latest ice age. The other is of softer granite, with a rough and crackled surface. The hard, smooth rock has not attracted the slightest trace of moss in thousands of years of exposure to drifting and alighting spores, while under the same circumstances the soft, rough rock wears a luxuriant pelt of the moss *Racomitrium aciculare*. That is the way of mosses on rocks in sun.

In rich, woodsy shade, within the native range of certain irrepressible mosses such as *Brachythecium* and *Eurhynchium*, any rock, rough or smooth, or for that matter any other kind of hard material—glass, wood, leather,

Plate 24. Stepway in the Japanese tea garden at Washington Park Arboretum, Seattle, Washington. Moss growing between and around rocks that are nearly bare enlivens this composition in the same way as that of moss growing on rocks.

metal, plastic, or bone—will serve as a foothold for the moss as it rolls onward. When I was a boy exploring the woods near my home, I chanced upon an oak wine barrel with a little purple ichor still in it, as I discovered when I turned the spigot. Hidden in the woods since Prohibition, which had ended a few years before, the barrel was totally green, overgrown by one or another of the above-named mosses for the place was within their territory. That picture of the swift authority of woodland mosses startles me to this day. I would not want to stretch out in a mossy woods and fall asleep for long.

CHAPTER SIX

The Camp Followers

OUR CONCERN here is not with the kind of camp followers that Billy Sunday might have beaned with a Bible. There are other sorts, among them those that come to us from the tribes of lichens and mosses. These plant tramps number only a few score, a paltry figure considering the base of thousands of moss and lichen species. But the few that trail us do so doggedly.

Traveling as spores, they follow us everywhere, settling in our farmyards and in our towns and cities to take up residence on the structures we build. They dote on aging fences, garden walls, roofs, stonework, statuary, and other firm surfaces of pleasant quality. Yet they do not disdain an abominably fertile sidewalk crevice in skid row. They are among the most opportunistic forms of life that slip into the human encampment, the vegetative counterpart of starlings, pigeons, and house sparrows, but nicer in being noiseless and in not making a mess wherever they land— at least not to the eyes of their admirers.

Once they have settled, these erstwhile vagabonds grow into being possibly the most effective landscape plants of all the primitive miniatures. Their landscape value, like that of any plant, lies in their tonic effect on the mood of people. By the sheer fact of their being everywhere in our midst, brightly alive and welcomely a part of our everyday world, the value of the camp followers perhaps exceeds even that of the famous Zen mosses

Plate 25. A self-made collage of lichens on a barn door includes usneas (bushy), parmelias (gray and papery), lecanoras (stain-like), and a lone *Candelaria* (dark yellow).

of Japan. Those are seen by relatively few people, who must pay admission and line up for the privilege, while city mosses and farmyard lichens are a gift of Nature available any day to most of us.

The tonic benefit of these plants comes not in such a visual rush as that provided by the tides of mosses in the temple grounds of Kyoto, but in countless encounters with mosses and lichens in small or even minuscule quantity: a rough emerald of moss at the base of a lamppost, medallions of lichen on a fence rail. Such plants, in greeting us on our daily rounds, give a little boost to the spirit.

All one has to do to gain this boon to well-being is to walk more slowly if one is accustomed to walking briskly, to examine, in a leisurely but keen manner, such smallnesses as these species, and to apply some play of imagination to them. It helps to have a sense of anthropomorphism. Then these plants are seen to be exemplary for their demonstration of some of the higher human attributes, such as daring and tough resilience, in the way they take hold and thrive in the harshest places. We may admire them as well for quite another human quality: artistry. The simple patches of color and texture that the camp followers make of themselves become, in creative viewing, abstractly patterned tapestries, collages, watercolors—for if ever pigments were activated by water they are those of a rain-livened moss or lichen. All in all, these plants are a triumph of holism, the makers and the media of art (Plate 25).

The great daubers-cum-daubs that decorate the walks and roofs and sundry other slab surfaces we inadvertently shape for them include such lichens as *Buellia*, *Lecanora*, *Parmelia*, and *Xanthoria*, and such mosses as *Bryum*, *Ceratodon*, *Grimmia*, *Homalothecium*, *Tortella*, and *Tortula*—names that translate into as many hues, ranging from orange through lemony yellow to russet, greens light to dark, silver, pewter, and antique gold, glowing softly.

Much of the mellowest of old gold belongs to the moss *Homalothecium sericeum* (Plate 26), British and European, with close relatives in western North America that are probably just as rich. In Britain, *Homalothecium* grows on dry stone walls totaling tens of thousands of miles in length, outlining roadsides, paddocks, and gardens. It grows on additional miles of old garden walls made of brick, with mortar moist and commodious. On such perches, this species outperforms and outnumbers all other clinging plants, imparting to the British Isles one of their characteristic colors of summer. The other colors, as I see them, are green in the world's greatest multitude of hues, assembled here mainly by the world's most industrious horticulture, rain-gray with intervals of blue, and at last a good long draft of late summer wine in the color of heather. The gold of *Homalothecium* moss is most pronounced on its outer branches, which are exposed to summer sun and drought. The sheltered interior of the plant is a middling green, and the entire plant greens up in prolonged rainy weather (Plate 27).

In examining this plant we engage in what seems to me a good workout at that purest form of gardening: gardening visually. That, as I would have it, is the process of looking at a plant profoundly, leaf and stem along with whatever attached jewelry, and assessing whether the plant—if it is wild rather than cultivated—is gardenworthy. Perhaps it has even made a garden composition of the place where it grows. Having seen all this, the visual gardener may smile a self-congratulatory smile, or at least feel a bit

Plate 26. *Homalothecium sericeum* in its dry-weather phase, as golden as can be, as demonstrated by a sprinkling of antique earrings upon the moss. This is one of the exceedingly few garden plants that are truly 24 carat in color.

radiant about possessing a fine degree of visual acumen, and then walk on well satisfied. Visual gardening, at its best, negates the need to garden physically. The adept visual gardener feels not the least compulsion to grow what is already growing so well. Just there, where it grows, the plant provides the viewer with that momentary reward which is the ultimate goal of all physical gardening (all of mine, anyway): that timeout for relaxed and appreciative viewing.

In our world of plants, all of it the visual gardener's realm, the camp-following mosses and lichens are especially helpful in being so at hand. With them we skip the effort of gardening and zoom directly to the goal— if we so wish to do. These are plants that, in growing, create garden views even in the most unlikely places. They can actually make a dismal industrial setting a garden experience for those with the eyes to see grandeur in these least of ornamentals.

Plate 27. Mossy wall in "Miss Roberts' Garden" (I quote the photographer, Pamela Harper) in England: *Homalothecium sericeum,* green in response to spring rain.

The Lively Roof

While out on a session of visual gardening, don't forget to look upward. Some of the grandest works of the camp followers are on rooftops. The primitive plants arrive here in space capsules, or more precisely as spores, perhaps having ridden the jet stream—circled the world—in numbers of meaningless vastness, as many as suns. Thousands of these microscopic voyagers touch down on rooftops, which are among the largest of landing fields open to them, places least contested by plant competitors. Certain complexities now figure, reducing the number of candidates for a life here to a few: The aerial sailor must be of a kind suited to existence on a rooftop, while the roof must be of a material suited to the sailor.

Happily landed, the spore opens and its contents spill out slowly as a pat of a plant, a vegetative tam-o'-shanter. Other spores arrive to form additional tams here and there on the roof. On a new roof the first comers are only slightly noticeable and of no great aesthetic moment. Years go by and, eventually, if the roof is especially supportive of life, the isolated plants edge together to form a fairly uniform cover—of moss, let us say, saving lichens for later consideration. Behold now the thoroughly mossy roof awakened after a rain, a strange, self-contradictory surface, at once amusing, solemn, mischievous, serenely silent and yet silently aloud with life (Plate 28).

Of course not everyone is an admirer of mossy roofs. To people of tidy mind, such a roof may seem a disgrace, a sign of decadence in the building and probably in the householders. But to certain individuals of artistic mentality (very untidy), a mossy roof is a natural splendor—even a national one in certain places in the world.

Entire nations tend toward a unity of response to moss overhead. In Scandinavian countries, where sod roofs are traditional, moss as a main component of the turf is received as a plant of good fortune, a household stork of sorts nesting benevolently on the roof top. In Britain or on the Continent, the plant on high is admired as a badge of Britannic continuity from old time, or of the *ancien régime* forwarded, of all that is wonderfully old and enduring in architecture and nationality. In Japan the majesty of roof moss is expressed in haiku such as this one by Ikiru:

On the shingled gate
Where in rain moss grows jade-bright
Earth and heaven merge.

Plate 28. Roof rug of *Racomitrium* moss, a full cover here for decades.

But in North America and in Australasia (where the topping is more usually lichen than moss), a lively roof is generally abhorred. The difference seems to be that while societies with long histories cherish the growth of slow plants on tiles and slates as a mark of noble antiquity, in younger places people are devoted to keeping brand-new surfaces pristine and resalable.

Auckland, New Zealand, where I write these sentences, is one of the world's youngest of large cities and is remarkably lichenous (but certainly not licentious). Ours is a tile-roofed suburban cottage in Auckland, a community of tens of thousands of tile roofs. Lichens love the tiles, particularly lichens of the cosmopolitan genus *Parmelia*, of which there are more than 50 kinds in New Zealand. These mainly gray-white plants probably have their world capital in Auckland. It is a place where parmelias fix themselves not only on roof tiles but on just about anything else that is firm and motionless for a sufficiently long moment. They take hold on the bark of any tree or shrub that is slow to exfoliate, on any leaves of woody or even of perennial plants retained for more than 2 years. The Auckland of various mineral substances is equally their home. Streetside parking lanes of asphalt, and whole parking lots as well, become magnificent with a solid silvering of *Parmelia* within about 4 years after being laid down. The stones of the city—graywacke and scoria in retaining walls, polished granite in graveyards—blossom with ruffly gray peonies of *Parmelia*. Even plastic plant labels stuck in the ground for a while will come into flower. (If this last example of Auckland's ever eager lichens seems beyond belief, I give evidence in Plate 29.) The alacrity, audacity, and abundance of *Parmelia*

Plate 29. *Parmelia* on a plant label in Auckland, New Zealand, city of opportunity for this genus of lichens.

condemn it in the eyes of most Aucklanders. In this setting, one of the world's newest services, the chemical poisoning and fire-hosing away of lichens, mosses, and anything else that grows on roofs, has found customers who will listen. Count me out, as I found myself having to do one evening.

There came a loud, authoritative knock on my door. I thought for a moment it must be the Law. But it was a salesman. "I notice that you have lichen growing on your roof," he announced. "Did you know that it produces an acid that will eat into tiles? We offer a service . . ." I stopped him with more courtesy than I really felt was due. What I wish I had said was, "Whoa, now. The tile roof has been up there 30 years and shows barely visible etching by lichen, where I've brushed it away to have a look. At that rate of erosion this house could still be a happy home for the plant and for people in about the year 2200."

Roof cleaning is a hot new profession also in the Pacific Northwest, in such young cities as Vancouver, Seattle, and Portland (all of which, like Auckland, were pioneered in the mid-nineteenth century). Some of the same Pacific Northwest jobbers who are now cleaning roofs were spraying insecticides in city and suburban yards, from grass level to tree tops, during the heyday of the fad for all-over poisoning some time back. The step from that to this has been a short one, with old equipment serving the new job.

The notion that mosses or lichens on a roof give it a disreputable appearance is a privilege of opinion. I would agree that an accumulation of tree droppings is unsightly. But the scare-your-pants-off portions of advertisements for some roof cleaning services are just plain hokum. Roof damage from acid rain—if such damage were real—could not be controlled unless the householder were to hose down the roof after every rainfall. Mosses and lichens do not cause roof leaks, and removing them will not prevent or delay the eventual leaking of a roof retained past its years of soundness. Roof cleaners have blamed moss for forcing up wooden shingles at their edges, and so admitting rainwater. That is not the way it happens. Moss takes refuge under wooden shingles or shakes already warped with age, but moss itself is incapable of causing such warping. Shingles made of asphalt may become heaved at the edges by moss, but if this occurs (as has been claimed but not tested) it is highly unusual even when moss has covered the roof for decades.

Plate 28 shows an asphalt shingle roof in place for more than 40 years.

From the start, *Racomitrium* moss (a seeker of sunny mineral surfaces) has been allowed or encouraged to cover the shingles, and for the past quarter-century the moss has blanketed the roof almost completely. There is not a single tiny leak in this old roof, whose shingles would seem to have been protected instead of damaged by the moss. And a commonplace asphalt shingle roof, ordinarily not worth more than a glance, has been converted by moss growth into a rather gloriously verdant vision.

Shingles and shakes cut from two Pacific Coast trees (the redwood, *Sequoia sempervirens*, and the western red cedar, *Thuja plicata*, noted for their resinous, decay-resistant wood, and nowadays shipped as premium roofing to places as far away as Japan, the British Isles, and Australia) make rooftop homes beloved of the moss *Dicranoweisia*, among others, which manifests itself there in mounds of a greenness as lively as tree frogs. These roof excrescences cause many home owners undue concern.

In my own historic experience, a roof of cedar shakes or shingles of the best quality cut from old-growth timber could be counted on to last up to a quarter-century with moss growing and multiplying steadily upon it, or to last about 25 years if kept scoured (as neighbors of mine used to do). My experience is historic in the sense that old-growth cedar is out of stock, almost out of planet, and that roofing cut from available younger trees lasts less long. But the principle remains: a roof of shakes or shingles that is cleaned and fully exposed to the harshness of sunlight, and all weather, decays (by curling, cracking, becoming brittle, and then flaking away) at least as rapidly as a roof that is left mossy. What is more, a good thick blanket of moss on any kind of roof provides insulation and may save on heating or air conditioning.

There I rest my case for rooftop mosses and lichens, sensing somewhat sadly that I will never convince anyone that these plants are beauties who has not been susceptible to their charms all along.

Afterthoughts. Several years have passed since I wrote the foregoing section of this chapter, years in which I have watched for mossy and lichened roofs where ever I have traveled. By now I have come to see that a lively roof is really far more in keeping with the traditional housing and edifices of Europe and Asia than it is with North America's architectural pasticcio. With rare exceptions, moss on the roof does nothing nice for suburbia's millions of speculator-built houses of oddly hybridized architecture.

There is exception in the flat roofs of certain modern-day carports on steep properties in the Pacific Northwest, roofs that extend shelf-like from the earth or stone of the hillside and that are covered handsomely with a natural growth of *Racomitrium* moss: ho-hum architecture made radiant. And there is that rich *Racomitrium* roof (Plate 28) presented earlier. That roof, too, is North American, located in North Vancouver, British Columbia, on a cabin built in 1929 in an area that was then forested. A dense suburb now surrounds the building in whose midst it emanates a kind of homely soulfulness that shows up a lot of the newer neighborhood as the architectural equivalent of Twinkies. Moss does that for the old place.

There are other structures in the New World, for example, wood-shingled gazebos or garden sheds whereon roof mosses work their spell, especially in a woodsy or rural situation. For many years a gardener in the farm country of Oregon's Willamette Valley maintained a more-than-mossy roof garden on the shingles of a garden shed. Polypody ferns as well as mosses grew there naturally. In addition, a number of kinds of *Sempervivum* had colonized the roof. The gardener had given them a start by simply tossing excess sempervivums from her terrestrial garden up onto the mossy shingles, counting on the plant's usually easy nature to do all the rest.

But it is in Asia, on tiles and on *Cryptomeria*-wood structures, and in Europe, on slate or tile, that the green, the ochre, the gray, and the blush of

Plate 30. The lichen *Xanthoria parietina* on a tile roof in Kent, England.

mosses and lichens most often enhance buildings and harmonize with the human spirit. Plate 30 shows an old barn in Kent roofed with terra-cotta tiles and with the lichen *Xanthoria parietina*. The building is right, the plants, compatible. In all there is a fusion of staid antiquity and of freshness. The lively roof has its place.

Diplomacy, Artistry, Funny Business

While tenderly the mild, agreeable moss
Obscures the figures of her date of birth.

from "Tombstone for an Actress," by Dorothy Parker

Tactfully, soothingly, the camp followers among mosses and other cryptogams obliterate that which we are better off not knowing or viewing. On stark, matter-of-fact surfaces of architecture, artwork, and artifacts that we construct and consign to the sun and rain and to these talented plants, they commence their work as diplomats and artists. We may observe them at their tasks on carvings in the garden at Villa d'Este (Plates 16–18), on a barn door (Plate 25), on rooftops, walls, steps, and pavements (Plate 31), on a totem of the Haida people (Plate 32), on a gravestone that Miss Parker probably never saw (Plate 33), and on a certain mossy homunculus (Plate 34).

This little fellow displays something more than the usual dual overlay of diplomacy and artistry that the cryptogams bring to surfaces. He shows as well their occasional third application, funniness, in this instance the be-mossing of pomposity. With his left hand he seems to be signaling, Stop your sinning! With his right he is surely raising a finger of admonition (the sculptor Mary Fuller calls this piece of hers *Admonishing Man*). Carved of a calcareous, tufa-like mineral, he stands just where I placed him in the 1970s, on a granite boulder in a watery basin within the garden of my friend Nancy Davidson Short.

The figurine, together with the rock and the basin below, demonstrate the choosy, sometimes crotchety selection by various mosses of different kinds of minerals on which to take up life. For reasons too subtle for me to know, moss refuses to grow on that deliciously moist and tasty concrete basin. This is in spite of all that I *do* know about mosses, which tells me that any one of a number of kinds would love it here and should have found this perch years ago. Meanwhile, the granite boulder, which was arid and barren when I placed it in the basin, has attracted a dense coat of one of the species of *Brachythecium* moss that dote on acidic mineral and wet-

Plate 31. Steel-and-pebble staircase, with a quarter-century's growth of mosses. Traction is always good since foot traffic keeps the greenery from growing on areas where people step. The owners, Ken and Phyllis Hollingsworth, enjoy this mossy-go-round and sometimes hose it down in dry summer weather just to see the mosses perk up.

ness while the statuette, rich in calcium, has fostered a slowly spreading pelt of the lime-loving moss *Tortula muralis*. The little troglodyte's mossy mane would cover his face like fur on a werewolf if I didn't scrape it off every couple of years.

Plate 32. Communal cushions of the moss *Dicranoweisia cirrata,* on a totem pole of the Haida people of British Columbia and Alaska.

Plate 33. *Caloplaca* lichen in a country churchyard.

Plate 34. The moss *Tortula muralis* forms a pelt on this roly-poly personage (*Admonishing Man* by Mary Fuller), the moss *Brachythecium* grows at his feet. In the garden of Nancy Davidson Short.

CHAPTER SEVEN

Moss Carpets

A CARPET of moss is a great awakener of the sensuous human being that I think every gardener must by nature be. At any rate, those of us who are susceptible have only to gaze at an expanse of this plant in order to go into a state of reverie and rare fancy. If we could purr as felines do we would now purr away. Visual contact with a moss carpet is, however, not enough for many of us, who will now get down close and stroke the inviting plant, eager to meet it with fingertips. A gentle touch will hardly suffice for some who feel compelled to shuck off shoes and socks for a tickly trip across the feathery carpet of green.

Moss of supine extent even has an amorous quality about it, or so it is perceived to have by minds alert to the notion. And the notion is an old one. For centuries, moss has appeared in amatory literature. Here are some tender words by Aphra Behn (1640–1689), who happens to have been the first woman to make a living as an author writing in English:

> Her balmy lips encountering his,
> Their bodies, as their souls, are joined
> Where both in transports unconfined
> Extend themselves upon the moss.

O magic carpet. This ultimate tactile meeting with the plant, even if only in imagination, may lie at the very heart of moss appreciation. If so, a moss carpet in the garden links today's gardener with pleasure gardening at its beginnings in the pleasance, that leafy redoubt of dalliance outside the medieval manor. Or, if it is no such cupidinous thing as that, a carpet of moss is at the very least a pleasure to behold.

Now down to the business of being the custodian of such a swatch. An expanse of moss, if planted by Nature (usually before the gardener comes into possession of the property), is easy enough to maintain. There is weeding to be done, in not unreasonable amount, and the picking up of debris. But perhaps there is no real need for maintenance at all, not in the moss garden of the gardener who feels no urgent compulsion toward tidiness. Nature will have provided a moss or mosses that are stalwart in the setting. The plants *au naturel* may look somewhat scruffy in places but will very possibly carry on for years without being fussed with in any way.

But a moss carpet planted by a *gardener* is not so self-sufficient as Nature's own, nor even sure to grow at all. Before deciding to plant, first consider whether or not the local climate is to the liking of carpeting mosses. They are creatures of coolness, of rain, dew, and fog. Most kinds are inhabitants of the shady forest that precipitation and high humidity sustain; the several kinds that grow extensively in open sunshine only do so in moist regions. Now then, while even a desert gardener might conceivably induce a carpeting growth of moss within an air-conditioned shade house with a misting system to produce the necessary high humidity, the gardener who lives in a climate that supports forest (which for most of us amounts to location in a grove of houses where there was once sylvan ecology) is the one more naturally located for the growing of carpeting mosses.

Within a region of forest bygone or existing, garden mosses will receive a vital supply of precipitation during fall, winter, and spring. When rain fails during summer, the gardener has a choice of keeping the carpet brightly green by watering or of letting it go dry and dull for the season. Shade, crucial to most carpeters in summer, can be that cast by garden trees, or the shady side of a house, garden fence, or wall.

There are five methods that I have tried and can recommend for the establishment of a moss carpet in a garden, and a sixth that I have read about but wonder if it has ever got off the printed page and into real gardening. In brief, the five I am sure about are simply waiting for the moss carpet to come down from the sky in the form of self-sown spores; encouraging "weed" mosses present in a weakening lawn to take over the ground from the grass; carpeting a garden area completely, and at once, with transplants of moss; setting out transplants at spaced intervals; and pulverizing certain willing kinds of mosses, scattering the bits, and growing them on into a full carpet.

The sixth, and perhaps mythical, method is the sowing of moss spores in containers, and a wait for a supply of plantable green moss to appear. I doubt that this has ever been done on a scale large enough to supply moss for a carpet. I go no further with it here but will give a recipe in Chapter 11, Bonsai Mosses.

Method One. Waiting for mosses to come skyborne calls for Faith and Patience, those patron saints of gardening of any sort. There is a distinct advantage in this method when it works. Wherever Nature in the fullness of time, say, within the passing of several years, supplies a moss carpet from self-sown spores, the ingredient moss or mosses will be the best kinds for the particular piece of ground in which they occur, the species Nature evolved for exactly the given conditions of soil, humidity, and lighting (Plate 35).

The mosses that arrive may not be the gardener's first choices but they are Nature's appointees, ones that the gardener would have to fight a continuous battle against in order to keep them from taking over the ground. Why not relax and welcome Nature's gift? After all, any kind of moss, even the so-called weed, when studied with perception undistorted by prejudice, cannot but be seen as good-looking and probably even an asset where it grows.

To prepare ground for an anticipated moss carpet, weed, rake, and perhaps roll the earth smooth and firm, although raking alone may iron out the grade to one's personal satisfaction (and the mosses will not ask for more). But before giving the ground its final refinement, place ornamental rocks or logs, shrubbery, or ferns to complete the garden picture, if you favor the use of any such theatrical props (I for one have a lot of fun with them). As a further option, a dusting of powdered sulfur over the soil to increase acidity, about 2½ pounds (1.1 kg) spread over 100 square feet (9 square meters), will help encourage the arrival of moss. A pH reading of 5.5 is ideal. Or dust the ground with skimmed milk powder or aluminum sulfate, or sprinkle it with rhododendron fertilizer, to increase soil acidity to a degree attractive to mosses; and then, if the weather happens to be dry and breezy, lightly hose any of these powders or granular materials into the ground.

Speaking of powders and potions, which I, as a chemical-shy gardener,

Plate 35. Carpet of *Mnium hornum* (a species native to eastern North America and Europe), self-sown from spores that have alighted beneath an old *Rhododendron* 'Matador' in the garden at Bodnant, Gwynedd, Wales.

do with some reluctance, soil poisons can be as conducive to the establishing of airborne mosses as can a fertilizer. To quote the English writer
on gardens, John Sales, in the symposium, *A Gardener's Dozen*,

> I once visited a garden where spraying with paraquat was the sole
> method of weed control among shrubs. This is not a practice that
> appeals to me particularly but the result was interesting. After two
> or three years the ground was covered entirely by moss and prim-
> roses [*Primula vulgaris*]!

Paraquat is a stuff that has been banned in recent years, has it not? But
other, available chemical killers of weeds and grass (including Roundup,
a product now as cosmopolitan as Coca-Cola), will promote the colonizing
of the ground by mosses by way of clearing the soil of competing plants.
The mosses then come into the barren ground fast and early, outpacing
plants that are more complex in the scheme of life. The invaluable carpeting moss *Polytrichum*, and also *Pohlia* and *Atrichum*, are especially apt
as first comers in soil cleared by poisoning.

With the ground prepared (poison possibly included in the regimen),
stand by while mosses generate and grow lush, but step in now and then
to keep weeds pulled and tree or shrub debris removed. How are you
equipped for patience? Good for a few years' wait? Within 2 years you
should begin to see areas of mossy green on the ground; within 5, a full
cover. If in the earlier years of waiting you do not see the beginnings of a
moss carpet, however, such absence will give evidence that Nature disap-
proves of this piece of ground as a home for mosses. That is not a likely
letdown, though. Depending on whether the ground is shady or sunny,
mosses with a preference for one or the other condition will usually appear. Nearly all the species are fastidious in their needs of lighting, and additionally, in a certain humidity and soil moisture optimal to the plant.

It is very nice that Nature computes all the evidence and then supplies
just the right moss. Sunny ground, especially ground that dries in summer, will attract such carpeters or patch-makers as the mosses *Polytrichum*,
Racomitrium, and *Homalothecium*. Soil that is sunny and marshy or merely
perpetually damp is, in some regions, the natural home of that gorgeous,
gold-green carpeter, *Calliergonella*, and is in other regions the home of *Aulacomnium*, a moss pale green in spring, tow-colored in summer. Ground
that is shady and damp may attract the eager, green *Brachythecium* (cha-
meleon-like, it can also be yellow, depending on its mood) or may bring

many other kinds of moss, for here is the place most conducive of all to the germination of airborne mosses in wide variety.

Yet mosses are often not the very first green plants to arrive and to cover shady soil. The pioneer of all pioneers may be algae, quite satisfactory visually for their time of being. In the gardens of Japan we see shady areas of bare earth that are kept neatly swept, and there algae often green the ground for a year or more before mosses arrive, if indeed they ever come, for the setting may not support these relatively complex plants. Being an algae gardener rather than a moss gardener is an alternative that Nature sometimes urges upon us wherever in the world we may garden, and it is not bad. The soil-inhabiting algae are far different from those repulsive stringy growths found in moribund bodies of water. Instead, they are a vegetative frog skin covering the ground with a finer green than any moss. (But possibly that apparent carpet of algae actually may be moss on the way, for in the life cycle of moss there is a primary stage, the protonema, of thread-like form that, en masse, appears very like an alga.)

Method Two. The second method is the establishing of a moss carpet by encouraging mosses already present in a weakening grass lawn (Plates 36, 37), coupled with the weeding out of the lingering grass. That may sound subversive. Moss, after all, is the conventional lawn enemy to be got rid of, a good idea in the case of one of those Edwardian lawns with a rolled-on pattern resembling mattress ticking in front of a formal, porticoed mansion. Yet there are other places where lawn grass is the wrong plant, and where the allowed moss would be just right: Wherever moss makes an earnest bid for some piece of garden ground in which grass just does not want to carry on no matter how much it is pampered, there, with great good sense, the gardener might pluck out the wan remnants of grass and greet the moss as friend.

There are a number of mosses capable of sneaking into grass lawns all over the world or nearly so, even capable of supplanting the grass under conditions that especially favor the moss. These are the so-called weed mosses, which, when treated with respect, can be turned into some of the handsomest of ground covers. Among these good-bad mosses are *Atrichum*, *Brachythecium*, *Calliergonella*, *Mnium*, *Plagiothecium*, *Polytrichum*, *Racomitrium*, and *Rhytidiadelphus*.

Acidness of soil is encouraging to the moss and detrimental to unwanted grass. Refer to Method One for a list of acidifying chemicals and instructions for their application. Aside from acidification, grooming is of help to the moss. Keep it weeded and raked clean of tree leaves and other smothering debris. (Detailed information on the maintenance of moss carpets follows discussion of the various methods of getting one started.)

Once the moss carpet has grown lush, covering the ground fully, it will, with a little care, carry on in the spot indefinitely. One can walk on ground-covering mosses; children can even engage in occasional rough-and-tumble on them. Yet they are not as durable as healthy grass, not by half. Speaking for myself as much as for anybody else, I can see that a gardener's psyche could lead to as much fussiness over the perfection of a moss carpet as over the proudest grass lawn. Easy does it. The scuffed carpet of moss will heal during winter when the children march off to school.

Shade is the usual domain in which the decline of grass and the advance of moss may take place to such a dramatic degree that a fed-up lawn keeper begins to think seriously of becoming a moss gardener. But sunny lawns, as well, may be overwhelmed by moss, of the species *Rhytidiadelphus squarrosus* particularly. More often, however, those sunny lawns that are colonized by moss settle into a balance of Nature established by the grass, the moss, and other "weeds" that may be allowable and even entertaining to gardeners of Whole Earth persuasion.

Such lawns are as much a part of the British gardening inheritance as are those of the preciously maintained Edwardian kind. The grassy-flowery-mossy lawn is the original, the direct descendant of natural meadow. It is in fact none other than meadow kept low by mowing. This eldest of British lawns is to be seen, walked upon, and studied (for such a lawn repays leisurely perusal) in the country's commons and parklands, and at certain manor houses.

There is a famous example in the garden at Chatsworth House, Derbyshire: the 3-acre (1.2-hectare) Salisbury Lawns that clothe the slope arising at the back of the manor. Deborah, the present duchess of Devonshire, lady of the house, has written a pleasantly peppery brochure, *The Garden at Chatsworth*, which covers the Salisbury Lawns. (The duchess writes as crisply as she converses. Perhaps you have heard her, as I have, in a television film tour of Chatsworth. "That wretched man, Brown," the duchess opines, referring to the celebrated landscape gardener Lancelot "Capability" Brown, with whom she is at odds for his vandalizing of classic British gardens, including the one where the Salisbury Lawns now repose.) To quote her brochure, "Myself, I greatly regret that the 4th Duke engaged

Plate 36. A natural transition underway, from grass to moss (*Mnium*), beneath shady maples.

Plate 37. Same scene (as in Plate 36) 1 year later, after my having cleaned up leaf litter and pulled out most of the lingering tufts of grass.

Brown to make such drastic changes in this part of the garden and would dearly love to see the terraces, parterres and waterworks as they were in the early 1700's." But in another mind the lady would seem to have come to love the weedy grass that replaced that formality in 1760:

> Since that time little or nothing has been done to change it and I am sure it offends people who like a billiard-table green lawn with no weeds. But since the fashion is now all for wild flowers perhaps it pleases more than it offends, as heather, yarrow, knapweed, ox-eye daisy, lady's bedstraw, mouse-ear hawkweed, cat's ear, birds-foot trefoil, sorrel, white clover, speedwell, tormentil, harebell, milkwort, dandelion, creeping buttercup, plantain and even the yellow mountain pansy as well as the usual grasses and plenty of moss grow on the lawns.

Lovingly, I have quoted the centuries' old English names for the weeds, a list that the duchess seems to have set down just as fondly. Lawn weeds are the nicer for being known by their historic titles. The duchess goes on to say, "When first laid down the grass was close-cropped by deer. It has been mown, except in wartime, ever since the deer were excluded from this part of the garden early in the 19th Century." The mowing is done with the mower blades set high, which protects the mosses and other meadow plants. No lime or fertilizer has ever been applied. Low fertility favors the meadow flowers and mosses by restraining the grasses that would tend otherwise to crowd out all those noble Britannic weeds.

Method Three. The third method is that of the instant carpet. A small area of ground, perhaps located along a shady wall or fence, a piece of ground, say, of about 75 square feet (7 square meters), not so big that the planting of it would require an unreasonable quantity of moss, can be mossed at once if the gardener has access to a woods from which mosses in considerable amount can be taken legally. Even if legal, their removal is, of course, in planetary terms, debatable as a moral issue. I have done the deed and have a picture to show of the result (Plate 38). It is of a patchwork carpet pieced together out of ruglets of *Pohlia, Plagiothecium, Drepanocladus, Mnium, Brachythecium, Calliergonella, Dicranum,* and other mosses. These were planted edge to edge at the shady side of the house of some friends of mine, in front of shrubbery and ferns that give the composition a woodsy frame.

Plate 38. Patchwork of many mosses in the shade of a wall. These were planted with the edges of each kind touching, to form a full carpet at once. Birds are kept at bay with fine nylon netting (invisible at this distance) held down with small stones.

I found these mosses locally, in another friend's woodland acreage a few miles from the garden that I was planting, where climate and other conditions are much the same as here at my garden friends' home—considerations all-important in the making of moss carpets. Best results come by using species native to the gardener's region and by planting them in a location where soil, lighting, and moisture are as similar as possible to conditions in their habitat. A sandy, humusy soil suits all sorts of carpet-forming woodland mosses. If necessary, soil acidity can be altered to their needs (see under Method One).

If, in my planting, I had overestimated the supply of protective shade and underestimated the amount of burning sun in the site I chose, the plants would have let me know at once of my error. In the first sunny day that followed the setting out of the mossery, the distress and imminent demise of the plants would have shown up in the bleaching or browning of their leaves. I speak from experience gained all too abundantly in other plantings.

During its first year in the garden, a planted moss carpet will need watering whenever rain fails and the soil surface begins to go dry. Apply water even in times of winter drought that first year. By their second summer, the carpeters should have settled in sufficiently to withstand dryness and should, in times of rainfall, show their contentment by the surest sign, growth. They will not need watering in their second year and thereafter but will love it. Rainfall alone would sustain the established carpeters, but if it happens that water from a lawn sprinkler reaches the mosses, they will drink up like the rounders they are.

Since the initial planting described above, a planting made 5 years previous to this writing, I have added ten or twelve more moss species, piecing them in among the original patches of moss. The community of mosses has grown somewhat turgid. I wish that I had devoted a more extensive spread of ground to the moss garden but that would hardly be possible now, since other plantings occupy the space that might have been mossed. The original planting of mosses extended, as it does today, about 3½ feet (about 1 meter) front to back and about 9 feet (about 3 meters) end to end. I should have made it twice that length. Had I done so I would not have had mosses enough to cover all the ground at once, but that seems not so important now. I could have left spaces between the patches of moss. If the spaces seemed too bare the ground could have been dressed with sand, or peat moss, or finely ground tree bark. Since the ground area is level, any of these toppings would have stayed in place fairly well, dressing up the soil and slowing down seedling weeds.

I had worried a bit that the more boisterous mosses would begin to overgrow less aggressive kinds. Five years on, I see the beginnings of moss wars (Plate 89) but not brought on at all by the kinds (*Brachythecium* and

Calliergonella) that I had thought would throw their weight around. Those mosses remain good neighbors to all the others. *Atrichum* moss, however, never planted but native to the property as sporelings that spread here and there, has appeared in the moss garden and has begun to muscle out some of the other kinds. The *Atrichum* is as beautiful as any, and I find its inroads to be acceptable. Not so with the moss *Polytrichum juniperinum*, which was among the first that I had planted. It has invaded its near neighbors by means of underground stolons. *Polytrichum juniperinum* pops up as single stems and in small clusters in the midst of neighboring nations of mosses soon to be taken over if the invasion is not stopped. I should never have planted the *Polytrichum* in the first place and must caution anybody who would plant any such cartographic layout of mosses as mine not to trust this species, nor probably any other large-size *Polytrichum*, anywhere near the community.

Now for the good news. Nearly all of the other mosses, first-comers and later additions, have grown in health and beauty. If a person did not know that there was anything wrong with what is here, there would not *be* anything wrong. It is an intellectual quibble, not a visual one. On sheer looks, the moss garden has developed into one of the several most interesting features of the whole garden property. Garden guests, even those whose central hobbies are far from gardening and remote from mosses, usually pause there for a long, amazed and admiring gaze, having never seen the like.

Method Four. This method involves the planting of moss sods at spaced intervals (Plate 39) and the waiting for them to grow together solidly. All the preliminary needs, such as likeness of the plant's native soil and that of the garden, acidification (if needed), accustomed lighting, and enough water, are the same as in the preceding methods. (Please take into account, as well, the values of soil toppings in level ground, as outlined under Method Three.) Method Four can be used in the installation of carpeting moss of any kind and is the usual method of planting that foremost of mosses for sunny sites, *Polytrichum*. Plants of this genus grow well in either leafy or mineral soils (if the latter, better friable than a dense clay) and are as much at home in hot sun and in soil that dries hard as they are in mostly shady, constantly moist ground. But such tolerance of one or the other condition—sun and drought, or shade and moistness—may be properties of individual sporelings that settled in the particular site and were

Plate 39. Moss sods set out with their centers about a foot (30 cm) apart. These transplants are summer-dry and shriveled but very much alive. With irrigation during dry weather they will grow into a full carpet within a year or two.

genetically gifted to make a life for themselves with what was there. At any rate, *Polytrichum* transplanted to a harsher site than that in which it grew natively seldom adjusts.

In digging *Polytrichum* or other terrestrial mosses, use a spade or a butcher knife with a long blade, as stiff and sturdy as that of a cleaver. Dig sods at least the size of an outstretched hand. If dug or divided any smaller than that, the moss is apt to die and in any case will partly die back at the edges of the sods. With a deeply rooted moss such as *Polytrichum*, take about a 2- to 3-inch (5- to 7.5-cm) depth of the native earth. With other, shallower mosses (Plate 40), take up all of the ¼ inch (6 mm) or more of soil or leaf mold that adheres in order to capture the plant's roots (rhizoids, technically) along with enough soil to keep the plant from drying. While mosses will withstand long-term drought in the wilderness, transplanted sods are subject to fatal desiccation. (By the way, in *Forests of Lilliput*, John Bland's invaluable and entertaining book on mosses and lichens, there is advice that in collecting mosses for the home garden one should carve away as much of the soil at the plant's base as can be taken off and still have the plant hold together. The perceived purpose is to discourage the moss sod

Plate 40. When digging moss take up all the soil that clings to the plant. A knife is handy in digging just a few sods. For dozens or hundreds, a spade is more practical.

from curling up at the edges when dry. In my own experience, the thinner the soil pancake, the more likely the curling.)

In digging wild moss, the gardener frankly violates Nature. To make amends, scoop up a handful of plant debris and use it to heal the gouge where the moss was removed. Within a couple of years, regenerating moss will usually close up such minor wounds in the skin of the earth.

Back home, plant the sods approximately 1 foot (30 cm) apart, measuring from the center of each. With this spacing, sods of the swiftest mosses, such as *Brachythecium*, will unite and cover the ground completely in as short a time as 1 year. But the many relatively slower growers, *Polytrichum* for one, will require 2 or 3 years to become full ground covers, if they will cover the ground at all.

In unsuitable places, starts of mosses may go on a sit-down strike. I know of a major job of planting in which *Polytrichum* largely failed to perform, probably for the reason that it was brought from a cozy place in the wild and transplanted into relatively trying conditions. On the fifth of June, 1984, I chanced upon two landscapers planting *Polytrichum* in the Japanese tea garden at Seattle's Washington Park Arboretum. I thought, What luck! Here's my chance to take a series of photographs over a period of years, of a moss planting from start to culmination as a lush carpet. The two landscapers on the job told me that the landscape plan called for 6000 sods on 6000 square feet (560 square meters) of ground. The men had collected the *Polytrichum* in the Green River Gorge of western Washington, a place that I, as a hiker, knew to be woodsy and moist. In the deep, shag-rug-like pile of its stem and leaf growth, the collected moss showed that it had come from just such a habitat. The men were planting the sods in poorish ground, in the hot sun of a new garden not yet blessed by sufficient tree shade. At the time, I was unaware of any mistake being made. But the moss knew of the error and sulked.

There is no point in showing the "before" picture of the moss planting I took on that day in 1984, for there followed no glorious "after" condition of established *Polytrichum*. That never happened. I went back year after year to study the progress of the planting. In 1988 I compared what I saw with what I had photographed 4 years earlier and noted that the moss had made almost no progress. Most of the sods remained separate and at a standstill. During those intervening 4 years, groups of student horticulturists and others had weeded the soil between the sods time and again, in quite a dedication of hands and knees.

Plate 41. "Weed mosses" (*Leptobryum, Pohlia,* and others) form a light green ground cover, filling in for a moribund planting of *Polytrichum* (dark green). Years before, *Polytrichum* had been set out all over this ground but failed to grow. The so-called weeds were just right for the spot, the planted moss quite wrong. (The text explains.)

In 1990 I looked once again and took a picture of the planting (Plate 41). The *Polytrichum* sods, the many that were not growing, had extended not a jot farther than in 1988. However, mosses of other genera had finally covered the ground between the dabs of *Polytrichum*. Surely, these other mosses would have completed the job of ground covering years earlier if they had been allowed. But for years the weeders considered them to be weeds cropping up among the rightful *Polytrichum* and pulled them out. Somebody new must have come along eventually, with a more ecumenical view that all mosses are good mosses, and given instruction to let these others be. By 1994 the other mosses had overcome and replaced nearly all the planting of *Polytrichum*. The unanticipated moss carpeting attained a handsomeness here that in its own way equaled anything the *Polytrichum* ever could have been.

Meanwhile, in a more shaded area of this same tea garden, only 50 feet (15 meters) away from those stultified sods, Nature provided a swift ground cover in the form of an attractive gold-green moss, *Calliergonella cuspidata* (Plate 42). Nobody planned or planted this other moss, either. It grew from spores that drifted in and took hold. The gold-green carpet appeared in the late 1980s, on bare ground at the base of rhododendrons, and for several years remained steady-on. Then in the early 1990s the moss *Rhytidiadelphus loreus* began to contest the ground where the earlier moss had grown as a pure cover. The two share the ground fairly equally, although the latecomer may one day take it all. No matter. They are of similar goldish appearance. Together they provide the tea garden with one of its most distinguished features at little cost of upkeep. Sheet-forming mosses such as these will overwhelm most weed seedlings and so will require only minor weeding.

Before we leave this discussion let us consider the object lesson in the tea garden *Polytrichum* that disappointed the best efforts of a renowned garden planner (Juki Iida) brought from Tokyo for the purpose, made a Laurel and Hardy of those two professional planters, and frustrated the dedicated "greenies" working in the garden. Compare all that with the countervailing example of those rather divine weed mosses, the best of plants for the location, planted there by Nature with the ease and certainty of a piece of work with God's own trowel.

Method Five. The fifth method is the growing of a moss carpet from crumbled fragments. This is rarely practiced though much touted in magazine articles on moss gardening. What is not mentioned is that in practical procedure only a few kinds of moss can be grown this way—those that propagate themselves in the wild by breaking up and scattering about. These include certain bun-forming mosses that are usually of no use in making carpets much larger than the extent of ground in a bonsai pot. Among the mosses that increase by natural fragmentation there are several mat-makers of garden importance, however, among them *Leucobryum*, *Racomitrium*, and in at least one horticultural episode, that more usual bun-maker on wood-shingled roofs and decaying stumps, *Dicranoweisia*. Aside from these mosses and a few others, the great majority of carpeters can hardly be said to be growable from fragments.

(A note of technical rebuttal seems in order here. In full truth all mosses are capable of regeneration into new colonies from minute fragments de-

Plate 42. A carpet of *Calliergonella cuspidata* soaks up water from a garden brook, to the benefit of a planting of candelabra primroses.

tached from any part of the plant. Even so, the majority of mosses usually propagate themselves by means of spores. In nature, the regeneration of these mosses from fragments would occur only after some accident had pulverized the plant, for example, the grinding action of ice or, in times past, the footfall of a *Seismosaurus*. The regeneration would take place with colossal wastefulness. One smidgen of moss in a thousand or a million might prosper while the rest perished. The same odds would prevail if a gardener tried to sow, in the open garden, fragments of mosses for which this means of propagation is hardly natural, as is the case with most species. A bryologist working in a laboratory might vastly increase the percentage of live plants to come from a batch of moss bits, however, by using a sterile jar, a sterile nutrient gel, and a moss plant sterilized and minced. Overall sterility is necessary to prevent the invasion of fatal molds from spores. None of this seems readily applicable to the making of a moss carpet. But for small-scale work and for entertainment, many kinds of mosses might be grown from branch cuttings inserted in peat and sand and kept misted.)

One year I tried Method Five with good result, using as the mother plant a square foot (300 square centimeters) of *Racomitrium canescens* collected during summer drought, when the moss was crumbly dry. After rubbing the brittle plant through a screen, I scattered the bits over two nursery flats that had been filled with a mixture of builder's sand and weed-free compost in equal portions. I placed the boxes in a fully exposed location and covered them with nylon netting to keep birds away. By the next summer, a full year later, the *Racomitrium*, one of the more rapid spreaders among soil- and rock-inhabiting mosses, had covered the soil surfaces of the flats fairly evenly.

I have read a number of accounts of the propagation of mosses that claim far quicker results from the same scattershot technique I used: a full green moss cover within weeks or several months at most. But my own findings don't tally with what I read. Neither does the experience of moss gardener Garry Savage, whom I have consulted. He propagated a grand sweep of *Dicranoweisia cirrata* from a stock of the plant that he had scraped from a cedar shingle roof, then fragmented and scattered. The moss is unorthodox for the purpose. Normally a maker of little mounds (we used to call them moss mice, we children who watched them turn from blackish and shrunken, to brilliantly green, cushions after a rain), *Dicranoweisia* is not at all a carpeter in nature. The propagator coaxed it into being one.

He first constructed timber frames in a sunny place for this inhabitant of open sky. Within the frames he spread a mixture of sand and peat moss, only 1–1½ inches (2.5–4 cm) deep. Upon this medium he spread cheesecloth smoothly and then dusted crumbles of dry moss over the cloth, which served as the finest of netting, helping to keep the moss bits in place during watering and rainfall. More than 12 months passed before the bits grew into lush carpets (kept green by frequent watering). At last the time came for transplanting. With the use of a really sharp knife, the moss, along with its attached cheesecloth, was cut into manageable pieces (as a cake in a pan might be cut into just the right size squares or oblongs) and was then scooped up with a spade.

Garry Savage says that he will make certain changes the next time he propagates moss by crumbling. He will not bother with the frames or with transplanting but will spread the soil mixture where the moss is to grow permanently. Then, as before, he will top the soil with the cheesecloth and scatter the moss. Although not relevant to Mr. Savage's next-time project, there are reasons, in addition to the one cited above, for using cheesecloth as an aid to propagation. It keeps the moss intact as a kind of fabric, preventing it from breaking up into little unmanageable pieces at the time of transplanting into open ground and helping secure the transplanted moss while it roots down.

Savage's one-layer use of cheesecloth may be distinctly his own. Some other moss gardeners place a layer of the cloth beneath the inch (2.5 cm) or so of growth medium, sprinkle the crumbled moss on top of the medium, and then place another layer of cheesecloth on top of the moss. Later, when the moss is ready for transplanting, the whole affair—the two layers of cloth, the growth medium in between, and the young turf of moss on top, the moss having grown up through the cloth—is lifted in one piece out of the container (conveniently a nursery flat) that held it all.

The details of this two-layer use of cheesecloth in moss propagation were first published in *Sunset* magazine, March 1967, in an article that includes a historical note too engaging to leave buried and yellowing in library stacks:

We first heard about it [this method of propagation] from a bonsai enthusiast who learned the technique in China during the 1930's. He reports that one elderly master of *p'en-tsai* (the Chinese precursor of bonsai) regularly raised 75 species of moss, and that many kinds could be bought in strips a yard [90 cm] long and about a foot [30 cm] wide.

I did not include cheesecloth at all in my propagation of the *Racomitrium* but never regretted the omission. The propagated plant held together well enough when I lifted it from the flats and stayed in place well enough where I planted it. I consider the cloth optional in small-scale work such as mine with those two flats of moss and more relevant in a sizable job of landscaping. A more detailed account of propagating moss from fragments is given in Chapter 11, Bonsai Mosses, since it is actually for use under bonsai trees rather than as a cover for open ground that moss is more usually propagated by this method.

Maintaining a Moss Carpet

The unanswerable question that I, as a moss carpet gardener and also as a mower and edger of grass, ask myself in moments of ebbing enthusiasm, is, Which plant is the more costly to keep up, time, labor, and money considered, the ground areas of both plants being equal? I would like to think that moss is not *more* costly than grass lawn, but in my experience it can hardly be less. A gardener's sense of recreation while working, however, of pleasure taken in the job in times of perky will, also figures in the equation. I personally find that while moss certainly requires care, the job seems to give back more than does the relentless routine of lawn upkeep. The work of moss gardening has an elitist quality that I must admit I find appealing. Every John and Jane grows grass. Only Nature's chosen grow moss.

One eminent moss carpet gardener, Gordon Emerson of Ohio, has written to me of cultivating white moss (*Leucobryum*), hairy cap mosses (*Pogonatum* or *Polytrichum*), and other kinds native to his property, summing up his many years of work in words of evident satisfaction:

> These plants are ideal for an area under large trees such as mature maples, where they provide year-around greenery with low maintenance. I use a variety of mosses for varied texture and pattern, adding some steppingstones, a few rocks, a couple of patches of ferns. I have one moss area approximately fifty feet by fifty feet [15 by 15 meters], and several other extensive patches. Moss makes excellent cover for fast-shrivelling spring flowers such as clintonias. [*Chionodoxa, Cyclamen, Dodecatheon, Erythronium,* and many

other bulbs, tubers, and corms thrive beneath a protective quilt of moss, increasing there more readily than in bare ground.]

But one must decide: moss or rodents. The squirrels and chipmunks won't leave moss alone. They dig it in search of fallen seeds. For years, I've box-trapped fifty or sixty chipmunks a season, and still I must repair their gougings (like divots in a golf course, the damages always look worse than they really are). Autumn leaves are no problem. Careful work with a wire rake gets them off. But the heavy seedfall from maples and ash requires hand-cleanup, tedious and time-consuming. One thorough early-summer weeding and degrassing is essential; after that, one or two light goings-over. Frequent watering promotes lush growth, and moss looks its best when wet. An elixir of manure is beneficial. Altogether, this amounts to really minor care for a considerable area of garden ground. The rest is moss viewing.

Moss viewing is no doubt one of the better endorphin-makers available to the human mind. Go to the temple gardens of Kyoto on any day and you may see monks and nuns of the Zen faith, seated motionless, gazing out over ancient mosses. Such delicious dreams as those the faithful conjure forth from the moss, that natural calmative, we too may enjoy.

But the spell must be broken with a spot of exercise. In my garden in the Pacific Northwest, with its winter of usually unfrozen ground, an openness of soil that coaxes up certain weeds as early as in March, I find that springtime weeding, as the first session of the year, is a better attack than the early summer weeding our Ohio consultant gives his plants. For leaf removal, Mr. Emerson and I, too, use rakes with wire tines. Other moss gardeners use rakes with tines of rubber or bamboo or use a garden hose to flood fallen tree needles away. Gardeners at Saihoji in Kyoto use a not-too-stiff, not-too-flaccid broom, devised especially for sweeping debris from moss and made by binding dried rushes to a stick. This produces a broom that greatly resembles the one used by the Wicked Witch of the West in *The Wizard of Oz*. But any of these tools, gentle though they are, will still cause minor tearing of the moss. In a cold-winter climate, wait for the ground to freeze before raking fallen autumn leaves; there will be less damage to the moss when ice holds it fast.

At any time of year, leaf-blowers are a swift (and noisy) means of cleaning tree droppings from moss carpets and are of special value in clearing away small conifer needles (such as those of hemlock, *Tsuga*), which are perhaps the most trying of debris in moss carpet gardening. Too small to be raked off, they drizzle down day after day for months. Carpeting mosses of loose and feathery growth (*Hylocomium*, notably) will absorb much of the rain of small needles, but most other carpeters will be inundated unless the needles are removed every few days. If left to build up into a layer, needles or any other kind of plant debris will smother the moss beneath, probably not totally but from place to place. Yet the process may be allowed by an especially relaxed gardener, Nature's disciple in this matter.

In wild woodland, Nature, with grand indifference, allows falling debris to smother much of the moss on the forest floor. The fate of mosses under garden trees often would be the same if things were left to follow their natural course: here and there, pure islets of mossy green, interspaced by drifts of tree jetsam. Wind and rain are the tidal agents that propel and pile the debris. Leaves and twigs, seeds and bark gather especially in hollows of ground. Even with some of the ground given up to jetsam, the overall effect of the moss carpet may still be pleasing in being more in tune with the natural world than if incredibly neat. Such pleasant imperfection is particularly in keeping with large-scale moss carpets.

Fertilizer applied to mosses affects them just as it does any other plants. They beef up like steroid athletes. Gordon Emerson of Ohio uses an "elixir of manure" (enchanting phrase). Some other moss gardeners never apply fertilizer of any kind. In fact, I have been told by several gardeners that fertilizing moss will kill it. Dry fertilizers, especially in heavy dosage, could be fatal by chemically burning the plant. But fertilizers in solution of weak to moderate tincture are harmless, I know. I have used them for years. Any sort of fertilizer compounded basically of nitrogen, phosphorus, and potassium can be sprayed on or sprinkled on and perhaps hosed into the ground to avoid any possibility of burning the moss. Rainy weather in spring or autumn is the best time to fertilize. If the compound contains trace elements in addition to the basic three, so much the better. But of course, fertilizer containing lime, death to most kinds of moss, should be avoided.

Once established, carpeting mosses can be watered as often or as seldom as you like, except for a carpet of *Racomitrium*, a moss that prefers to sleep dry in droughty weather. For all others, the water works as a quick face-freshener, brightening the carpet's shade of green and fluffing its texture. The rest, as the man said, is moss viewing, but maybe there could be more, as recommended at the beginning of this chapter.

Companion Plants

There is something of a paradox about mosses in the company of other plants. Any kind of plant, from a tulip tree (*Liriodendron*) to a tuberous *Begonia*, is visually improved, settled in its surroundings be they acreage or a flowerpot, by the companionship of moss. But moss itself is not necessarily enhanced by the proximity of just any kind of plant. Plants companionable to carpeting moss add body to its flatness, and add to its uniformity the piquancy of differing textures and colors. Such visual spice is to be used sparingly. The carpet of moss should be allowed to remain the principal understory plant in a tree-shaded garden, enhancing the peacefulness inherent in absorptive greenery, soft light, and shadow. *Touches* of color, such as woodland wildflowers provide, are harmonious in a mossy garden. But the aforementioned tuberous begonia and nearly all other hybrid flowers (colors cosmeticized, corolla enlarged as if with silicone, soul of the wild thing deflowered) may seem out of place. All that, however, is merely a matter of taste, about which I am no more an arbiter than the next person. I can only recommend those flowering perennials and other plants that I, for one, consider to be compatible with carpeting mosses, both in appearance and for the practical fact that the companion plants are considerate growers that won't take up too much of the garden.

My suggestion that wildflowers could well be added to the moss carpet presumes that moss is already there, along with shade that supports the moss, if it is indeed the shady kind. But if you are starting out from ground zero, nothing but dirt, no trees for shade—and tree shade is wanted for the moss or mosses you would grow—observe whether those varieties are found naturally beneath conifers or deciduous trees. Then plant the tree that suits the mosses' needs. This or that kind of moss is often specific to either hardwoods or conifers and is unable to live under the wrong tree. It is a matter of the moss wanting shade in winter or not wanting it. *Leucobryum* moss breaks rules in being equally at home beneath hardwoods such as maple (*Acer*) or beech (*Fagus*) and at least one kind of conifer (*Cryptomeria.*)

Oak (*Quercus*), tupelo (*Nyssa*), tulip tree (*Liriodendron*), ash (*Fraxinus*), and maple (*Acer*) are especially accommodating to mosses of many kinds growing at their feet. Conifers, while providing shade and shelter, are brutal friends of terrestrial mosses. Mosses exist beneath those trees precariously, as described heretofore. But if the gardener removes the needles from the moss (and in an overly dark woodland garden removes lower limbs from the conifers to let in brighter light), the mosses will be given vital advantage. In that case almost any conifer, even one known to be especially repellent to moss growth beneath its crown, will make a serviceable shade umbrella. For example, while hemlock (*Tsuga*) is to mosses one of the most inconsiderate trees, there is a certain hemlock-shaded garden in which carpets of *Mnium* and *Plagiothecium* mosses grow as thick as fleece. The gardener uses a leaf-blower constantly.

Among the many shrubs well suited to the moss garden are shade-tolerant members of the Ericaceae, such as *Enkianthus, Kalmia, Rhododendron*, and *Vaccinium*. These are compatible with moss both in their appearance and in their fine rootlets, close to the surface, which delight in undisturbed soil covered with moss. Some other shrub candidates include *Abeliophyllum, Aucuba* (a green-leaved form is generally the more color-compatible with green mosses, but one of the gold-spotted varieties, used together with a carpet of a gold-green moss, could make quite a visual melody), *Buxus, Danaë, Euonymus, Fothergilla, Fuchsia magellanica, Hedera* (the minor varieties), *Hydrangea quercifolia, Ilex crenata, Mahonia, Nandina, Osmanthus, Prunus laurocerasus* in variety, *Ruscus, Sarcococca*, and *Viburnum*.

Of the possible thousands of perennial species (wildflowers gathered from around the world) that will go nicely with carpeting mosses, the following are among the best of all: *Anemone nemorosa* (a colonizer that will need a few feet of ground and that will especially enjoy a moss blanket over its shallow rhizomes), *Arthropodium, Asarum, Aspidistra, Bergenia*, bromeliads, *Camassia* (made to order for a *Sphagnum* carpet), *Campanula poscharskyana, Carex, Cimicifuga, Convallaria* (a spreader but not too much for a large mossy garden), *Cornus canadensis* and related creeping dogwood species, *Cyclamen* (all kinds revel in moss, and several such as *C. coum* and *C. hederifolium* will naturalize there from seed), *Dicentra, Disporum, Dodecatheon, Epimedium, Erythronium, Fragaria vesca* (a prolific self-sower, perhaps a slight danger but a delight), *Francoa, Galax, Galium* (will need at least a few square yards), *Helleborus, Hepatica, Heuchera* (the woodland species), *Hosta* (especially the miniatures), *Iris foetidissima, Jeffersonia, Kirengeshoma, Leucojum, Linnaea, Liriope, Luzula, Mentha requienii, Ophiopogon, Oxalis, Pachysandra, Primula vulgaris* and other primrose species, *Saxifraga stolonifera* and *S. umbrosa, Sedum rupestre* (good with mosses on the ground or atop stone), *Shortia, Smilacina, Streptopus, Thalictrum, Tiarella, Tolmiea, Trillium, Viola* (the violet species will self-sow agreeably, except perhaps for *V. rupestris*, a spreader all too willing to be admitted to a moss carpet at all small, but good in a mossy acreage), and I must not leave out *Waldsteinia*, with its handsome, leathery strawberry foliage, a plant deserving of the few feet of ground it will need and maybe even the annex ground it will happily take unless edged back.

Finally, and foremost of all companion plants for mosses, come the entire tribe of ferns. The stay-in-place kinds (those of shuttlecock form) suit the small garden. A large area of moss will accommodate the colonizing species.

All told, there are more good companions for carpeting mosses than any one of us can possibly employ. They are a part of modern horticulture's embarrassment of riches. And new plants keep pouring forth in daunting quantity from that cornucopia, the nursery industry. Even the modest lists of plants I give here may seem intimidating to a beginning gardener. I well remember the frightfulness of so many unfamiliar names when I, myself, was starting out. Avalanched, one may doubt having any talent as a landscaper, as a selector and organizer of plants. But take heart. For this task of selecting companion plants that are to be placed within or bordering a moss carpet, one utilizes an ability almost as basically human as standing and walking. It is the sense of harmony with which nearly all of us are endowed (but which may be in need of cultivation). Any person capable of selecting a coordinated outfit of clothing for the day will certainly be able to combine plants agreeably. The selfsame ability serves both the art of the ensemble and that of the garden. And if somebody makes a snide remark about a personal outfit or about a garden outfitting of yours that you are happy with, what does that snickersnoot know anyway?

Moss Edging

Mosses make first-rate edging plants. Where they grow along the banks of brooks and ponds, beside pathways in parkland and gardens, and to the fore of beds of shrubbery, they provide fineness, an intimacy in what one views, a visual comfort. In contrast, more distant views—at their farthest, panoramas—may be inspiring, humbling, or only isolating, or all that at once, but at times isolation and an attendant loneliness prevail in a world seen distantly. It may be that landscape gardening is in essence a defense against the too-bigness of the outdoors, a reactionary response to a hidden undertow of agoraphobia that is perhaps nearly universal in human make-up. A world more closely viewed, in vignettes of landscape that we discover or plant for ourselves, is a world made more cozy. Mosses up close are large on fellowship. Nothing else of greenery is more companionable at the near edge of our universe. As cases in point, see Plates 43–45 and 51. Plate 38, additionally, is a good one to review at this juncture. The photograph was presented previously as an example of instant carpeting (described under Method Three), yet it shows mosses in place as edging just as much as anything else.

Plate 43. *Polytrichum* at pathside. Used as edging in thousands of Japanese gardens, this moss is freshly distinctive wherever employed.

Plate 44. A colony of the moss *Hygrohypnum luridum* on the margin of a brook.

Plate 45. *Pohlia* moss, as an edging plant, provides lilt in this garden vignette of stone, gravel, and a ground cover (*Pachysandra termi-nalis*) of lilt-less personality.

CHAPTER EIGHT

In Alpine Gardens

NOT EVERY alpine gardener welcomes those mosses that would surely come on their own. To allow or not to allow them; to plant or not to plant others less forward, are matters of controversy. I present the opinions of three alpine gardeners: myself, whom you already know to be a dedicated defender of mosses wherever they grow; and two expert witnesses whose appraisal of these plants as garden alpines is not as sanguine as my own.

Perhaps I should start by defining a field of horticulture that remains little known. An alpine garden is a sanctuary for the smallest and most delicate plants that can be grown in the open ground. Most alpine garden plants are actually hearty miniatures with no special propensity to pine away. If only they were a few inches bigger they would lend themselves nicely to routine treatment in a rock garden. But in fact they are too small for that, all too easy to lose because of their smallness. The usual location of an alpine garden is in a space kept clear of encroaching branches and roots, a place perhaps in the midst of, but not too near, shrubbery on a slope, or an open area within a large rock garden. The alpine garden may be mounded above the mean of the surrounding terrain to give it prominence. In any case, the garden is always a design for the better viewing of small plants that grow near soil level, and a device for the separating and saving of those plants from the more aggressive shrubbery, the mounding perennials, and the sweeping ground covers in the surrounding garden's bounding main.

Almost any moss transplanted into an alpine garden is visually pleasant and (in my opinion) perfectly harmless. Certain volunteer mosses can even be of vital assistance to many of the garden's flowering miniatures. In growing closely about, the moss provides insulation that may make all the difference in these little flowers' staying in the garden or leaving it. However, a few kinds of volunteer mosses can be troublesome invaders of the very bodies of the littlest alpines. More on this in a moment. But let me emphasize, the vast majority of alpines, inches larger and stronger growing than the potentially moss-ridden kinds, are not at all bothered by mosses, neither the volunteers nor those purposely planted.

The mosses a gardener might grow in an alpine garden easily amount to hundreds of species. I can see no limitation except that imposed by the mosses themselves. Will they or will they not grow? We are in an experimental field, we who would plant them here. In the words (mostly) of a celebrated split infinitive, We boldly go where no gardener has gone before (true of so much of moss gardening.).

First, one pays heed to moss gardening's most basic rule: one selects either sun-loving or shade-loving kinds to correspond with the exposure of the garden. Both soil-inhabiting and rock-clinging moss species make suitable alpine garden candidates. Also worth a try are those mosses that grow on nurse logs or fallen branches. Brought home on some transportable part of their wooden crèches, these will add foresty character to a shaded alpine garden, provided that they adjust to their new environment. (Speaking of bringing them back alive on their native wood, one moss-alpine gardener I have met believes in going for broke. She has had a massive, 20-some-foot (6-some-meter) cedar (*Thuja plicata*) log, mossy but sound, hoisted by crane into her shady garden. While showing this colossus to me the gardener remarked, "This is my mink coat," meaning that she had decided to put her money in the furry log instead of the garment. That is what I would call style beyond style. But surely nobody would buy a mink coat these days.)

Beside mosses, other primitive miniatures such as lycopodiums and selaginellas will fit into an alpine garden, these plants being "alpines" one and all. The word alpine, in garden usage, really needs quotation marks, for along with the thousands of bona fide high-mountain cushions, tufts, and matlets that are grown in alpine gardening, there are additional thousands of miniatures that arrive not from alpine zones but from woodlands, prairies, deserts, and rock outcrops almost anywhere on earth where rocks jut forth and are inhabited by plants.

Given the small size of its plants, an alpine garden no bigger than a blanket, when compactly planted, may equal in variety a ¼-acre (0.1-hectare) home garden. Alpine gardening is a lapidary art and craft requiring a fine hand in composition, and fingertip meticulousness in upkeep.

Maintenance is really one of alpine gardening's defining features and deserves emphasis as a matter of pride with those of us willing to take it on. Let it be said, then, that the alpine garden takes its place among the most carefully groomed and guarded patches of ground in the horticultural world. Among its few equals in finical needs, golf greens come to mind, and also a few small-scale landscapes that have come down to us seemingly spellbound from ancient Japan. There is, for example, Daisenin Garden, with its famous stone boat plying a pebble stream from whose course, century after century, any superfluous sprig of moss or fallen leaf has been whisked away instantly. Knot gardens made of various kinds of culinary herbs, which require a precise trim about once a week during the growing season to keep the knot from unraveling, might also quality as garden locations of maximal maintenance. But I know of nothing in garden art that exceeds an alpine garden's need for one's presence at gardener's prayers: knees on the ground, head bowed, hands reverently, delicately employed at weeding. I try to get friends with longish fingernails to help out. In alpine gardening, such talons are the best of pinching tools to pluck out weeds in the seedling stage before they root down, spread out and spoil the miniatures. If I cannot find anybody willing to jeopardize a manicure, I go at the weeds alone, using a dinner fork or the blade tip of a paring knife.

Of the several sample gardens I have to show, the first is a mossy alpine garden of my own, located in North Vancouver, British Columbia, planted between and beside stepping stones on a rise (Plate 46). Here I grow, along with flowering alpine plants, a variety of sun-tolerant mosses, lycopodiums, and a selaginella. All three kinds of plants were collected nearby at elevations near sea level and as high as 4000 feet (1200 meters). The mosses include a compact, montane form of *Polytrichum piliferum*, *Ceratodon*, *Dicranum*, *Hookeria*, *Pohlia*, and *Racomitrium heterostichum*, a petrophyte brought home on its rock.

Aside from the last-named species, all plants grow in a warm, sandy

Plate 46. Mosses and flowering alpines on a sunward garden slope in North Vancouver, British Columbia, seen here on a cloudy day, best for photography.

loam under day-long sunshine in a garden location watered every several days throughout the summer, whenever the adjacent lawn is sprinkled. To compensate for the constant leaching of food elements caused by the generous watering of this steep garden growing in porous soil, I pour on fertilizer about every 3 weeks springtime to autumn, using any combination of nitrogen, phosphorus, and potassium (for example, 5–10–10, 5–15–10, 18–8–4), preferably with added trace elements. In my experience, complete fertilizers of any concoction bring similar improvement in growth and flowering. Of course, I avoid using any fertilizer that contains calcium, a death knell to most kinds of moss.

But for many years, in my alpine gardening, I used no fertilizer at all and placed much faith in the humus and loam content of the soils I blended for the plants. In newly made alpine beds I would get a burst of growth for two seasons, or three. Afterward, a progressive wizening would take place in the plants, due I now know simply to starvation. In short, the lesson I have finally learned is to fertilize, frequently.

Plate 46 shows a substantial portion of my steppingstone alpine garden superlatively groomed for its photograph, possibly cleaner than it has ever been in everyday life. The rock at lower right, 1 foot (30 cm) across, sets the scale. The flowering alpines I have used here are of kinds that experience has taught me to trust in the vicinity of demure mosses that could be run over easily by swifter rock garden plants. The alpines are safe enough as companions for the mosses but still need occasional control by pruning or edging them back. Left to right, across the middle of the picture, is *Hebe pinguifolia*, bright gray of leaf; the moss *Racomitrium heterostichum*, on the stone above the *Hebe*; *Vaccinium vitis-idaea* var. *minor*, with red berries; a small-growing form of *Vaccinium moupinense*, bronzy-leaved; *Lycopodium alpinum*, just above that bronzy shrublet; next, toward the right, *Sedum spathulifolium* 'Cape Blanco', with gray, spoon-shaped leaves in flattened rosettes; *Sedum dasyphyllum*, gray-violet and tiny of leaf; *Androsace sempervivoides*, green-rosetted, growing in a V formed by two steppingstones; *Sisyrinchium idahoense* var. *macounii* 'Alba', an iris family member with little grayish green blade leaves; and above, at a topside edge of the same rock against which the irid grows, the gray mound of a miniature variety of *Saxifraga paniculata* (synonym, *S. aizoon*). In random places grow *Androsace sarmentosa* var. *chumbyi* (gray, furry rosettes, ruffled around at soil level with last year's leaves, which are browning off) and an *Armeria* hybrid (green, grassy hummocks) nearly like *A. caespitosa*, a parental species.

The miniature flowering plants in this composition are among the best of alpines for use together with sunny mosses and other primitives. Hundreds of other flowering miniatures, equally good for the purpose, are to be found in the catalogs of nurseries that specialize in rock garden plants, but a certain amount of trial and error goes with the finding.

Onward to Seattle, Washington, 150 miles (240 km) to the south, where gardener Florence Free grows alpines in nearly all quarters of the large city lot that surrounds her home. A small part of her planting covers a shady bank (Plate 47). Here, mosses commingle with certain alpine ferns and flowers that in the local climate perform best where protected from sun of any strength. They prefer patterned shade and sun and, in the Free garden, receive it from a south-side picket fence backed with open-branched shrubbery. Among the alpines at home here, in soil spongy with humus, are the heathlets *Cassiope*, *Phyllodoce*, and *Pieris nana*; several species of *Cyclamen*; a condensed form of maidenhair fern, *Adiantum*, from the Aleutians; the European mountaineer, *Soldanella montana*; *Polypodium*

Plate 47. Mosses shelter the roots of delicate shrublets and dwarf perennials in Florence Free's shady alpine garden, Seattle, Washington.

ferns; and *Shortia uniflora* and *S. soldanelloides*, both from Japan, two of the world's most exquisite wildflowers, two notorious garden snarks, apt to fade away. But in this setting, these two shortias are as vigorous as in the wild, benefited by the mosses that protect their roots, crowns, and winter buds from drying winds and frosts—mosses that do as much for all the other alpines in the garden.

Sphagnum moss shows up brightly in this photograph. Patches of live sphagnum (dry and bleached, sleeping through a spell of low humidity in late summer) balance the garden's preponderant greenness with notes of near whiteness. Never planted, the sphagnum elected itself to the garden, arriving as spores. Florence Free explains that she likes the looks of the plant in this location, but since hers is an inch-by-inch garden, and the sphagnum a foot-by-foot grower when it gets going, these young cushions will soon be transplanted to a place where plant neighbors are not so small and likely to be overwhelmed. The other, green-colored mosses on the alpine bank were set out by the gardener, who used old-fashioned black wire bobby pins to fix them to this steep ground.

Two mosses, *Atrichum undulatum* and *Pogonatum contortum*, are especially favored by Florence Free for use with shady alpines. The Seattle gardener prefers *Pogonatum* to other closely related hairy cap mosses of the genus *Polytrichum* because the former does not grow as tall for her as do the latter. Any species in either genus is greatly variable in height, however, in the case of *P. contortum* 1–5 inches (2.5–13 cm) tall, depending on the lusciousness or poverty of living conditions and, I have a hunch, on genetic predetermination, an evolutionary response to environmental influences. (If you require a hairy cap moss of foreshortened form suitable for alpine gardening, seek it on a sunny, windswept mountainside or prairie.)

Atrichum moss comes up generously as a volunteer in Florence Free's garden and is almost always helpful and attractive just where it grows. But where it seems weedy, this sketchily rooted plant has a compensatory charm in being "easy to pull out where you don't want it." I quote our hostess, who allows that for many years she has nurtured a love-hate relationship with mosses, mostly loving them on her shady bank of alpines, roundly hating them in her sunny scree garden. In the latter grow hundreds of species of the tiniest alpine bun plants, and of the most compressed alpine mat-makers, typical among them *Dianthus microlepis* and *Raoulia australis*. Mrs. Free writes that she spends a lot of time weeding out certain unbidden mosses that invade such plants:

For example, the moss *Racomitrium canescens,* which is soft and fluffy. It can be too damp in winter for the alpine plants which like a freeze-dry condition then. Or any *Polytrichum* which makes a deep, hard mat that can out-grow alpine plants. Or *Brachythecium albicans* that creeps into and over low, openly stemmed alpines such as *Penstemon rupicola.*

This gardener's experience with moss in a sunny alpine garden is contrary to my own and comes partly as a result of our planting alpines of essentially different strengths. Her specialty is in collector's prizes, the littlest alpines, which are often the hardest to keep. Even worm casts may bury them, let alone the actions of volunteer mosses. My own specialty is in the easier alpines. Among them I have planted mosses that in cultivation usually do not hop about on their own, to show up in unexpected places. Then, too, I find it beneficial, in a garden of mosses and flowering alpines to grow them all fast, not restrained as in a lean scree but in light, warm soil with plentiful moisture and fertilizer. This will speed up the growth of mosses somewhat while speeding up alpines greatly, enough that they would, if allowed, overpower the mosses I grow, not the other way around, mosses over alpines. My method also helps alpines gain an advantage over any "weed" mosses that appear spontaneously.

Onward again, to Branklyn Garden in Perth, Scotland, where *Polytrichum* moss (an airborne pest in the estimation of the Seattle gardener we met) is a welcome arrival on "peat terraces." These are an invention of British horticulture, to be found here and there in gardens throughout the British Isles and also occasionally in North America. Peat terraces are a kind of alpine garden made of sized blocks of bog peat stacked a few feet high against a slope, or sometimes as a free-standing, stepped construction. In place, the peat blocks provide staging and a rooting medium delightful to many small-growing flowering plants while supplying evaporative moisture that heightens the humidity about plants that, if topographically true to the alpine zone, remember the melting snow that humidified them and dote on cooled and constantly moistened air (so, not incidentally, do many kinds of mosses brought down from mountains).

Britain's garden terraces of peat perform their moisturizing function well enough in the climate of England but they are better in Scotland, with its naturally moister summer air, supportive of the evaporative peat moss, and are at their best in Branklyn Garden. There I found an alpine garden vignette, a composition as much happenstance as it was a calculated planting on a peat terrace, a party of miniatures obviously on the move and probably not now as they were. In alpine gardening, the year-by-year movement of plants, the going ahead or going back, which is normal in any garden, seems intensified in taking place in so small an area. But we have these plants happily together at Branklyn at this photogenic moment (Plate 48): *Primula poissonii*, a parent plant and its offspring in flower, no doubt with more generations to come from seed that will drop and incubate within the nursery mat of *Polytrichum* moss that covers most of the ground area; hart's tongue fern, *Asplenium scolopendrium* (synonym, *Scolopendrium vulgare*), with its long, lingual leaves, another self-seeder in *Polytrichum* moss; as is the shrublet *Arctostaphylos myrtifolia*, whose branches of little round leaves enter the picture from the left.

The *Polytrichum* moss unites this garden and unites it as well with peat gardens everywhere. Any garden planted on peat soon attracts the aerial arrival of *Polytrichum*, which most peat gardeners consider to be a helpmate of alpines and attractive in itself. But add to such approbation this note of caution, from a letter written by R. J. Mitchell of Branklyn House:

> The moss growing on our peat is almost certainly *Polytrichum commune.* Here at Branklyn, where rainfall is only 30" [76 cm] (although we do irrigate), this moss is not a problem—in fact it enhances the planting. But in high rainfall areas this moss grows very strongly, especially from peat blocks, and can easily choke the less vigorous plants. In essence be wary of it.

(In support of my having said that Scotland is moister than England, and the better country for peat gardening, humidity at Branklyn is higher than the moderate rainfall would indicate. It is high enough to support several *Meconopsis* species, a glory of this garden and a group of plants passionately in need of abundant moisture in the air.)

Plants suitable for peat gardens include those same species that grow, as noted before, on a shady bank in Seattle, and hundreds more such as gentians and small-growing primulas from the Himalayas, and among still other miniatures in great array and of worldwide origin, small-growing rhododendrons and other midget members of the heath family, many of which are inhabitants of peaty ground in the wild. If there is a plant of central interest in peat terrace gardening, it is the heath named *Cassiope*, in all its species and hybrids. (The crossbreeding of these tiny flowers may

Plate 48. *Polytrichum* moss (almost certainly *P. commune*) insulates an alpine garden community on a peat terrace at Branklyn Garden, Perth, Scotland.

by now have been done to redundancy. Perhaps hybridizers with an eye for tiny results will turn their attention next to the mosses.)

There in Scotland, peat terrace plantings usually perform best in the full, but tempered, sun of that northerly country; in England, part shade is needed by many peat plants as a defense against the more eager sunshine of the south. This same equation is operative in western North America. The nearly alike climates of Portland, Oregon, and Seattle, Washington, are said (by British expatriates who garden in these cities) to resemble that of England south of London. Ergo, a peat garden in Portland or Seattle should be located in part shade.

A Pacific Northwest climate comparable to that of Scotland is coexistent on the coastal slope of British Columbia 100 miles (160 km) or more north of the international border, or anywhere in the Pacific Northwest at an elevation above 2500 feet (750 meters) or so. Here, peat gardens enjoy sunshine. Not only is the peat garden of more northerly or montane location more acceptive of sun, it will support a greater variety of mosses and flowering alpines than will a garden in a warmer, drier climate. Yet even Californian gardens at low elevation could grow many alpines on peat terraces within shade houses. So could gardens located all across North America.

In areas where excavated blocks of peat are not available, compressed bales of peat moss have been used successfully in constructing peat terraces. The only difficulty they present is in wetting the peat. Thorough moistening of an unbroken bale of moss, necessary before planting, takes almost enough water to float an orca.

Onward once more, to Auckland, New Zealand, to examine just one rock, yet it is an alpine garden in itself, a stone so alive with lichens that it seems to be growing along with its plants. Located at pathside in the garden of Muriel Fisher, this lively stone (Plate 49), a Lilliputian mountain 18 inches (46 cm) high, has stood here for years while its lichen forests have grown deeper and richer and have never needed any care at all.

Like the summer-whitened sphagnum we saw earlier, lichens make fine fresheners in the alpine garden, eye-catching for the gray-white brightness of many species, worth a closer look for their filigreed fineness. Lichens found growing in open ground are usually easy enough to transplant if they can be moved with a solid chunk of their native soil and got home with that soil still attached. Lichens that inhabit bark and rock are easier still to acclimate in a garden when they are brought home on the branch

Plate 49. The size of a hefty watermelon, this lichenous rock is an alpine garden in itself, with its lacy *Stereocaulon,* papery *Parmelia,* and proboscidian *Cladonia.* In Muriel Fisher's rock garden, Auckland, New Zealand.

or stone to which they were born, placed in their accustomed lighting, and tilted or leveled to their old way of growth.

One other kind of alpine gardening has become increasingly popular: trough gardening, in big, blocky containers usually made of concrete but often saved from clumsiness by the lichens and mosses that arrive to clothe their crass sides (see Chapter 10, In Containers).

CHAPTER NINE

Mosses and Lichens in Winter, A Photoessay

O FTEN dormant in other seasons, the mosses and lichens wake up truly in an open winter. Now they are born-again cryptogams, eager to get on with growth and procreation, as in the following winter scenes.

Plate 50 shows an old apple tree with a winter coat of cryptogams. The plants are mainly the moss *Homalothecium* and the lichen *Parmelia*. All through the dry weather of summer and autumn these bark-dwellers remained dull and shrunken. I scarcely noticed them on this tree in my family's Finn Hill garden in Washington state. But now in winter, with the tree leaves fallen and with recurrent rains that keep the mosses and lichens bright, they become an important feature in the landscape. The apple, by the way, is a 'Yellow Transparent'. The tree and I began our association when we were both young, the tree as an unfailing source of an applesauce tart-sweet and exactly right without added sugar, and I as the tree's harvester and pruner, not entirely reliable. But we have kept the bargain reasonably balanced for nearly 50 years. Nowadays, I look up at the tree, and look at myself in the morning mirror, and see that we are taking on a kind of brotherly corrugation and gnarliness. The mosses and lichens, too, are as brightly active on me in winter as they are on the tree, spiritually speaking.

The mosses *Dicranum* (on the rocks) and *Eurhynchium* (on the ground) add their own winter freshness to a garden group of evergreens at the edge of an easy lawn of wild grasses (Plate 51). This area in our garden is not watered in summer, which is just fine with all the plants pictured. Beside

Plate 50. An old apple tree with a winter coat of cryptogams. These bark-clingers are hardly noticeable during other seasons. But when branches are bare of leaves, the mosses and lichens they wear become a garden feature.

the moss, there is a low-boughed Engelmann spruce, *Picea engelmannii*; an ivy, *Hedera helix* 'Carolina Crinkle'; holly-leaved *Mahonia nervosa*; heart-leaved *Epimedium versicolor* 'Sulphureum'; and marbled *Cyclamen hederi-folium*. The foliages of the *Mahonia* and the *Epimedium* have been burnished to a bronze-red by the winter sun. The cyclamens, with their foot-(30-cm-) wide span of leaves, are about 20 years old and have lately borne scores of flowers nearly all at once in early autumn. This species, along with other kinds of hardy *Cyclamen*, delights in ground that dries and bakes in summer. In such conditions the *Cyclamen* tuber is capable of living more than half a century and of growing bigger than a bagel. To return to the mosses on the rock and on the ground: Would this garden composition be half as effective without them? Without their contrasting, furry fineness and enriching green?

Ceratodon purpureus emerges from snow in Plate 52. The upright spore cases of this moss rise to 1½ inches (4 cm) above the leaves. *Ceratodon* is

Plate 51. Mosses add their own winter freshness to a garden group of evergreens.

Plate 52. *Ceratodon purpureus* emerging from snow.

one of the many mosses that begin forming spores in a rainy autumn. With *Ceratodon*, even when covered by winter snow, the case and its contents go on developing throughout the season. Then, during warm, dry weather in spring, the spores in their browning cases are ready to emerge and sail away on a breeze.

Plate 53 is from a photograph taken on the nineteenth of January, during a mild winter in the west of Washington state. *Crocus tommasinianus*, earliest of early-bird bulbs in this region, has pierced up through a protective mat of mosses (mainly *Brachythecium*) to pop open its first flowers. Also in this scene: leafy *Bergenia*; *Sedum rupestre* (lower right), a volunteer in the moss mat, as it is in the midst of all sorts of terrestrial and rock-inhabiting mosses in our garden, always attractively; and—look closely!— a ladybird beetle that has climbed up from hibernation beneath brown leaves into the day's balmy sunshine.

Plate 53. The nineteenth of January, during a mild winter that coaxes crocuses up through moss in the first days of the year.

CHAPTER TEN

In Containers

CONTAINER gardening makes possible the growing of a host of mosses, lichens, and other primitive miniatures that are too delicate for garden life in the open ground or are entirely unequipped for terrestrial existence. If the container is sizable, say, at least as big as a soup bowl, it is big enough for more than one kind of miniature. Place several kinds of little plants in a container in a way that pleases and one has a landscape garden in little, or at least an entire little pleasure garden if there is not much heroic landscape in it. But one kind to a pot is probably more practical since the life needs of that plant are uncomplicated by those of others, and there are no competitors for space in the container. Yet consider the alternative: the endless possibilities for garden design within a container by using a variety of mosses or others among the least of ornamentals, perhaps together with any of a world's worth of other miniatures, ferny, coniferous, or flowering.

True, the combination of several kinds of plants in the closest of quarters juxtaposes their plural needs and independent natures. The miniature garden grows as willfully as the large one and requires guidance—grooming and pruning, that is—just as does the landscape garden of full scale. Yet the miniaturist makes much more use of thumb and forefinger than of back muscles and biceps in maintaining the composition. Then, too, rewards of container landscaping are of the same kind as those of gardening grandly in the open ground but are *not* scaled down. There is constant surprise in that for me, a gardener of acreage and also of inches of soil in containers. I am always discovering that the smallest of gardens can bring in the full pleasure of gardening (along with its full component of exasperation and the usual nagging need to do better).

What shall we call our works of garden design in containers? The efforts are sometimes classifiable as dish gardens, sometimes as *saikei* (miniature landscapes) or as bonsai, but at other times, none of the above. Among our opuses are some that turn out to be so astonishing that naming them would require new terminology; perhaps "dadaist" or "surrealistic" or "impressionistic" gardening would do.

I believe that in order to turn out works as sophisticated as these, a gardener must remain in some resort of mind a lively child, nothing the like of a faux-naïf artist but a true little hellicat of tender years, given to pranks as well as to sessions of wonderment. If any actual children are to be found in the gardener's vicinity, as family or friends, then the making of a garden of little plants in a container can become a perfect point of communication between the generations. One longtime moss gardener, Faith Mackaness, tells me that her single greatest pleasure in a lifetime of gardening with plants of all sizes has been the making of mossy container gardens in collaboration with her grandchildren.

Another moss gardener, whom I met once years ago, was an amazingly well maintained boy in the disguise of a septuagenarian. The container for his garden was a junk-treasure he had found: an old bicycle seat, its metal rust-brown, its leather mummified. On its saddle he had placed a little soil and had then pressed mounds of a bright green moss. He was apologetic about showing me this (dadaist or surrealistic) fantasy landscape of his, probably expecting me to scoff. In fact, I was speechless. I only nodded to show the sympathetic interest I felt. If I had had words for it at the time I might have told him how much I admire such manifestations in grown-ups of the puerile imagination, as up-and-coming as springtime in some lucky people, in others so early-atrophying. What a loss when it goes. For this is the essential imp within, the impetus for the creation of gardens on any scale and of any worthwhile surprise, from bicycle saddle to parkland.

Pots and Non-Pots

Since moss gardeners are especially rejuvenescent of mind, it follows that the containers they use to hold mossy or lichenous landscapes are extraordinary in variety and inventiveness. Commonplace terra cotta and plastic plant pots may be used in a pinch, but other containers range to almost anything firm and even slightly hollowed with means of drainage. The inventory includes natural stone, concrete, wood or bark, shells or shoes, and even rarer surprises. (Add to that genre to which the bicycle-saddle moss garden belongs, an extemporaneous container of my own shown in Plate 54.)

Whether of conventional pottery or of one-of-a-kind originality, the con-

Plate 54. The moss *Philonotis fontana* in a seashell.

tainer need not provide a soil depth of more than 1 or 2 inches (2.5–5 cm) for mosses and other primitives native to mineral soils in sun, better 2 or 3 inches (5–7.5 cm) for woodlanders found in duff. If plants higher on the scale of life (treelets, shrublets, tiny flowering perennials) are to be grown in the container along with the primitives, however, a soil depth of 5 inches (13 cm) or more is preferable. In trough gardening the usual depth is about 1 foot (30 cm). The container must have one or more drainage holes or a drainage channel, as in a plantable rock.

Gardening in troughs has become an increasingly popular variety of container gardening. The idea originated in Britain, where the earlier gardens were made in old farmyard troughs of hard sedimentary stone shaped with mallet and chisel. The demand for the genuine troughs has turned them into costly antiques, rarely available on the market. Concrete troughs, supposed to resemble the farmyard artifacts, are now being made commercially or made by home gardeners for their own use. The recipes for the concrete in the troughs often call for an addition (or overlay) of finely chopped dry peat moss, particles of which help provide toe holds for certain mosses, such as *Bryum*, *Ceratodon*, and *Tortula*, that float around the world as spores and land gratefully on mellow concrete in lieu of their native stone. In time, 5 or 10 years, these clinging plants disguise the awfulness of the fake trough by furring its sides greenly and decently. (Their growth can be hastened by fertilizing the sides of the trough with potions described in Chapter 5, Mossy Rocks.) The furry-sided trough is a willy-nilly moss garden whether or not mosses are ever planted in the soil placed within. Of course, mosses can be planted there, too, along with flowering alpine plants, to fine compositional effect. All that has been said here of mosses goes for lichens as well. They often join the mosses as clingers on the trough sides and are also perfectly at home *in* the trough.

Of all possible containers for a garden of mosses, lichens, et alia, one of the most genuinely naturalistic is a receptive rock, a rock whose rough or hollowed surface will support the growth of these plants. The rock may already have been planted by Nature and exist as a ready-made garden of mosses or lichens or the other lowlies that grow naturally on rocks for preference or necessity, open ground being inhospitable to them. Their chosen rock is all the container they require, providing them adequate sustenance and a grip on the world. The gardener need only bring the natural rock garden home, provided that is allowable and the rock liftable, and place it in a location wholesome to its plants.

As a moss garden scout I keep a lookout not only for the rock already planted but also for the barren one that presents possibilities as a receptacle for a garden of mosses and sundry miniatures. Such a rock may be found under water, on shore, underground, or covered by other stones, situations that have prevented spores from finding such a potentially excellent perch.

One of the choicest of receptive rocks that I have ever turned up was a slab of lava (from underneath others), creviced and hollowed deeply enough to hold soil for mosses. I planted it mainly with that cosmopolitan species *Hypnum cupressiforme*, olive-green in hue, together with minor tufts of a darker green moss, *Encalypta ciliata*, also of worldwide range. To establish upon the rock these habitués of stones and mineral soils, I pressed wads of sticky clay loam into its crevices and then pressed the mosses onto the soil. Natural clingers, they took hold readily, and in the case of the *Hypnum* began spreading on the rock within weeks. A highly satisfying episode of gardening was this adventure (recorded in Plates 55, 56).

I hate to say, but after several years of steady growth and improving appearance in its location on a deck railing, this container garden came to grief. Some bird, a thrush I suspect, for they are active in the neighborhood, pulled most of the moss off the rock and flew away with it. This happened one morning during the nest-building season, apparently at dawn. I noticed my loss when I went out after breakfast that same day. I forgave the thrush, a bird I have observed paying for any damages by catching snails in the garden, clamping its bill over a doorway edge of the shell, dashing the shell to pieces against the garden sidewalk, and then gulping the contents. Anyway, I have only myself to blame for the loss of the mossy rock garden. I knew the risk. I should have known of it well enough to have kept netting over the rock (see Chapter 13, Bugaboos).

The Soil

The usual nursery potting mixes made up mainly of humus in the form of peat moss, ground-up tree bark, or rotted sawdust, perhaps mixed with sand, fertilizer, and vermiculite or perlite, are usable—if they can be kept moist. Such mixes tend to dry out too quickly since the particles of the materials of which they are made are often airily separate from each other and are too coarse to maintain sufficient moisture near the soil surface where it would refresh such shallowly and skimpily rooted plants as mosses. If one decides to use any such product, an addition of water-

Plate 55. A rough and pocky rock, the kind that mosses dote on.

Plate 56. The same rock as in Plate 55, planted with (mid-green) *Hypnum* and (darkish) *Encalypta* mosses.

absorbent polymer crystals (described below) will help conserve moisture. And if the fertilizer in the mix contains added trace elements, good, except when that moss killer, calcium (sometimes listed as a trace element), is among them. Mosses and other primitive miniatures that are grown in a mix that came with added fertilizer will require at least an occasional light feeding after about the first year, after the original fertilizer has been used up or leached out. (For more information see Chapter 11, Bonsai Mosses, under the heading, From Out of the Blue.)

Available in some communities are potting mixes (or bedding mixes) that contain loam, actual soil, in addition to humus and sand. As long as such mixes are acidic they may be perfectly wholesome to mosses and adequate in container gardening with these plants.

However, the natural substrates in which mosses are found may represent the best of all media in which to grow them. When gathering mosses or other primitive miniatures for container gardening, I often include a sufficient quantity of their native medium, but only if this material would seem to be hospitable to the plants when grown in containers. In fact, the stuff may not be usable on its own. It may be a fluffy leaf mold or a rotted wood too airy to be kept moist in a container (except under a mist), or it may be clay, which tends to become waterlogged when used in a pot, leading to damping off.

But even if the native substrate is too light or too heavy for pot gardening, I still leave a small quantity attached to the plant since complete removal would likely cause damage. I then settle the plant along with the attached substrate into a container filled with a homemade mix, a general-purpose soil for container gardening compounded of friable, acidic loam from the open garden, builder's sand, and humus (the leaf mold or rotted wood in which I found the plant growing, or peat moss, or any commercial mix that is mainly rotted sawdust or manure but that contains no lime) in proportions of one-third each, blended together with water-absorbent crystals.

This mixture is suitable for container cultivation of all kinds of terrestrial mosses and other ground-dwellers among the primitives, and also for their companion plants (listed below) except for succulents such as cacti and other dislikers of constant moisture. (Cacti, grown in a container, perhaps with moss or lichens that cling to a rock, need an especially airy soil. I use two parts coarse sand, and finely crushed rock, loam, and humus, one part each. Other growers prefer hen grit or pea gravel to sand and use up to nine parts of one or another of these crunchy minerals to one part humus but no loam at all.)

But suppose, now, I find that the natural stuff in which the moss is growing is neither too light, nor too heavy, but just right for container gardening. In that case, I bag it up, rub it through a screen with ½-inch (13-mm) mesh or break it up finely with my fingers, and use it unadmixed with other ingredients except for a sprinkling of water-absorbent polymer crystals, which, to an old-time container gardener such as myself, seem the greatest invention since watering cans. The crystals are an asset in growing, as container plants, all the terrestrial mosses and other ground-inhabiting primitives, and whatever else you plant with them, with the exception of cacti and certain other moisture-intolerant plants, as mentioned.

The crystals come in three grades: large, medium, and small. I use medium for nearly all pot gardening, small only in tiny or shallow pots. (Medium, often the only size available, can be crushed into small with the use of a rolling pin or a cylindrical bottle.) With water, the medium crystals expand from the size of coarse sand grains to that of coarsely crushed ice. They become a glassy-appearing but wobbly water gel 300 times larger than when dry and give up the absorbed water slowly.

The crystals can be used dry or hydrated and fully expanded, more easily when dry. Add about 1½ teaspoons (7 ml) of dry crystals to every gallon (3.8 liters) of soil and mix thoroughly, or about 2 teaspoons (10 ml) to the gallon if the container is to be placed in an especially droughty location. As an extreme measure of protection against dryness, in addition to mixing crystals in the soil as directed above, place a layer of crystals in water-engorged condition (they are now blobs rather than crystals) ½ inch (13 mm) deep at the bottom of the container.

With the use of water-absorbent crystals, plants in small or shallow containers will remain healthily moist for 2 or 3 days between sessions of watering while plants in large or deep containers will stay watered for at least 5 days or, with the bottom layer of crystals, up to several weeks. But water daily for the first 2 weeks or so after planting any new container garden to which the crystals have been added since it will take some time before roots reach out and avail themselves of the water in the blobs of gel. Manufacturers claim that the gel remains effective up to 5 years, after which it biodegrades. I can't say from my own experience, having used the crystal-gel for only 2 years, during which time the substance has continued doing its job. Water-absorbent crystals allow the gardener to leave for at least a couple of days with the expectation that plants will stay safely moist. But when I am home I still water my container gardens almost daily, if only to keep myself in communication with my plants.

Some mosses and other primitive miniatures require special treatment when they are grown as container plants. Among these are *Sphagnum* mosses and petrophytes of any classification. *Sphagnum* in a container wants a hydroponic life with enough fresh water to keep it saturated, along with timidly dilute fertilizer but no soil. (For more information, see Chapter 14, Portraits, under *Sphagnum*.) The culture of petrophytes in containers is a matter either of adding them to a container landscape along with their mother rock or of planting willing mosses on a suitable rock, as discussed above in this chapter.

The mosses, lichens, and liverworts that grow on trees, logs, or lumber usually will not live if parted from their native wood. Bring them home on their branch, bark, or bit of board and place them (whether in or out of a container) in the same posture—vertical, at an angle, or horizontal—in which they grew naturally (Plate 57). Restoring them to their accustomed posture is usually important to their continuing health.

Location

Sun for the sunny mosses, lichens, and others, shade for the shady, of course. A raised location on the railing of a deck, terrace, or balcony, or on an outdoor table, naturally gives a better view of the container composition than does placement at foot level. The composition that contains "higher" plants in addition to any lesser cryptogams is also *safer* for being raised up, out of the way of many of the appetites that lurk in the open garden at soil level.

Maintenance in Summer

Whether or not water-absorbent crystals are used when planting, most sun-loving species of terrestrial mosses are better with frequent watering when they are grown as container plants, while woodland mosses will enjoy a douse every day during dry weather. Watering almost daily will come as a welcome happenstance in the case of either of these kinds of mosses when they share their container with treelets, shrublets, or tiny flowering perennials, plants that in most cases must be kept moist. But with a container

Plate 57. *Claopodium crispifolium,* one of the world's many bark-inhabiting mosses, carved, bark and plant together, off a fallen, decaying fir tree and displayed on a cross section of log.

in which thirsty plants grow at the base of a rock that bears sunny mosses or lichens sleeping in time of drought (and wanting not to be awakened until cool, rainy weather comes), water selectively by removing the rose from a watering can and directing the stream toward the plants that need it, avoiding the rock with its peaceful sleepers.

Feed the container garden by applying a liquid fertilizer at about 3-week intervals from springtime until early autumn. Use a 5–10–10, 5–15–10, or other fertilizer in moderately potent dilution. (Further suggestions about fertilizing are given in Chapter 8, In Alpine Gardens.) But rock mosses of condensed, mounded habit (*Andreaea, Grimmia,* and others) must never be fed and thereby seduced away from an austere life, rather like that of holy hermits on their rocky perches. With feeding, those plants tend to fatten up, lose their grip on the rock, and blow off in a windstorm. However, other petrophytic mosses of generously spreading growth (such as *Homalothecium* and *Hypnum*) will not mind being fertilized. They don't need it especially, but it won't harm them.

Maintenance in Winter

The mosses, lichens, and other primitives native to a frosty climate stay at their healthiest when exposed to all the wind, rain, and snow of winter, along with the winterish weather of late autumn and early spring (these transitional weeks of chill rain and dampness are main growth seasons for the plants). A container garden that is to be wintered on a balcony in a frosty region is best made up of such hardy plants in a hardy container. If any of the plants are dubiously hardy, however, winter weather can be tempered by covering the garden with a tent of clear plastic or by placing it in a glassed-over box and keeping it shaded to prevent heat from building up in what is now a little greenhouse. Hardy primitives, as a component of the garden, really would rather face the fullest weather but will come through winter in such a cool, shaded greenhouse, although probably with some stretching of stem and softening of leaf.

If ground area is available, empty any winter-susceptible garden from its container on an autumn day before frost comes and plant the garden for the winter in a sheltered place away from sun and drying wind: at the shady side of the house (but rain or applied water must reach and thoroughly dampen the soil there throughout the season), beneath the low-sweeping boughs of an evergreen tree, or in a cool greenhouse or cold frame. In either of the latter two locations the glass may provide enough protection to keep containers from breaking. That would make depotting unnecessary, but don't forget to water.

Usually, a container garden of plants that have been growing together for a summer can be shaken or lifted out of the container easily and intact. Intertwined roots hold the soil mass together. But if the garden does not leave the pot readily, run a knife blade around the inside rim to loosen the soil ball, an operation like the excising of a muffin from a baking pan. This is the time to root-prune any shrublets or flowering perennials in the container garden that have grown tightly congested of root, to be done by using a stiff-bladed butcher knife or a cleaver to slice away 1–1½ inches (2.5–4 cm) of the garden's enmeshed root and soil mass (the larger cut suits the larger garden), all around the sides and at the bottom.

Into the earth now with the root-pruned container garden, at a planting depth that places its soil surface flush with that of the open ground. Come the next spring, the garden is to be lifted entire from the ground (a single plunge-and-pry with the garden spade usually does it) and is then to be repotted in last year's container, with perhaps a replacement of soil at bottom and sides to fill in where earth and roots were pruned away the previous autumn.

The wintering of a garden of mosses or lichens growing on a rock in a container *without* other plants is a much simpler procedure than that just detailed. Take the plant-bearing rock out of any container that would be broken by frost and leave the rock on the railing or outdoor table, or wherever else it summered. Store the pot, and reassemble the container garden the following spring. Of course, if the container is frostproof, or the climate frostfree, the garden ensemble can be left as is for the winter.

Companion Plants

The combining of higher plants, those higher on the evolutionary ladder, with the primitives is not really necessary but is enriching. While mosses, lichens, liverworts, lycopodiums, or selaginellas are capable of carrying a container garden artistically without the inclusion of companion plants, with them the garden gains the capacity of being almost infinitely variable for there are hundreds of the higher-ups, obtainable from nurseries or from Nature, that will fit in companionably.

The prerequisite for any such plant is that it be of a growth habit that will not crowd out mosses and others from the garden. The companion may either be taller, with foliage that forms a slender sheaf or a crown that spreads out well above the low-growers, or the companion may be somewhat moss-like itself, small-leaved and huddled into a bun shape, or of creeping habit and of modest or moderate growth. Whatever its habit, the companion should be a plant not so active as to overwhelm its shipmates in the vessel.

Ideally, the gardener proceeds with knowledge of the potential growth of every plant that goes into the container garden, since plantings assembled without such knowledge almost always contain a thug or two, plants that seem safely small when added but that turn out to be aggressors. In truth, however, I have never known a container landscape gardener (myself included) adequately equipped with knowledge and sensible restraint in selecting plants to be composed in a pot. Such sterling qualities go against the free spirit of the hobby. Our more usual method is to plunge ahead with a bunch of irresistible little plants, little when bought and supposed to be reliably small. Since nursery catalog descriptions are often misleading, we get fooled rather often. It takes years of trial and error in composing plants, and weeding out one's mistakes, before the gardener gains facility. But in the meantime, new and seductive plants come on the market, and thereby the veteran container gardener is made an eternal novice.

Fear not, for I have a number of classic plants to recommend, the names of species I have worked with for years and have indeed found to be workable in containers with mosses, lichens, and other lowlies. Taller plants, with foliage that will nicely clear the lower growers in container gardens, include bonsai trees and shrubs, dwarf conifers, *Hebe lycopodioides* and other whipcord hebes, small heaths such as *Cassiope*, cacti and other succulents of upright habit (and of kinds that can be wintered outdoors in the gardener's climate), and *Nandina* in its extremely dwarf varieties (there are about 200 of these in Japan, a number of which have been imported to North America and Europe).

Companionable miniature perennials include many an alpine bun and creeper, such as *Acorus gramineus* 'Minimus' or *A. gramineus* 'Pusillus', *Allium cyaneum*, *Androsace sempervivoides*, *Antennaria dioica* 'Minima Rubra' or *A. dioica* 'Nyewood', *Bellium minutum*, *Bolax gummifera* (synonym, *B. glebaria*) 'Nana', *Campanula chamissonis* (synonym, *C. pilosa*), *Carmichaelia enysii*, *Equisetum scirpoides* (a spreader), *Genista villarsii*, *Globularia repens* 'Nana', *Iberis pruitii* (synonym, *I. candolleana*), *Lewisia columbiana* subsp. *rupicola*, *Lysimachia japonica* 'Minutissima' (a plant that seeds about both welcomely and unwelcomely, requiring some roguing), *Phlox subulata* 'Ronsdorf Beauty', *Potentilla nitida*, *Primula* ×*forsteri* f. *bilekii*, *Salix alpina*, *Saxifraga hypnoides* 'Densa', *S. paniculata* (synonym, *S. aizoon*) 'Baldensis', and *S. paniculata* 'Minutifolia', *Sedum nevii* and others of the smallest of sedums, *Sempervivum arachnoidium* and other small growers in the genus, any of which will need edging back if they deign to grow (they do not always, for obscure reasons), *Silene acaulis*, *Soldanella alpina* and *S. villosa*, *Solidago multiradiata*, *Thalictrum kiusianum*, *Thymus cilicicus*, *T. serpyllum* 'Minor', and other dwarf thymes, along with *Hypericum yakusimense* and *Viola verrecunda* var. *yakusimana* 'Nana', two from the Japanese island of Yaku, a treasury of little plants such as these.

The list represents only a tiny fraction of plants in catalogs, which are of a stated size that would suit them to our work. As I have said, often we can't really know without tryouts. "Ya pays yer money and ya takes yer chances."

All in the foregoing list of miniatures will survive a hard freeze, most of them down below 0°F (–18°C) when the garden is properly stowed for the winter in a sheltered place (as discussed above, under Maintenance in

Winter). For gardeners in a frostfree climate, who keep their container gardens out in the fullest weather year-around, the repertory of miniatures good with mosses or lichens (especially) includes *Tillandsia*, any of the smaller-growing species in this genus of tender bromeliads. The tillandsias don't like to have their roots in soil but handle well when wedged between rocks, a practical use for lichen-bearing or moss-bearing stones. Rootless tillandsias (plants of the miniature species often come to market without roots, which they seem not to need for any sustenance-gathering purpose, and may never form) are just as usable as rooted individuals. Wedge the basal part of the rootless *Tillandsia* rosette between rocks in the container or glue the plant onto a bare part of a rock by applying almost any kind of waterproof household adhesive to the rock and to the bottom of the rosette, if possible a little to the side of its bull's-eye center, from which roots may yet appear in several years' time.

Another boon, but unhardy, companion for the primitives is *Haworthia fasciata*, one of the steadiest of container plants, capable of dozing along for a quarter-century in a pot without being divided and requiring no more water than does a lichen on a rock, which is to say that rain and dew alone will sustain the *Haworthia*. And when drought comes, this is a plant that will smilingly sleep through weeks of total dryness in full sun (in a desert, however, part shade suits it better). Then there is the tender *Alternanthera ficoidea* 'Magnifica', with tiny, bronze-red leafage especially effective in a container with gray lichens on an upthrusting rock. The *Alternanthera* is a spreader and somewhat of a puff-up, to be kept in bounds by clipping it down to size.

Where any plant I have listed above bears a third name, such as 'Magnifica', after the genus and species names, the third appellation designates a cultivated variety of a species also found in larger versions not to be tried with any hope of compatibility in a miniature container landscape with other plants in close quarters.

For 7 years, winter and summer, I have kept the mossy rock (a fragment of lava) illustrated in Plate 23 in a supposedly unbreakable stoneware pot on a garden railing in North Vancouver, British Columbia. The rock mosses, *Grimmia*, blackish when dry and, after a rain, as bright as green jasper in a brook, are of growth so slow that it seems plausible, from their present size, they were born on this rock 30 or 40 years before I picked it up in arid, scrub juniper country in central Idaho. I count the rock one of my luckier finds in a long career of searching for shapely stones inhabited by mosses and usable in container gardening: Its form suggests the menhir monoliths in Chinese gardens, limestones apparently solidified in tai chi postures. At the base of my Sino-Idaho stone, in lean and gritty subsoil, grows a cushion of a *Tortella* moss brought down from a mountain that overlooks Vancouver and planted in lean, gritty subsoil from its higher home.

The mosses and lichens in my container gardens are all mementos of the near or far places where I found them. A trip to northern tundra remains a living memory in the form of a bushlet of reindeer moss (*Cladonia rangiferina*, Plate 72) that I grow on a receptive rock, a blue-gray block of ancient clay compressed into a stone of exceptional hardness, flat at bottom and slightly saddle-scooped at top. The lichen was surely old when I brought it home to the same deck railing where I grow the *Grimmia*, for at its present 10 inches (25 cm) in diameter the plant shows an increase of only about 2 inches (5 cm) in the decade since I found it. The *Cladonia* is among the most rewarding and troublefree plants I have ever grown, in a container or in the open garden. It is a garden plant sufficient in its oyster-white brightness and in the intricateness of its filigree divisions. I have never felt shorted by the fact that no gardenias will ever pop forth from its branches.

About 7000 miles (11,000 km) to the south I grow other rock lichens in pots on another garden deck railing. The locale is Auckland, New Zealand, where the climate is Mediterranean, with only the lightest of frost, nothing that would break pottery. For 12 years a container garden featuring the lichen *Usnea* (old man's beard) has remained secure on the railing. The plants grow on their native rock (Plate 58), a wedge shape of lava from one of Auckland's many extinct volcanic mounts. (Old lava flows, wherever in the world, are likely places to find petrophytic lichens and mosses.)

Several of the original *Usnea* plants that clung to the rock when I brought it home more than a decade before taking a picture of it still cling. Gusty winds have broken others away as they have reached the end of a normal life span of about 15 years. Infant usneas have sprouted to take the place of departing oldsters. Coming and going, the plant will be capable of perpetuating itself on the rock indefinitely, as long as it is provided with sunlight, pure air, rain, and perpendicularity. Usneas are danglers in midair, like the long beard their English name commemorates, or like the well-known Spanish moss (*Tillandsia usnoides*), which is named after *Usnea*. As to the identity of this particular *Usnea* species, one of a genus of plants so

Plate 58. A hanging garden of beard-like *Usnea* lichens on lava. Companions in the pot include *Cotula* (with feathered leaves) and a gray succulent, *Echeveria elegans.*

similar that even lichenologists often come up from their microscopes unsure, perhaps only another *Usnea* needs to know.

Plate 59 provides an example of a type of container gardening with the most minute of mosses, *mame* mosses, as I call them, adapting a term from the lexicon of bonsai art. A *mame* (pronounced ma′mae) is a bonsai of tiny proportions; at maturity it may be as small as 1 inch (2.5 cm) tall, or not

Plate 59. *Mame* mosses, named and described in the text.

more than a few inches. A *mame* moss is one small enough to fit comfortably into a *mame* pot, a moss perhaps best displayed as a *mame* although not necessarily in a traditional Japanese container.

Even so, the pot in the photograph is an example of classical *mame* crockery, 3 inches (7.5 cm) in diameter (interior dimension). Within it grow four mosses: *Barbula convoluta*, a bright yellow-green tuft, here less than $\frac{1}{16}$ inch (1.5 mm) tall, and no bigger around than a lawn daisy; *Ditrichum heteromallum*, broomy of leaf, with plover-billed spore cases; a *Tortula* species, its leaves (with brief hair points) in starry, *Sempervivum*-like rosettes; and *Bryum argenteum*, with silvery scale leaves pressed against branches that are like stubby, reptilian tails.

The combination of a silvery gray plant and a yellowish one is horticultural heresy, of course, a bilious color mismatch, except perhaps if you are an artist with liberated sensibilities. Ordinarily, I would be too tame to go in for such a fauvist combination. But that is the way the plants came from nature. They were all growing, just as you see, in one small sod, in hard ground and hot sun, at the edge of a garden path. It is unusual to find as many as four mosses growing companionably in so small a ground area. Two or even three may alight and grow chockablock, but four, almost never.

Finding them special, I lifted them as one with my collecting knife, taking them up together with a deep piece of their substrate, the better to minimize the curling of the sod when planted in a pot and allowed (for reasons given below) to become dry in dry weather.

The four neighbors were placed, as shown, in the *mame* pot, bedded in with a little extra of their native soil, a fine gravel with a minor component of clay that I had bagged up and brought along. Toward the rim of the pot, where the moss did not quite fill the space, I sifted in (from the tip of a teaspoon) some selected, relatively weighty grains of the fine gravel as a top-dressing for the soil beneath to keep it from being blasted out of the pot by hard rain. Natural precipitation is all of the moisture that the mosses in their pot ever receive. They are used to summer drought and may require it for their well-being. In winter wet and cold, this pot garden has sometimes become icy, yet the pot has survived the freezing. I think that the gravelly porosity of the soil within the container helps prevent ice pressure from building up, as does the shallowness of the pot.

As containers for *mame* mosses, I also use commonplace red clay saucers of the kind one buys at garden centers and ordinarily places beneath flower pots to catch excess water. Before being planted with mosses these saucers must be drilled to provide a drainage hole ½–1 inch (13–25 mm) in diameter. I must confess that I am too much of an elegance snob to use plastic saucers, which would work even better, in that they are usually frostproof and are certainly easier to drill than terra cotta.

Once, I made a *mame* moss container out of a 2-foot (60-cm) length of a thick board that had floated ashore as driftwood, eroded, sculptured, and silvered by its knockabout life. The conversion of board into planter required a woodworker's chisels and mallet (borrowed), with which I gouged into the board five free-form pool-shaped basins, provided them with drainage holes, and connected the basins in several places with narrow channels. In three of the basins I arranged small stones bedded in soil. Finally, I planted the soil around the rocks and in the other basins with *mame* mosses. Results: not bad. If I were to overcome false modesty I might even say, Wonderful! The annual tree growth lines in the silvered board suggested ripples in water or sand; the stony and mossed areas, islands and peninsulas.

I had made this *mame* moss planter with the thought of giving it to a gardener friend who I knew would appreciate it. But I got to liking it so much that I hated to part with it and had quite a few bouts with myself,

Kid Generous versus Kid Gimme, which went on for weeks until the nice guy finally won out.

After having written the above paragraphs on *mame* mosses I read an article ("Creating a Miniature Landscape with Mosses," *Bonsai Magazine*, January–February 1995) concerning a related type of moss gardening carried on in Japan. In 22 color plates this article shows the completed compositions of five artists in tray landscaping entirely with mosses, a branch of *saikei* gardening. The making of one such landscape is shown step by step.

None of the compositions portrayed uses more than three kinds of moss, the idea being to present a cool green tranquillity that would be upset by the more jazzy employ of many mosses. The three mosses are not named, but *Bryum argenteum* appears to be the main species in all the *saikei* gardens in view. Scattered tufts of *Polytrichum* moss are used are stand-ins for tree groves, and I believe I see occasional domes of *Leptobryum* bearing spore capsules, the stemmy presence of which, in this setting, imparts to the moss the size and presence of shrubbery.

Clumps of the three moss species are fitted edge to edge in the shallowest of bonsai trays, about 1 inch (2.5 cm) high, oval or rounded in form, about 7–13 inches (13–33 cm) in diameter. Within the container, moss clumps are pressed onto a mixture of sphagnum and a pelletized clay called *akadama* soil. The sphagnum, dry and finely chopped, is sprinkled over a basal bed of akadama, watered, and washed down among the bits of clay. In order to fit the mosses in the shallow tray, the collected clumps are first turned upside down and pared free of much of the native soil that clings to them. For this the artists use a miniature, spatula-like tool with a sharpened edge.

Now, all of this evokes in me an affection and an awe for Japanese artists in bonsai, and maybe even for the traditionalists around the world who follow them; their finicky practices fascinate me. Yet I know from my own work with mosses as bonsai ground covers and in *mame* compositions that a gardener usually does not need to remove soil from collected moss, except perhaps to pare an especially thick plant to fit an especially shallow container. Nor is there, in my experience, any particular need for akadama and sphagnum, if instead you can find and use a porous, fast-draining soil or can make one of sand, loam, and humus (as discussed above, under The Soil).

To return to the sampler of container gardens of my own making, Plate

Plate 60. A bowl of water surrounds a rock island forested with the moss *Distichium capillaceum*.

60 shows a mossy rock in a bowl of water, a container garden that makes a good taking-off point for the viewer's meditations on the immensities. For the garden is a sweep of the planet, watery, mineral, and green, in a small package. I keep this little world atop a low wall in community with the rush *Cyperus alternifolius*, with ferns, and with *Selaginella kraussiana* (between the stones of a stepway that leads to the wall. I wish I had a more protected place for the garden, a screened porch perhaps. Where I have it, out in the open, Murphy's Law is always ready to pounce. Birds perch on the rock or on the bowl rim and drink, or they hop down in and take a bath, which does the moss no good. Mosquitoes drop their eggs in the water, evidenced by the sudden manifestation of their wigglers. Algae delight in the nutritious soup the water soon becomes, greening both bowl and water. I can control algae and mosquitoes by changing the water frequently. But the birds will finish off this garden the day one of them decides to start picking at it. It is only a matter of time. For protection, I would have to keep the garden covered with netting, which would ill suit this particular

opuscule of mine. Netted, it would not look like anything, except maybe a miniature Christo artwork. My resolution of this dilemma is to relax and enjoy the garden while it lasts. But the saving grace of photography will help out. Having a picture (Plate 61) to see and to show makes any garden, in a sense, permanent.

The Mossy Terrarium

Mosses, lichens, and other primitives brought from the woods are sometimes capable of living for years (even of growing) in a terrarium kept outdoors in shade. A shady balcony or porch is perfect, in providing a safe platform for the container and a convenient one for the gardener while serving up shade steadily the year-around. In a sealed terrarium kept outdoors, one can try any of the feathery mosses and others that fail in the open-air garden because of insufficient humidity.

Before I go any further with encouragements, however, I must tell the whole truth by identifying the great enemy of terrarium gardening with native woodlanders, for there is one: mold. One may be able to discourage the growth of mold by keeping the garden only moist, not overly wet. If mold does appear one *may* be able to control it by using a fungicide. But most terraria (especially those kept indoors) are of limited life and eventual demise due to mold. (Photographs we see in garden literature, of plants bright and healthy and compactly growing in a terrarium, are usually of inmates that have been assembled hours before the picture-taking.) Still, there can be an entirely satisfying garden adventure in the making and viewing of even a short-lived terrarium garden.

A large container is best for a terrarium garden, say, one of about fish tank size. A container the size of a fish bowl will also work, but one any smaller will not work well. The need is for air space within the terrarium. An insufficient breathing space tends to cause the drowning of plants in excessively wet air and fosters the growth of mold. The air needs to circulate somewhat in response to changing temperature, condensing its moisture, taking it back, altering humidity by a wholesome degree.

A couple of inches (5 cm) of any light and airy commercial potting mix (that is lime-free) can be placed at the bottom of the container before arranging the plants. Such mixes, while not the best for open-air gardening with mosses, are perfectly good in a terrarium. Or use leaf mold or compost that has been thoroughly heated in a microwave to kill hidden insects. But if the terrarium garden consists principally of mosses deep with their

Plate 61. Mossy rocks, container gardens in themselves, arranged as a sculptural baluster at the head of an outdoor stairway.

old browning stem portions, no additional rooting medium is needed. Crushed charcoal, mixed in generously with any made-up rooting medium, is helpful for its ability to absorb excessive acidity and detrimental gases formed by natural decay in the medium.

If mosses are collected in moist condition, the terrarium probably will not require added water; if the mosses seem dryish, add 2 or 3 tablespoons (30–45 ml); and if they are totally dry, add about ¼ cup (70 ml). Then, seal the container, using plastic wrap if there is no lid. Next morning, and the morning after that, examine the terrarium for heavily beaded, excessive moisture condensed on the inside walls of the container. Wipe it away, and reseal. On the third morning there should be a remaining light coating of condensation on the upper half of the container's walls: this is the correct amount of water with which the plants will sustain themselves, probably for the lifetime of the garden. But if, after a few weeks, this light film of moisture is not there in the morning, add water. Easy does it. The plants are better for being a bit dry than too wet. Take special care that an outdoor terrarium garden is not overly wet during frosty winter weather since the formation of ice could shatter the container.

While, as I have claimed, a terrarium garden kept outdoors is capable of long life, an indoor terrarium, at least one planted with woodlanders from North America or elsewhere in the world's temperate zones rather than from the tropics, makes a short-term hobby. Such a planting is usually good for 3 weeks at most, after which the stretching of plant stems (somewhat controllable by using fluorescent lights), the growth of mold, and decay may take place rapidly.

But the first week or two of the indoor terrarium can be magic, especially for children. Once, a niece and a nephew of mine helped me plant a terrarium to be displayed in the family's living room. We used mosses, lichens, and yearling ferns we had found on a hunt for such minikins. We had marched along a woodland trail while singing "A-hunting we will go," to the disapproving chatter of chipmunks. Back home, we arranged the plants in a bell jar. During the 2 weeks that followed, the children (I am told, for I was not on hand) stood still for actual minutes every day to study the plants. Call it moss mesmerism, the minutes of which are worth hours of television.

After a couple of weeks in a warm room, the mosses and ferns had etiolated considerably. The children were excited over this change, seeing it as healthy growth, but of course it was not. I suggested that it would be great fun, now, to liberate all the plants. And it was. The three of us went back to the woods and restored the flagging ferns and mosses, and the stoical lichens, to their original places, as nearly as we could find them. If we had had a place to keep the terrarium outdoors, some of those plants might still be prospering within it these years later. The magic might still be there for me, but for those children, entering childhood's sobering old age, I wonder, Have they been blessed with the gift of rejuvenation? That gift is the best toy I have ever had, and an essential tool for the landscape gardener.

CHAPTER ELEVEN

Bonsai Mosses

WITH THE addition of a compatible moss, the bonsai tree in its container becomes settled and soothed in a green landscape, seemingly suspended there for a long interval without human intervention (Plate 62). Ground-inhabiting or rock-clinging mosses of especially low, dense habit and minute foliage are the best for use as ground covers beneath bonsai trees. The mosses *Antitrichia* (Plate 63), *Bryum, Homalothecium, Hypnum, Leptobryum,* and *Pohlia* are among those that have been tested and have won approval by bonsai artists. Many other kinds that are almost sure to be suitable remain untested. Such mosses are to be found in almost any setting, fields and glades, pathsides or mountainsides, even in the city. Look for them especially on rather bare ground of low fertility, where competing weeds or native plants are sparse and dwarfed, leaving sunny space available to the mosses. Sun-loving mosses are the kinds usually needed in bonsai culture, the exception being the moss companion for the tree kept in shade. The other need is for a kind of moss that, in the fertile living conditions of the planted bonsai pot, will remain for a year or more small enough of leaf and compressed enough of stem to enhance, rather than dispel, the bonsai illusion of arboreal stateliness in petite scale.

In the city, look for joggers' mosses. These are as good as any and better than most for bonsai culture. Joggers' mosses? A bonsai artist friend of mine (now deceased) invented the term and specialized in these plants, using them beneath many of her dozens of potted trees. Joggers' mosses

Plate 62. A moss meadow (*Dicranella heteromalla*) and a lone hemlock (*Tsuga*, a pre-bonsai) in a driftwood boat that sailed away. In actual fact, it was pirated: somebody walked off with this garden (Chapter 14 tells all).

made the perfect bonsai carpeting, according to her lights, and to find them my friend Connie would follow the hard-breathers, not too closely, along their chosen paths and sidewalks, to gather patches of *Bryum* and *Leptobryum* that had been hammered down by sneaker-shod feet to the thinness of a graham cracker (attached soil included). Connie would scrape them up in pieces as large as she could manage to keep intact, using a spatula from her kitchen, or, for prying mosses out of crevices, a paring knife. The more compressed the moss patch, the better Connie liked it as a ground cover beneath her bonsai trees. Her reasoning was that the lower the moss, the more visible the impressively thick part of the bonsai trunk toward soil level. The moss, liberated from a sidewalk life of constant thumpings, would fluff up to a height of about ¾ inch (20 mm). Connie never let her bonsai mosses grow higher than that. She kept them pruned, using manicure scissors. With pruning, the plants' container life and good looks could be prolonged for years.

My friend never saw eye to eye with me on the suitability of some of my own bonsai bryophytes; they seemed to her too coarse. Every time she

Plate 63. Maple grove mossed with *Antitrichia curtipendula,* one of the neatest species for use beneath bonsai. In place 2 years, it has grown only ½ inch (13 mm) deep. The maples (*Acer palmatum*) are siblings that I collected as seedlings some 30 years ago, from beneath a parental tree in our garden, and then planted together. The conifer grove in the background (*Picea glauca* 'Conica') is composed of 62-year-old trees, the tallest of which peaks at 13 feet 3 inches (4 meters 4 cm).

dropped by to see what I had been up to with my bonsai trees and mosses, she would give me a cluck-cluck critique. In these trying moments, I would call her Banty, an old-time country-American name for a pint-size but pugnacious breed of chicken properly known as bantam. For while the physical Connie stood less than 5 feet (1.5 meters) tall, the verbal one rose as a tower fortified with slings and arrows of outraged opinion. She (who got even by calling me Mr. Shag, or simply Shagmeister, heartless plays upon my surname along with reference to the mosses I used) especially could not abide my use of the moss *Polytrichum piliferum* beneath a grove planting of bonsai maples. In my list of approved bonsai mosses at the beginning of the chapter, I omitted this one out of deference to dear old Banty, but I still use an especially compact, alpine form of the species that I collected in the early 1960s and have propagated by division ever since.

Even with pruning (I use household scissors), *Polytrichum piliferum*, like my friend's beloved joggers' mosses, and probably all other kinds one might find and use, eventually grows too tall for bonsai work. When the time comes, the moss is to be peeled from beneath the tree and replaced with younger, tidier material. In removing established moss from a bonsai composition, often I find that rootlets of the tree or trees have grown upward into the moss. This is not a problem, but in this circumstance the moss cannot be peeled off. Instead, the tree roots, together with the living moss and the turf of older, decayed moss beneath, must be clipped away, using pruning shears. The minor loss of roots incurred in this operation has never harmed my bonsai. I usually perform the surgery during a moist time of early spring before the bursting into leaf of the tree's winter buds. (This business is not the same as that of the major root-pruning of bonsai, which is done by clipping away roots from the bottom and the sides of the root mass, not from the top. My own preferred time for that job is in autumn.)

Connie wintered her trees in their pots and with their moss intact, within a cold frame. My method of winterization is quite different. I de-pot my trees along with their mosses and plant the two as a unit in the open ground for the winter, burying the root mass only up to the level of the moss in the case of such hardy trees as maples, but deeper, sacrificing an edgewise inch (2.5 cm) or so of moss in burying the roots of a bonsai less certainly root-hardy. Another of my bonsai, of the juniper clone named *shimpaku*, a treelet known for hardiness, grows in a frostproof container (a large, concave rock) with the mosses *Dicranum flagellare*, *Pohlia* (of some kind), and

Plate 64. *Shimpaku* (*Juniperus sargentii*), 30-something of age, surrounded by a parterre of the mosses *Dicranum, Pohlia,* and *Polytrichum piliferum* (with spore cases). Placed here as sods 3 years before, they have grown about as high as an index finger is deep when plunged down into them, but are not yet out of scale with the tree and the container, a 27-inch- (69-cm-) long, concave stone. The use of more than one kind of moss would perhaps be too busy in a smaller container, but in this rangy composition, with a tree-in-training that is not yet very grand, the moss garden beneath provides about one-third of the show; the rock, one-third; the tree, the remaining third.

Polytrichum piliferum as ground covers. The ensemble of rock, tree, and mosses is displayed year-around on a terrace railing (Plate 64).

Mosses help protect the roots of bonsai from frost and drought, but the mosses themselves drink up a great amount of water. The gardener must be lavish in watering to be sure both tree and moss get enough. Check on this by lifting the tree out of its pot. How is the moisture supply toward the bottom of the root mass? Of course, one can make this test only with a bonsai tree and accompanying moss that are well enough established in their container that their underground parts form a soil-clutching mass.

The arrival of *Marchantia* or *Conocephalum* liverworts on the moss turf is bad news. Remove these pests with tweezers or the tip of a knife blade, the sooner the better. They would spread and take over. These particular liverworts are ones that you may all too soon come to recognize. Their pad-form leaves sprawl flat on the soil surface or on top of mosses, to their ruin.

Propagation from Fragments

Certain bonsai mosses can be increased into pot-covering quantities from mere fragments of their leafy stems. There are two methods: by sowing or by slurrying.

Sowing. Sowing works best with those mosses that, when dry, crumble readily into bits. *Bryum* and *Leptobryum*, among others, are likely candidates for such propagation. Suitable mosses, if moist when collected, can be spread out on newspapers indoors and left to dry. Use them soon after or, if need be, store them. I have found that desiccated mosses of the kinds named above, and others that live in sun or part shade and dry out to a shriveled condition in hot summer weather, can be stored indefinitely. As an experiment I once collected samples of such mosses, sealed them crispy dry but not pulverized, in plastic bags, and stored them in a box within a room heated for human comfort. One year later I took them outdoors and planted them. They quickly greened up and grew. I have a hunch that the interval of estivation could have been stretched into years. But in the same experiment, a variety of shade-loving woodland mosses fared less well. Most kinds were dead or damaged after a year of desiccation.

The propagation of moss from fragments usually takes at least several months, even a year or more (as discussed in Chapter 7, Moss Carpets, under Method Five). If the site of propagation is in the open air with all its weather, the best time to sow moss fragments is at the beginning of a cool, rainy season, which will stimulate growth: in autumn or spring, or right through the winter, as well, in a region where the season is usually not icy and growth-stopping.

The job calls for a screen with a mesh of about ¼ to ⅜ inch (6–10 mm) through which to rub the moss, a nursery flat or some other shallow box with holes or a slot for drainage at the bottom (or in the case of propagation on the smallest scale, a flower pot or two), a moistened rooting medium (called soil hereafter), an empty jar or something else to flatten the soil in its container, and enough cheesecloth to cover the soil. (But there is another way of using cheesecloth, an older Chinese method. See Chapter 7, Moss Carpets, under Method Five.)

Use as soil one or another of the kinds—commercial, native soil, or homemade mix—that are detailed in Chapter 10, In Containers, under The Soil. If adding polymer crystals, the small size is preferable to the medium. Avoid any commercial potting mix that contains vermiculite or perlite, materials that cause the mix to be too loose and scatterable to be good for propagating moss from tiny bits, which are all too easily knocked about. Spread the soil in the flat or box to a depth of about 1¼ inches (3 cm), after compression. That depth is perhaps the minimum that can be kept moist by watering manually whenever rain does not do the job. But in propagating moss within a cool greenhouse where a misting system is used, a shallower depth of soil, about ¾ inch (2 cm) or even less, is practical and preferable in that the propagated moss will make a shorter ground cover for the bonsai tree. Flatten and lightly compress the soil within the container, using a mayonnaise jar as a roller, or a bit of board, or a book you don't much like (not this one, surely).

Spread a single thickness of cheesecloth (obtainable at stores that specialize in fabrics) smoothly on top of the soil and secure its edges by poking them down into the soil all along the inner edges of the container. Then give the cheesecloth and soil a final flattening, making sure the two are everywhere in contact. Scatter the pulverized dry moss generously over the cheesecloth. A peppering as thick as that of sesame seed on a bun would not be too much.

Place the prepared container in half, or full, sun (for any of the sun-loving mosses, which are usually the ones most suited to bonsai). If placed in the open air the container may receive pelting rain at times, causing some of the moss particles to be dashed away, but the moss that remains will be neatly shortened by wind and rough weather, an asset in bonsai culture. Or keep the container in a cold frame, or a cool, well-ventilated greenhouse, or on a sunny indoor windowsill if the window can be kept ajar so that a certain amount of weather reaches the moss.

Water the newly scattered moss gently to keep it from washing away.

If the irrigation is done with a watering can, use a fine rose, or better yet, use a mist-maker (for delicate watering I use a misting bottle that I reclaimed after the bug-killer that came in it had been used up). In the daily watering or frequent raining the moss must receive, the cheesecloth helps prevent the majority of the moss particles from being blasted away during those sensitive first weeks before they take firm root.

Possibly within a year's time or even less, the growing moss will become dense and durable enough to lift as a green sheet ready for transplanting. With scissors, cut the green sheet to fit the bonsai composition, and press the moss upon the soil within the bonsai pot. On steeply sloped soil, secure the moss with toothpicks, the flat wooden kind, bent double into V shapes.

If bonsai trees are grown in a cool greenhouse, there is a shortcut to all this from the start. Merely dust the pulverized moss liberally over the soil surface at the base of the bonsai in its container, water gently, and wait. If the dusting of dry moss is thick enough, there will not even be a wait for effect. With the first watering the moss will green up instantly, will at once seem almost a natural carpet and will soon enough become one.

Slurrying. Slurrying is the method by which to fragment and propagate bonsai mosses that do not break up easily into bits. It will work with some, not with others, but is worth a try with any. For slurry propagation one needs pieces of a suitable moss totaling at least the size of a pancake, a large jar with a lid, a few blobs of a specially made mud, a kitchen blender, and maybe a piece of cheesecloth and several bricks (both these materials will be used in only one of the alternative methods of planting described below).

Start by placing in a jar a pound (0.4–0.5 kg) or so of finely particled leaf mold (no chunky stuff), or acidic garden loam, or decently old barnyard manure. Fill the jar two-thirds full with water, screw on the lid, and shake the jar. Wait briefly for solids to settle and floatables to rise. Pour off the flotsam together with all the murky water, keeping back the muddy material at the bottom.

Next, stuff the moss, thoroughly moist, into a kitchen blender. Add about a cup (280 ml) of the mud from the jar after carefully separating from it any pebbles. By using a spoon to dig not too deeply into the mud in the jar, lurking bits of rock can be avoided, for such will tend to settle to the very bottom. Blend the moss and mud briefly. The mixture should be pourable but not too thin, about like pancake batter. If necessary, add water and blend again.

That is all there is to the making of a moss-mud slurry, except perhaps for a need of privacy. I for one would want to be alone in the kitchen for the performing of this dirty work, and after having rinsed the blender ever so thoroughly would say not a word about what I had been up to, not to anyone who uses the blender for more orthodox products.

Now the mud and moss mixture can be spread thinly on the soil of the planted bonsai tree in its pot and then kept gently watered. With growth, the moss will form a seamless cover. Or, the mixture can be spread on top of bricks, the unglazed kind, which should then be kept in shallow water within a pan. The idea is for the brick to draw water upward, constantly supplying the regenerating moss, with no need for watering from over-head. A layer of cheesecloth placed between the brick and the mossy mud at the time of planting will help later in transplanting the full green pelt of moss from the brick to the tree base. Merely peel off the live fabric and plant it as handy pieces cut to shape.

Propagation by Spores

Nature has maintained constant renewal in each species of moss these many millions of years by counting on perhaps one spore in a million, in the yearly outpouring, to catch hold and grow. The rest are all sacrificed to chance. Any artificial means of germinating moss, and maturing it until it reaches a plantable stage of growth, is likewise chancy. The project is a lot less likely to end in success than is the raising of beans from seed.

One can go about the sowing of mosses with clinical care, as bryologists sometimes do, by using nutrient gel as a medium for spore germination, test tubes for containers, and fluorescent tubes for lighting. Or one can go about it with a more rustic low technology, relying on soil and sunshine, as I have done and recommend doing. A procedure that, for me, has brought success in several tryouts (although not with a uniformly high yield of plants each time) begins with legwork in the wild. The spores must be found, since they can't be bought. None of the right kind is for sale, it seems. I have studied the sales lists of all the mail-order nurseries I can find (six) that sell moss spores. Their offerings included nothing suitable for bonsai.

Once spore-bearing mosses that one would like to use under bonsai trees are located, use scissors to clip off the spore capsules, drop them into a jar (which should be perfectly dry on the inside) and put the lid on it. The spore capsules must be ripe and yellowing or browning, but not too old and empty. Tap a few of the capsules with your fingertips. If the spores they hold are ripe and ready for harvest, tiny spore clouds will emerge for an instant before dissipating. Early summer is the harvest season for the spores of some mosses, autumn for some others.

At home, pour about ½ cup (140 ml) of dry sand or dry, pulverized soil into the jar with the spore capsules, cover, and shake the jar vigorously. Then shake out the contents over a soil-filled container.

Container, soil, cheesecloth, location, the watering and the await, the cutting to shape with scissors, the placing of the spore-grown moss in the bonsai composition, all is the same as in the production of bonsai moss by the sowing of dry fragments. Except that moss gardening here reaches its greatest finesse.

From Out of the Blue

Surprise: All of the fiddling fine work outlined above in this chapter may be avoidable. There may be—no, there is, in an especially moss-inducing climate and garden—a way to be-moss bonsai effortlessly, by relying on the aerial arrival of moss by spores. It is a process that grabs my imagination mightily. Elsewhere, I have spoken of moss spores as sailors in space vessels. But here, given the fey ethereality of bonsai art, they seem more a kind of heavenly host. From out of the blue, moss spores come down like microscopic angels (countless thousands will fit on the head of a pin). Having arrived, they metamorphose and eventually green-garb the soil beneath one's bonsai. Sometimes this works even better than the best human efforts, in supplying, with superhuman niftiness, just the right moss.

Some bonsai artists rely altogether on the aerial arrival of moss. It is either the heaven-sent article, or none. Such artists, including many professionals with hundreds or thousands of potted pre-bonsai (young trees in early stages of training) to take care of until they are sold, find no time or inclination to moss their trees. They merely let whatever moss or mosses will come, come on their own. Sometimes these arrive soon enough; at other times and places they never show up. If heavenly mosses are ever to grace one's trees, the first traces of mossy green will usually begin to appear on the soil surface at the base of the bonsai within about 6 months after the potting of the tree. The full greening of the soil will probably take 2 years.

One commercial layout of pre-bonsai in pots, thousands of trees-in-training at the nursery of Marilyn Beauregard and Robert Hearst, supports no fewer than nine kinds of heavenly mosses (none has been planted). These range in size from nicely small, in suitable scale (*Antitrichia, Barbula, Dicranella, Hypnum,* and *Leptobryum*), to somewhat oversize in the circumstances but probably acceptable to some eyes (*Atrichum*), to decidedly too big and boisterous in growth to companion a small potted tree (*Polytrichum juniperinum* and *Rhytidiadelphus loreus*), to downright messy (*Ceratodon*, massed over with spent, brown stems carrying spore capsules).

In this nursery, the fullest, most effective development of these mosses as ground covers has taken place at the base of pre-bonsai potted several years before and maintained on tables in a lathhouse within a sunny clearing surrounded by tall trees that help keep humidity high. This setup in daylong patterned shade and sun is clearly ideal for the inadvertent attraction, and lasting health, of mosses of many kinds.

Certain other growers, who tend collections of magnificent, decades-old or centuries-old bonsai, also count on the divine mossing of their trees. It is the means relied upon almost exclusively, for example, in the upkeep of the finest display of bonsai in a public garden on the West Coast of North America, the Pacific Rim Bonsai Collection, located on Weyerhaeuser Company acreage in Federal Way, Washington, south of Seattle. The curator of the collection, David J. De Groot, finds that the local naturally mossy, maritime climate, plus the constant application of fertilizer to the potted trees, stimulates moss growth sufficiently that manual mossing is rarely necessary.

The Pacific Rim bonsai are maintained in pluperfect health by methods that are as modern and technological as the means still employed by many growers in Japan are traditional and charming. In Japan, the trees may still be grown in actual soil, even in a miniaturized profile of natural soil, subsoil toward the bottom, topsoil appropriately on top. There, the trees may still be fertilized with little soybean custards placed on the moss at the base of the bonsai, where they remain for months in moldering dabs ever so remindful of bird droppings.

But at Pacific Rim all that has been scrapped: no such quaint, catch-as-catch-can fertilizing, and no soil at all. The trees are grown with a science that is halfway like hydroponics. The medium about their roots is made up, 40–60 percent, of conifer bark ground up finely, and the rest of it of builder's sand and crushed lava in equal parts. For some trees, clay, fired and crushed, is used instead of lava. The trees are fertilized once a week from March through October, a span of seasons within which, in the local climate, late-winter frosts are few and oncoming autumn frosts have hardly begun. The feedings are light, about one-third the dosage usually recommended for houseplants. Pacific Rim gardeners use a water-soluble commercial fertilizer containing a small amount of nitrogen along with phosphorus, potash, and added trace elements to which the gardeners add extra potassium (potassium nitrate) and also lime (calcium nitrate). Several mosses that are known calciphiles or are apparently lime-tolerant come in and thrive beneath the trees, among them *Bryum argenteum, Leptobryum pyriforme*, and a *Pohlia.*

It seems a good bet that many other mosses, very possibly most kinds, could be cultivated and kept in fine fettle by essentially the same rooting, feeding, and watering methodology outlined above. Bark (or sawdust or peat) and grit of some sort, water, and fertilizer as needed, are, after all, the recipe by which the nursery industry grows almost every kind of plant ever brought into cultivation. Mosses will almost certainly prove just as growable by these slim means, which will serve gardeners who disfavor natural soils for container gardening or who have no ready access to them. For the majority of mosses, just leave out the lime.

But you should see the response to that element by those several lime-guzzling mosses at Pacific Rim, especially in the silver of the silvery *Bryum*, which takes on a brighter burnish there. Curator De Groot admires this moss above all others for its year-around neatness in pots with bonsai (other mosses tend to puff up during spring growth and spore production) and for its silvery sheen, so complementary to gray-green conifers.

The Pacific Rim Bonsai Collection is one of a number of outstanding public displays of bonsai in North America. Among the others are the National Bonsai Museum at the U.S. National Arboretum in Washington, D.C., and the collections at the Jardin Botanique de Montréal, Canada, and the Brooklyn Botanic Garden, New York. Heroic little trees are maintained in all these places, where one may find effective mossing of the bonsai by both heavenly assist and the mundane, manual techniques described here.

CHAPTER TWELVE

Transportable Trophies

MOSSES, lichens, and other cryptogams, collected on a trip, make elegant souvenirs of travel. No little gimcrack replicas of the Eiffel Tower or of Mickey Mouse, these. Rather, they are tokens rare and tasteful beyond price (Plate 65). In fact, you could not buy them if you tried. And so, bits and pieces of any likable, lowly plants that one discovers in trekking the world are apt to be wrapped in a tissue and pocketed, or (in the case of the premeditative, prepared collector) plastic-bagged and satcheled. We collectors must, of course, take care to prevent the importation of pests along with our trophies. We must, as well, give the plants protective care during the trip and afterward at home.

On motor trips during summer, mosses and any of the other primitive miniatures that have been collected when dry and dormant should be left dry for the trip and kept away from heat as much as possible. Then, too, they must be kept in a place where they will not get crushed. Where to put them? If one travels with friends or family in a vehicle packed to the gunnels (the usual situation), there may yet be one remaining spot of available space and safety: beneath the front seat. This happens to be one of the better places even if the vehicle is not crowded, a location insulated from direct sun and below the worst of the buildup of heat when the vehicle is parked with windows closed. But be sure, before placing plants upon it, that the floor does not heat up with the running of the engine.

Plants that are to be stashed under the seat should be closed in bags or

Plate 65. Ten little cryptogams—mainly mosses—gathered on a trip, planted with leaf mold in a shallow ceramic pan (at lower right). Above the mosses is a bowl in which water fern (*Azolla*) floats. Arching over the water are the ferns, *Adiantum aethiopicum* and the palm-like *Sticherus flabellatus* (synonym, *Gleichenia flabellata*). Ferns and mosses make boon companions.

wrapped in newspaper or cloth to keep any draft from reaching them, since a breeze from the vehicle's air vent or air-conditioning could be damaging. On arrival home, the summer-dry plants, set out in the open, will wake up quickly and start growing (or start thinking about it) as soon as autumn rains have begun.

Mosses and other primitive miniatures collected in *moist* condition are especially sensitive to heat during travel. Seal them in plastic bags and place them on ice in a portable food cooler, if you can squeeze them in. Small hope, so I find in my own travels with friends. Soft drinks or wine and cheese take precedence. In that circumstance, my only recourse has been to place any moist plants under the seat.

Interstate Shipment and Importation from Abroad

Primitive plants, collected dry, boxed up, and shipped by mail or a parcel service, are usually unharmed even by a month or more of travel time. Plants in moist condition may be safe in a box for a week or so (if not over-heated anywhere en route). They fare better if they are only slightly moist rather than wet.

According to the letter of the law, plants sent interstate or driven across state borders are supposed to have been inspected and documented as being free from disease and pests. California, Arizona, and another state or two, as I recall, stop all vehicles at their borders (as you perhaps know full well) and ask if any fruit or plants are being carried. The essential concern is over crop plants such as oranges, apples, and cotton, along with certain ornamentals, such as *Mahonia*, known to harbor pests and diseases of particular danger in the state. The inspector might let other, apparently innocuous plants go through—or might not. Much depends on the judgment and disposition of the person one deals with.

Customs declarations of many countries bear plant import restrictions that are similar to those of each of the United States. But what specific regulations may apply to gardeners who enter the United States from another country carrying mosses and the like, I can't say. But I did try fairly hard to find out. I sent a letter to the people in charge: the Animal and Plant Health Inspection Service, Hyattsville, Maryland. The letter read, in part,

> I would like to be able to inform my readers about the legality of importing these plants from other countries into the United States. Mosses collected from woodland usually have leafmold adhering

to them. Will it be legal to bring this in with the plants? Other mosses (and liverworts and lichens) grow on stone and usually cannot be removed from it without killing the plant. Is it legal to import these plants on their native rocks? Will an import permit be required?

Such inquiry would seem worth a reply, would it not? But none came. After waiting 6 months I sent the same letter again. Additional months passed with still no reply, and none expected by now.

Another mosserian, Michael Fletcher of Reading, England, author of the *Moss Grower's Handbook*, reports a similar lack of concern among civil servants in his own country: "I once enquired at a Customs office about getting an import license for live mosses. Someone made a remark (I think a facetious one) about checking the regulation for fungi, but otherwise aroused no interest at all."

I have an inkling that the answers may not be in the books, since the questions may never have been raised officially. We seem to be on our own when it comes to sending or bringing these plants home from abroad. Should we declare them on package labels or to customs people? Yes, indeed, we should. Some travelers may feel inclined to keep mum about carrying plants as small and apparently harmless as mosses—but that very well may be dangerous, as I show below. As for myself, when I confront customs I turn into a twitching suspect, even when I have nothing to conceal. If I were to try to sneak in some little thing, I am sure my state of mind would show as if spelled out in flashing neon: Guilty! Guilty! So I attempt not the least infraction.

Coming home from England once, I decided I must declare the mosses and lichens I had with me, sealed in plastic bags. Forthrightly, I ticked off the appropriate box in the "yes" column on the customs declaration, where it said, Do you have plants, seeds, et cetera, et cetera, with you? Having landed, I was directed to a special line where I told the examiner that I had some dried specimens of mosses and lichens, and showed him the bags. "No problem," he said, glancing at what I held. Without further ado, I was sent on to freedom.

But there *were* problems in those bags, the possibility of which I anticipated and took precautions to guard against. I left the plants sealed in the bags when I got home and kept watch on them. After a week a single fly of a small species hatched out from a pupal case evidently hidden in the brown, lower stem portion of a clump of moss. And after 3 weeks a small moth hatched out in another of the bags. I dispatched both insects and waited a few days more to see if any other animal life would show up. Nothing. I then planted out the parched mosses and lichens, which, with rain, readily came back to animation.

Since both those insects were single and unmated, there was really no danger of getting them started as invasive pests. But had male and female of a species hatched out together they might, conceivably, have started a reign of terror in agriculture, horticulture, or forestry.

The treating of one's imports with insecticide would be more effective prevention than quarantining them in plastic bags as I did. I would suggest immersing the plants in a jar filled with a dilute bug-killer and leaving them for several hours, time enough for trapped bubbles of air to find their way upward from the recesses of the plants while the killing potion finds its way inward.

In that there comes an end to the business of this chapter. But how wretched to exit on the subject of toxicity and last gasps. Let us adjourn while thinking of the trophy instead. Handled well, it will be with you for years, a living memento of a faraway forest, or seacoast, or mountain, or of wherever you found it on such a splendid day.

CHAPTER THIRTEEN

Bugaboos

IN GARDENING with mosses and other miniature cryptogams, bugs are seldom a problem at all and rarely a problem of any severity. As a rule, nothing that wears chitin, and nothing that leaves a slime trail, shows more than the slightest interest (an experimental nibble, no more) in these plants of ours. If bugs there are not, there are still a few bugaboos that may beset our plants. Air pollution, drought, damping off, weeds, excessive sun or shade, birds, and certain rodents are all but one of the items in the bad-news list insofar as it is known to me. The remaining malefactor is the misunderstanding human, to be introduced shortly. Everything else in the list has been at least mentioned in other chapters, and all are now brought together for convenient reference and emphasis on a few points that may be relevant to every aspect of moss gardening.

Air pollution in concentrated doses, such as the exhaust fumes a planting beside a highway or parking lot might receive, can be fatal to nearly all mosses. Smokestack industries located up the wind stream are destructive to mosses (and lichens) of most kinds. However, several mosses of garden value are highly resistant to aerial poisons and are capable of healthy life even in industrial cities. Among these species are *Bryum argenteum*, *Ceratodon purpureus*, *Leptobryum pyriforme*, and *Tortula muralis*, the *Tortula* being perhaps the toughest of all.

Weeds are a universal problem in moss gardening. Even if the planting soil is completely weedfree, weeds will come in as airborne or bird-borne seeds. New plantings of moss need frequent weeding; established planti-ngs, two or three weedings between spring or early summer and fall.

Drought will damage newly planted mosses of most kinds, even those collected within the gardener's own property and completely drought-tolerant where found. (The intolerance of drought shown by new plant-ings is in contrast to the ability of many mosses to live through long-term desiccation when the plants are closed up in bags and stored away, as de-scribed elsewhere in this book.) Give mosses that have been transplanted in spring, summer, or early autumn enough water to keep them moist until autumn rains take over. Mosses planted in winter probably will be moist-ened well enough by rain or snow. But in case of winter drought, make up for it by watering. By the time of their second summer in the garden, mos-ses will have established themselves (if they are capable of doing so where planted) and will probably withstand weeks or months of dryness. During dry weather, established mosses of certain kinds, such as *Polytrichum*, crin-kle their leaves and appear to be as dead as ashes and clinkers but are ac-tually peacefully asleep. The first rain or hosing brings them back to a blaz-ing green liveliness.

Copious watering is helpful to terrestrial mosses, with the possible ex-ception of *Racomitrium*, which never needs watering, not even when newly transplanted. But watering, especially in dry weather, can cause fungus infection and damping off in certain mosses named in Chapter 10, In Con-tainers. As preventative medicine, withhold water from those plants.

Too much sun can kill a moss planting in 1 day; too much shade may prove fatal in a few weeks or months. When collecting mosses, note the exposure in which they grow. A sunny habitat dictates a sunny location in the garden; a shady place in nature, a like situation in cultivation. Mosses collected in sun will usually transplant successfully into as much as half shade (with some loss of compactness resulting from the stretching of stems and enlargement of leaves), however, while mosses found growing in part shade will accept somewhat more or less of it in the garden. But those found growing in full shade will probably not take any sun at all and would show their abhorrence by quick death. A knowledge of habitat pro-vides the means of imitating Nature well enough to satisfy the plants. (But if you don't get it right on the first attempt, try another spot in the garden, or try another kind of moss.)

Birds, squirrels, and chipmunks adore scratching at garden mosses but can be deterred by several means. The rodents can be live-trapped and taken for a long, one-way ride, which may rid the garden of their kind for as long as a year. Birds are a menace particularly in the spring nesting season, when many species collect mosses as building material. And at any time they are present, such birds as thrushes (including the American robin), towhees, sparrows, and all others that scratch at the ground for food recognize the fine, concealing fabric of mosses as a likely hiding place of little comestible creatures. It is all too easy to lose a small moss garden entirely to birds, to have it ripped up and scattered in tatters. The situation is different from that in a woodland, where the sheer extent of mossy acreage disperses the attacks of birds so that the plant receives minor damage here and there, and none at all over much of its spread. In contrast, a garden moss patch often becomes the target of all ground-feeding birds in the neighborhood.

I have found that making the moss garden appear dangerous to the birds reduces their attacks substantially. To the avian brain there is danger lurking about mosses that have been planted between large rocks a foot (30 cm) or more in diameter with a rise of 6 inches (15 cm) or more from the soil surface. It may be that the birds fear an enemy lying in wait behind the rocks and decide not to land, or perhaps their good sense tells them that landing there amid obstacles could be injurious. Planting mosses between rock garden shrublets that are fairly close to each other will also help turn away birds. A carved or cast figure of an owl or cat may be even more frightful and effective, especially if it is moved a few feet every 2 or 3 days.

Mosses in the open ground can be completely bird-proofed, and rodent-proofed almost as certainly, by covering them with fine nylon netting. This material is available in garden stores for the more usual purpose of covering fruit trees and other fruiting plants in time to fend off hungry birds or for use as pea vine support. Blackish nylon netting of about 1-inch (2.5-cm) mesh and almost as fine as horsehair is the best sort for covering mosses. In use, it is nearly invisible and lasts for years before rotting.

Moss gardens in containers can be bird- and animal-proofed by covering them with this same netting or with shade cloth stapled to a frame of 1- by 1-inch (2.5-cm) or 1- by 2-inch lumber. If shade cloth is used, a kind that provides about 70 percent shade is ideal, not only as a bird-stopper but as a means of growing some kinds of shady mosses in a sunny garden. But sunny mosses will not tolerate shade cloth. Use the fine netting on these; it blots out very little sun.

Quite another approach to the foiling of birds (although perhaps not of rodents) is to select for your garden certain mosses and moss-like plants that are fibrous enough to resist birds' feet. These include *Drepanocladus*, *Polytrichum*, *Lycopodium*, mossy selaginellas, and no doubt many others (that I have not tested). The most bird-resistant specimens of these various plants will be found in open places in the wild, where the plants, in reaction to sunshine, have grown compactly, with an increase of cellular toughness. Dig these miniatures with a layer of attached soil 2–3 inches (5–7.5 cm) thick, take them home, and plant them firmly in sunny ground.

Misunderstandings

There are definite moss-haters among humankind, who, as a rule, do not like lichens either. There are many such people. They make the worst enemies of mosses in gardens and their enmity comes, I think, in large part from misunderstanding.

Consider the case of moss abduction that I was engaged to solve by a Japanese-American friend. He asked me, in my capacity as the landscaper of a condominium apartment building where his aunt resided, to intervene as tactfully as possible in the not so mysterious disappearance of a much loved patch of moss from the small allotment of ground where his aunt gardened at the back of the building. (Her garden patch was one of 16, as many as I could fit into the limited ground area outside the apartments. These allotments were snapped up by former homeowners who had been open-ground gardeners and who wanted to carry on.)

The aunt, classically Japanese, planted Kurume azaleas, placed some stones that measured not much bigger in length and breadth than this book, and edged the ground with that most Japanese of ground covers, *Polytrichum* moss. Her garden neighbor at one side of her allotment was another woman, seventyish or eightyish, of European ancestry. She had planted zinnias, in the midst of which reclined a fawn made of fiberglass or some such material.

Cheerful little gardens were those of both women. Unhappily, the fawn gardener was also a moss-hater. Or it could be that her fawn was responsible for the disappearance of that plant—ate it up, perhaps. Howsoever, the moss was totally gone when the aunt returned after being away a few days. Shocked, she kept her composure and asked her garden neighbor if she had seen anybody walking off with her beloved *himesugigoke* (*Polytrichum* moss). The fawn gardener replied by launching into a lecture about the dangers of moss growing in the vicinity of one's garden. Awful stuff, moss. Whatever had happened to it, she for one felt relieved that the moss was gone. It would have jumped over into her allotment and mugged her plants in no time.

I got all that from my friend, the moss gardener's nephew. Immediately, I wrote the zinnia grower a polite letter on my business stationery, introducing myself as the landscaper of the premises and explaining that the moss her neighbor had planted was completely harmless and forever incapable of invading her annuals or anything else she might plant in future (an assertion *almost* certainly true). I continued with a budget of facts about *Polytrichum*, a wonderful plant to the Japanese. People of European origin, as well, had come to admire it lately and actually paid to have it planted in their gardens.

I never had a reply from her, nor did I expect one. I don't know that my letter was instrumental in changing her attitude toward mosses. However, I later learned from the nephew that his aunt had replaced the moss and that no enemy had attacked this second planting.

The case of the mossy grotto, an event that took place one summer long ago, did not turn out as happily. I happened to be at the scene because my girlfriend lived there, in an apartment building with a basement garage that car-parkers entered by way of a verdant grotto reminiscent of those at the Villa d'Este in Italy, the next best thing, as far as I was concerned, when I drove in after work to call on my friend. The verdure was a natural growth of the mosses *Homalothecium* and *Tortula* that had built up, no doubt over a period of many years, on two moist walls of concrete (to the right and left of one's car) that led down to the garage and embanked a lawn at the front of the apartments.

Late one afternoon I arrived to find the building superintendent at work, whistling merrily as he scraped away at the magnificent walls of moss. I never said a word to express my dismay. I suppose I could have leapt out of my car and delivered an oratory as bathetic as "Woodsman, spare that tree," only changing the words a bit. But he would have considered me loony and gone right ahead. Besides, I needed the fellow's assistance in order to get into the garage at times.

During the next two evenings, hobby time for him, he continued warbling and working, taking a wire brush to the moss, sluicing the de-mossed walls with bleaching fluid, and returning the concrete to a gleaming gray newness. And still I never said a word. He and I were so far apart in our views of the world no words could bridge the gap.

But the case of the moss carpet killer might have been averted by reasoning if only we, a friend and I, had known his intentions and talked to him in time about the worthiness of moss in the world and the garden. He was, after all, a nice guy, bright, and adaptable enough to listen. But he was also deluded, propagandized by the advertisements of such anti-moss factions as the grass seed and chemical industries. His attack was upon a backyard carpet of *Brachythecium*, notorious as one of the "weed" mosses but in this location a plant of shocking beauty, a swale of glowing, yellow-green down, bigger than a good-size living-room rug and the perfect landscape answer there in the shade of a large maple. This was at the back of a house owned by the friend I mentioned, in which his mother lived. The moss-killer was her well-meaning son-in-law.

The *Brachythecium* carpet formed a nearly flawless cover marred only by a few remnant strands of a grass lawn that had nearly given up as the shade of the maple deepened year by year and the moss burgeoned. My friend and I had been intending to weed out the last of the grass but left it too long. Enter the son-in-law. In his thinking, moss was the enemy one was supposed to get rid of, right? He bought a killing potion at a garden store and gave the *Brachythecium* a dose. It died 100 percent. Then he raked it away. The result was garden alopecia: wisps of grass spiking at odd intervals from otherwise bare ground. Within a year, even those died. Grass just did not want to grow in the shade of the maple even without competition from the moss. And there, a sad finale.

What is this misunderstanding of mosses that addles so many people? Is there a conspiracy behind it? Something of the sort prevails, as evidenced in the considerable agitprop instigated against mosses by commercial interests, and by garden writers as well. But that is only a partial source of the malaise. Other contributing factors are an instinctive unease with moss that I think most of us share even as we admire the plant (explanation below) and an all too commonplace environmental illiteracy, an unpreparedness as a reader of the natural world. The poorer readers fear all mosses the same way they may fear all moths that bumble into the house, even such a regal creature as a luna moth. Kill it quick before it gets into the clothes closet. But of course there are moths and moths, mosses and mosses, with neither tribe categorically evil nor wholly good. Even so, both moths and mosses are enlisted overwhelmingly in the camp of friendly life forms: those innocuous to human concerns.

To the groundskeeper at a golf course, however, an invasion of such a moss as *Rhytidiadelphus squarrosus* (bane of banes of the greensward) would be an oncoming disaster, necessitating all-out chemical warfare. Likewise, to the home gardener who is bent on producing grass of plush perfection in the British model, "weed" mosses are for the poisoning. But many of us moss gardeners tend to look upon our plant as never bad whatever its identity and wherever it grows. Moss weaving its way through the grass lawn? Charming. Let it elbow out the rest of the boring grass.

Heresy. After all, The Lawn is one of the Western world's Sunday religions of major rank. Many are the souls who spend more time and passion on the upkeep of grass than on the maintenance of deity, which is perfectly fine with me, a books in brooks, sermons in stones type. Apart from the sanctification of the lawn and the subsequent condemnation of moss as a lawn devil, there exists a far more ancient and fundamental human adversity to mosses, and lichens, too. In their progress over soil, stones, and tree trunks, these plants are seen to stifle the world. At a certain level of mind, mosses and lichens are allied with owls, toads, bats, and things that go bump in the night, are in league with Nature in the downturn, at one with decadence and demise.

There was a time, many hundreds of years ago, when even the Japanese, nowadays fervent admirers of mosses and lichens in the garden, considered the growth of these plants on stone a mineral disease, requiring control by scouring it away. Such response is primitively human and, as we have seen in the actions of that superintendent, perfectly contemporary.

Admiration of mosses and lichens, and interest in cultivating them, represents the attainment of a certain wholeness of the civilized mind, a roundness in understanding our environment. Even while we see these plants as a part of finality, we see them also as early-arriving life (Plate 33), a part of Nature freshening and on the rise. The message of mosses and lichens is, Thumbs up!

CHAPTER FOURTEEN

Portraits

NOW COMES a collection of word pictures and color plates—a gallery of moss species and other, moss-like cryptogams that gardeners, myself included, have grown with success and satisfaction. Here, too, are a few especially desirable wish plants, growable by some gardeners but not by me. You may have just the right place for them, where they will flourish. Many of the plates in this chapter include part of a grass blade 1 inch (2.5 cm) long, placed at lower left, provided to demonstrate scale. Plants are listed alphabetically by genus (consult the Index of Mosses and Other Bryophytes for the common names of those few that have them). In addition, there are entries under Lichens, and Liverworts (divided into Leafy Kinds, and Thallose Kinds), with more information on those plants.

Acarospora. *Acarospora chlorophana* is a crustose lichen found on shady cliff faces and beneath overhangs in mountainous and desert country around the world. In the arid coulees of Washington state, and along the Columbia River, *A. chlorophana* colonies older than Luxor's colonnades have spread over vertical acres of columnar basalt cliffs: soft yellow on stone of bruin-brown colors (Plate 66). *Acarospora*, transported from a cliff face in a desert to a maritime climate on a chunk of its native mineral will require vertical positioning in an airy place protected from most rain and sun, but it will enjoy a little of each, as of early morning or of evening sun,

Plate 66. Small but centenarian plants of *Acarospora chlorophana* (yellow) and *Xanthoria elegans* (red) on basalt in a desert. One of the rewards in studying such lichens in situ is in discovering their compositions in abstract expressionist art. See also Plate 25.

and of mist or wayward drops deposited on the plant by a breeze. I have in mind a location beneath eaves.

Amblystegium. If mosses of the genus *Amblystegium* had egos they might believe they own the world, for they occupy the planet from the subarctic to the subantarctic. There are many species, much alike and in a state of flux both as life forms and as taxonomic beanbags. The amblystegiums are finely textured, mat-forming plants, inhabiting moist logs and tree bases or lying flat and close to the ground. They move along, hiding beneath the foliage of taller vegetation, such as woodland plants or the grasses of meadows and lawns, and then show up in open areas as a neat soil cover of dark or light green.

In one property, that of Stockton, California, gardener Lem Hagopian, an *Amblystegium* moss developed into a superb shade-garden carpet. For many years Hagopian maintained an expanse of this moss, approximately

45 by 75 feet (14 by 23 meters) in measure, that had planted itself beneath redwoods *(Sequoia sempervirens)* that *he* had planted. The *Amblystegium* grew originally on the lower part of trunks of native oaks that bordered the garden and, as the gardener recalls, eventually "jumped down" to the ground beneath his redwoods and filled out as a nearly flawless cover, but one that required the almost daily hosing away of fallen redwood needles.

Andreaea. *Andreaea rupestris* is one of a small genus of rock-clutching mosses, a species that ranges around the globe, from near sea level to 10,000 feet (3000 meters), keeping always to acidic rocks. As with other mosses of both lowland and lofty habitat, the higher the place where *A. rupestris* grows, the more compressed its growth. Colonies that inhabit outcrops in an alpine zone hunker there in dwarfed form and with amazing spunkiness. In all this they are a match for those acorn barnacles that cling to shoreline boulders well above almost all of the year's tides, and seemingly above the possible.

The color of the *Andreaea* varies, in differing locations, from greenish brown to russet to blackish red. The reddish phases are typical of plants found in harsh sun at high elevation, where the plant's red pigment shields its leaves from harmful ultraviolet rays. *Andreaea rupestris*, especially in high alpine form, is an exceedingly slow-growing, sullen-seeming plant, somehow fascinating as a garden possession. For years I have grown this species on its native rock, kept on a garden table in fullest sun, and never watered or fertilized. Such abstinence is crucial to the garden life of the plant.

Antitrichia. Moss spores do get around and have got *Antitrichia curtipendula* around to residency in Europe, North Africa, Greenland, Patagonia, and western North America (Alaska to California). A similar species, *A. californica*, shares *A. curtipendula*'s western North American range. These two are mat-forming mosses, green of varying lightness or darkness, with fine leaves, and a neat, pressed-down branch habit. They are patch plants on rocks, logs, and especially on the trunks of deciduous trees. They have a special ability that refutes cautions I make above about mosses not welcoming change in their angle of growth. To change almost any vertical tree trunk moss, for example, to a horizontal container plant can be fatal. But the *Antitrichia* mosses are so adaptable that in falling off tree trunks, as they often do, they readily take root on the ground beneath; they are just as accommodating when peeled off a tree trunk and planted in a pot (Plate 63).

You may have the luck of finding *Antitrichia* growing on a little-used sidewalk (this moss will not take much foot traffic) beneath trees from which it has fallen and has grown into a pad that can be lifted off as if it were a tortilla. It is just that thin and flat and delicious (in an ocular sense). It is a great find with all kinds of uses as a stone cover, log cover, ground cover, and bonsai scarf; give the plant part, or full, shade.

Atrichum. *Atrichum undulatum* is a moss of European and North American distribution. This species is one of seven similar North American atrichums, from all but one of which (the virtually indistinguishable *A. selwynii*) it differs in having wavy leaves rather than straight ones. In the Pacific Northwest portion of its range, *A. undulatum* (Plate 67) may be more common in suburbia than in the wilderness. It seeks newly disturbed soil and shows up within a year after bulldozer or shovel work, forming handsome green patches in any scrap of ground left fallow. It is a neat-grower, a low colony of upright tufts that are like so many twig ends of a short-needled conifer, but much reduced. In that feature it is also like *Polytrichum* moss, to which *Atrichum* is related. But the needles of *Atrichum* are broader

Plate 67. *Atrichum undulatum,* stretching up its cormorant-head spore capsules.

than those of its relative, less firm, of thinner, translucent tissue. The color of the plant in new growth is a bright, light green, which darkens with age. The spore capsule display is one of the most attractive among mosses, a dense flock of green cormorant heads (maturing to a blackishness) on curved necks, held high on reddish stems.

Colonies of *Atrichum* are transplantable with care, for they tend to break up into bits all too easily. The plant is perhaps best enjoyed in situ, as an attractive and perfectly harmless patch of greenery almost anywhere it decides to be. However, it is often misunderstood and apparently feared. Once I visited a garden and paused to admire the *Atrichum*, which had clothed bare ground magnificently between concrete pavers set in a shady side yard. The gardener caught me at it, thought me strange (if I read his expression correctly), muttered that he hated moss, and was going to poison the lot of it. Too bad. It was the liveliest thing in his garden.

Aulacomnium. *Aulacomnium palustre* (Plate 68) is a moss of eye-catching coloration, a pale greenish yellow in spring; in summer, a beach-girl blond (or, if my reader prefers, a beach-boy of the same hue). This plant is a world-circler in both the northern and southern hemispheres, and a settler in sunny, watery places, such as on banks of basic mineral earth seepy with spring water, and in marshes, where its short, broomy-leaved branches often intermingle with *Sphagnum*. The *Aulacomnium* is a determined invader of any other moss it may meet. So it is not suitable for patchwork plantings but is valuable on its own. Easily transplanted, it is easily kept happy in cultivation as long as it is kept moist. Grow it in a pot or in the open ground. After some years, a single transplanted sod is capable of expanding broadly. Many transplants on a steep, seepy bank may grow into a goldish curtain.

Barbula. *Barbula* (Plate 59) has narrow little leaves held down tightly, as a rule, in tufts and cushions. The many mosses in the genus *Barbula* grow on sunny ground, rocks, mortar, and asphalt shingles, and can be scooped off their native places and used as ground covers in container gardening. Therein, they spread with satisfying moderation, being neither too slow nor overwhelming. Old plants may die at the center but are easily restored to fullness by plucking out the brown portion and planting green bits of the same species in the bare space.

179

Plate 68. *Aulacomnium palustre* in its relatively dark, springtime color phase.

Brachythecium. *Brachythecium* (Plate 69) is a moss genus of worldwide range. Many of the species in this large group are so similar that their identities pose difficulties even to specialists. Typically a moss flat-growing and speedy, a sheet of fine foliage, of a delicate, clear green, or soft yellow-green, it is an attractive cover for shady ground. Several of the species readily shoot through lawn grasses at soil level and drive grass purists mad.

Plate 69. *Brachythecium asperrimum,* on a decaying log in woods.

Brachythecium is easily (if temporarily) got rid of by using any moss-killing product sold at garden centers. But beware of clearing shady ground of moss in the hope that a scrappy grass lawn lingering there will fill in healthily. It may not. (More on this appears in Chapter 13, Bugaboos, under Misunderstandings.)

Bryum. *Bryum* is a huge genus, containing about 500 kinds of mosses worldwide, half a hundred of them in North America. Many are like green velvet, tight against the ground; these will make container garden carpeting of the finest texture.

Bryum argenteum, silvery green of leaf, is a world-circler that settles down in town as often as in country. It is a species that prospers even beneath our city feet, in sidewalk cracks, where it may be hammered down to a thinness of ⅛ inch (3 mm), the living and the decaying, underneath portions measured as one. When collecting sidewalk moss of this or of any other kind for garden use, it is best not to look too closely at the plant in hand. But if one cannot help doing so, now that the suggestion has been diabolically implanted, close examination will reveal that the plant has been feeding on an awful humus cake made up partly of the flake-away particles of passing humans and of the libations of furry and feathery creatures. The hair of *Homo sapiens* is the most evident ingredient in the humus. Sidewalk moss mats are actually bound together by a meshwork of human hair of many hues, hair that has fallen during an interval of 5 or 10 or 20 years, the moltings of many transient scalps at just this spot on the sidewalk. Here, as everywhere, moss functions as a skillful capturer and engulfer of any trifle that blows its way, and that it hopes will be digestible.

In addition to its common occurrence in sidewalks, *Bryum argenteum* often grows naturally in the soil seams between garden pavers (Plate 70), making a bright improvement in a routine area. The *Bryum*, and other mosses as well, can be transplanted into such seams if these plants are too slow in appearing on their own. Wide seams give the mosses their best chance to take hold, as does planting them with their surface a little below that of the pavement. But beware of planting an area too big to be weeded by hand, the only way that it can be done since herbicides would kill the moss.

The use of sand can be of help in weeding, as it is in the Bellevue Botanical Garden in Washington state. The garden features a broad entry plaza made of concrete pavers interspaced by hundreds of yards of the silvery *Bryum* in narrow lines. The pavers were set in sand, and within a year or two after their installation the *Bryum* arrived and entirely filled the seams in between. No other moss competes with the *Bryum* in this sunny location. Weeds, as weeds will, drift in as seeds and sprout in the seams. Loosely rooted in the sand, they are easily enough pried out by hand while they are still small, hence they "have never become a major maintenance problem." The quotation is from a letter written by Nancy Park, curator of the garden, who goes on to say that fresh sand is swept into the seams periodically throughout the year. In icy winter weather, the entire surface of the plaza is lightly sanded. Neither salt nor de-icing chemicals are ever used. Apparently the *Bryum* comes up through the sand in the seams or restores itself into unbroken lines of silver-green from patches of moss left uncovered. For there it is—perhaps the most extensive realm of this particular moss in public view anywhere.

Bryum argenteum withstands months of total dryness in full sun with no hardship whatsoever for the plant. This easy tolerance of long-term

Plate 70. Silvery green seams of *Bryum argenteum* between garden pavers.

drought makes the *Bryum* especially useful in container garden compositions of xerophytic plants such as cacti, desert *Cheilanthes*, or other rock
ferns. This moss species is also one of the major bonsai ground covers.

Bryum capillare, cosmopolitan in range, is at home in countryside and
on mountainside, often in soils of low fertility barren of higher plants.
Here the *Bryum* mat may be only ⅛ inch (3 mm) deep in its living, green
layer. Add to that measure the plant's underlying strata of brown stems
and leaves, which accumulate at a rate of about ⅛ inch (3 mm) for each
year of growth. In digging a saucer-size mat of the *Bryum* (perhaps 7 years
old), one finds that it is still a compact ground cover less than 1 inch (2.5
cm) deep.

Buellia. Lichens of patriotic import in British gardens, plants of the genus
Buellia grow spontaneously on pavements (Plate 71) and walls, and with
such nationalistic spirit that they almost seem to be singing "Rule Britan-
nia." One does not quite hear that anthem, of course, but sees it and feels

Plate 71. *Buellia* lichens and waterlilies at Wisley, England.

it within the lichens in all their solemn dignity. In other words, these lichens help sustain a sense of national security and continuity, as demonstrated in the mellower features of the gardens of Britain. Lichens are
major suppliers of that ease of garden and mind, none more effectively
than *Buellia*.

Buxbaumia. Bryologists, hunched over their microscopes, rise to flights of fancy from time to time. Some do, at any rate, and among them is A. J. Grout. He examined *Buxbaumia aphylla*, a tiny moss in its spore-capsule-bearing stage, and christened it bug-on-a-stick. The name caught on with some of his colleagues and has even been given credence in an *Encyclopaedia Britannica* article on mosses. Grout had in mind the true bugs, Hemiptera, and perhaps the bedbug in particular, for the flattened capsule of the moss (rising on its stick above scanty foliage) is very like that onerous creature. *Buxbaumia aphylla* grows coast to coast in Canada, in the northern United States, in Europe, in New Zealand, and elsewhere. Other buxbaumias, similar bugs-on-a-stick, occupy parts of that same range. These plants can be kept for a time in a jar, as we children used to do with beetles and caterpillars, which we later released. Or grow *Buxbaumia* in a terrarium. Or best of all, make this moss a "belly plant"—one of those minutest of species that wildflower watchers get down flat on the ground the better to see, and then leave the little life alone to get on with living.

Calliergon **and** *Calliergonella.* *Calliergon* and *Calliergonella* are two small, similar genera of mosses that grow as bounding ground covers in sodden places or on damp ground. *Calliergonella cuspidata* (Plate 42) is typical, a gold-green romper, covering yards of ground in a few years. Worldwide in range, it is a major "weed" moss, actually one of excellent landscape value. It is easily transplanted by peeling it off the ground as a sheet and then by pressing this moss fabric onto the surface of the soil where you want it to grow. *Calliergonella* closely resembles another gold-green weed moss, *Brachythecium*.

Caloplaca. A big, worldly group of crustose lichens, some caloplacas inhabit tree bark, coloring it yellow. Others—in many shades of yellow, orange, and red—glorify rocks in Nature, as they do stonework in gardens and at graves (Plate 33). Certain bright yellow caloplacas grow typically on seaside boulders, so close to the water that they are splashed by waves in rough weather. These shoreline lichens may need the salty douse, or more certainly the nightly dews of the littoral; they will not live if taken far away from the shore.

Campylopus. *Campylopus introflexus* (Plate 73) is one of those mosses that arrive in a garden after it is a few years old. This one comes in, fits in, and elbows out nothing. We have welcomed this good-guy volunteer in our Auckland garden, where it has appeared, and slowly increases, upon century-old, silvered railroad ties of *Eucalyptus* wood that we have used as retaining, and on ground surfaces of crushed rock left undisturbed for years.

It is a southern hemisphere native that somehow has found its way north, perhaps as spores on the wind, or on the feet of migratory birds, or about the roots of imported plants. By now it is well established from place to place in Europe and North America but is nowhere a pest. As I say, it fits in. Moreover, it offers considerable entertainment to the keen-eyed connoisseur of mosses as gem plants.

Campylopus introflexus grows as a tuft, spreading its pale greenery not much and usually standing no more than an inch (2.5 cm) tall. Nevertheless it is a noticeable and intriguing plant, even when the observer looks down at it from the great distance of head height. Each of its upright stems appears to bear a delicately leggy spider at top—or make that a long-rayed star, twinkly with reflexed light. These effects derive from the nearly ¼-inch- (6-mm-) long, white, hair points (actually as colorless as clear ice) on the plant's narrow, needly leaves.

When *Campylopus introflexus* is rained on, its hair points radiate straight out. But when the plant is dry, the hair points bend at a near-right angle to form a whorl rather than a star (the observer must look closely to discover the shape), a whorl whose hair-fine filaments point counterclockwise. That is the way of the plant in its Down Under range. Only an extensive investigation of those colonies of the moss that have shown up in the northern hemisphere will answer the question, Do the hair points of this antipodean species reverse their direction, and now bend clockwise in accordance with those same planetary influences that cause water to twirl left-handedly or right-handedly down the drain, depending on where in the world it twirls? Science awaits the answer. This might be worth a sizable grant.

Cephalozia. See Liverworts—Leafy Kinds.

Ceratodon. Ceratodon purpureus (Plate 52) is a plant of remarkable march over the world, in habitats as diverse as tundra, rotting logs, the mortar of brick walls and the grime on rooftops at the heart of big cities, rocks in deserts, gravelly poor soil on mountainsides, sodden ground along the margins of marshes, hard ground between tufts of stunted grass in starving lawns. In ground too infertile to sustain taller competitors, *C. purpureus* may become the dominant vegetation over as much as several acres, and yet even where it is abundant it is a self-effacing greenery, hardly noticeable, especially so in dry weather when the plant becomes blackish and shrunken. But then for some weeks in springtime this unimpressive moss has its season of glory. It sends up green spore capsules that ripen into a russet color, on longish stems of wine-red, glossy and shimmery in the sun. Where this plant grows in large tracts it becomes in its season as colorful and magical as any field of spring wildflowers. And it is easily grown in a container garden.

Cetraria. A circumpolar genus of lichens, as a group *Cetraria* is a kind of portmanteau including both fruticose and foliose species. Typically, the cetrarias cling to the bark of tree branches and twigs, from which they dangle in ruffly clusters that resemble oyster mushrooms, sea-green, yellowy, or oystery in color. Brought home on a twig and kept dry, any of these plants retains its color and shape indefinitely.

For many years I have maintained *Cetraria juniperina* as a houseplant, rarely watered. During all this time it has retained the powdery, pollen-yellow tint of its branches, and the chestnut-brown of its disk "flowers" (apothecia). The dry *Cetraria* coordinates well with other houseplants, particularly ferns and succulents. But of course any dry bouquet (which, in a sense, describes this household lichen) becomes a bore in time. And then I put the *Cetraria* away in a drawer, perhaps for as long as a year. Eventually I reinstate it as decor, freshly interesting.

I don't ask too deeply whether or not the lichen is actually alive. In any case, when the *Cetraria* is soaked briefly in a bowl of water, as we do for entertainment every once in a while, it provides a spectacularly lively show, puffing up from the size of a sleeping kitten to that of a startled marmoset. The moistened *Cetraria* gives off an aroma that suggests still other mammals or things mammalian—a blended whiff of suede worn by an equestrian, and of the horse, sweating. It is a good-bad-intriguing scent, probably with pheromonal powers, and of the sort that is used as ballast in the making of a perfume. I would not be at all surprised if an essence of this plant is eventually stirred into some concoction with a name like The Devil's Dew, to be dabbed on by would-be Dionysians.

Cladonia. The lichen genus *Cladonia* contains some of the most garden-worthy of any of the lesser cryptogams. The cladonias include the many species of goblet lichens (Plate 10 shows an example), of British soldiers

Plate 72. Garden on a scow-shaped stone features the nearly white reindeer lichen (*Cladonia rangiferina*) along with deep green *Grimmia* and chartreuse *Racomitrium* mosses.

(see *C. floerkeana*, below), and of reindeer moss (see Chapter 10, In Containers, under Companion Plants). Technically, there is only one, true reindeer moss species, *C. rangiferina* (Plate 72), but there are a number of others closely alike and deserving of the name. Reindeer will certainly eat them if they find them.

Cladonia evansii is one of the showiest of the world's filigree lichens, that is, of lichens of the reindeer moss type. These are usually associated with northerly regions, yet *C. evansii* is a feature of pine woods in parts of the American South, notably in the vicinity of Cocoa, Florida. In its southern stations this species multiplies into colonies containing thousands of individuals, even filling entire woods at ankle height. The plants are of a whitishness, size, and mushroom shape that suggest large cotton bolls or small soufflés. Their web-work structure contains even less substance than that of a luffa sponge, allowing light to stream through the plants. *Cladonia evansii* in the wild is a sight worth journeying to see. And like other filigreed cladonias, it makes a great show pet when grown in a container.

Cladonia floerkeana of Europe, *C. cristatella* of North America, and the many allied species within this lichen genus, found in both the northern and southern hemispheres, are British soldiers, all. So named for their red caps (fruiting bodies) of pinhead size atop battalions of greenish gray stalks ½–2 inches (13–50 mm) tall. Their bright carmine headgear earns these lichens their place as perhaps the most popular of all miniature primitives. Every child who roams their range knows them by sight (Plate 73), and most of us who have been brought up in English-speaking countries come to know them early on by their common name as well, for it is truly common property on both sides of the Atlantic, and also in Australasia.

British soldiers grow on decaying wood, on peat, and on the crust of soil baked for years in the sun, in places too infertile to support taller plants that would shade them out. They are difficult to transplant, but only because their colonies shatter easily into bits that do not survive. British soldiers are easy enough to transport, if not transplant, when they are found growing on a handy piece of wood, and if the red caps can be kept from being crushed en route (by placing them in a box, perhaps with wadded-up paper which will prevent the wood from knocking about). Once British soldiers are safely home and properly stationed (in sun and fresh air), red caps will keep forming year after year on newly arising stems.

Plate 73. British soldiers (red-capped *Cladonia* lichens) in company with the moss *Campylopus introflexus*.

Climacium. Popularly known as tree moss or umbrella moss, a grove of *Climacium* (Plate 74), with its little arboreal heads held a mere 2–3 inches (5–7.5 cm) high, nonetheless has sizable powers to fascinate and discomfit. This spiky thing, apparently half animal, has so clearly scuttled forth from some steamy marsh in the Mesozoic.

Plate 74. The tree moss *Climacium dendroides* on the margin of a pond. Note the "tree" with the visible trunk, located upper right. At lower left, for scale, is a chip of bark an inch (2.5 cm) across.

There are two species, *Climacium americanum* and *C. dendroides*, identical twins with slight differences that only a mother (Dame Nature) or a moss specialist might notice, the most apparent being the long, tapered tips of the leaves along the branches of the first-named plant, compared with the ovate leaf tips of the other twin. *Climacium americanum* grows throughout eastern North America, from Canada down to the Gulf states; *C. dendroides* rounds the northern hemisphere and is also found in New Zealand. The North American range of *C. dendroides* covers Alaska, Canada, the West, the Great Lakes states, and the East, southward to Virginia.

In Nature, these twin mosses seek wet soils along the margins of streams or marshes, in shade or nearly full sun; or damp, rotting logs in woodland; or moist bottom-land meadows open to the sun, where they hide away at the base of grasses whose leaves provide a miniaturization of lath shade. When collecting tree moss, lift it with a thick clod of the substrate in order to capture the plant's deeply placed runners along with its visible, aboveground portions. Tree moss slowly adjusts to transplantation into wet soil toward the edge of a sunny garden bog; or into a moist, shady bed; or into a pot, watered well.

Conocephalum. See Liverworts—Thallose Kinds.

Dicranella. *Dicranella* comprises a group of mosses velvety fine and dense of foliage (with exceptions), in tufts and patches. About a dozen members of the genus inhabit North America. Of these, *D. heteromalla* (Plate 75) is typical and is especially abundant within its broad range, which covers most of the American continent and much of the remainder of the northern hemisphere. In western North America it is often found on sunny stream banks and on the raw soil of roadsides not yet claimed by leafier vegetation. Here it grows as a compressed mat as low as ¼ inch (6 mm) in thickness. In Europe it is commonly a woodland plant, as tall as 1½ inches (4 cm). In the eastern United States, as on the other side of the Atlantic, it frequents woods and is oftentimes a volunteer in woodsy gardens. A prime example of such is the shady hillside property of moss gardener David E. Benner of Pennsylvania, where *Dicranella heteromalla* (together with *Dicranum scoparium* and *Thuidium delicatulum*) grows as a carpeter.

My own experience as a grower of the *Dicranella* has been in container gardening, especially in a certain memorable composition (Plate 62). In that photograph, taken 2 years after I made the planting and a few weeks

Plate 75. *Dicranella heteromalla* interstitching fractured granite on a mountainside.

before its disappearance forever (a caper to be examined in a moment), the container in view is a fragment of mountain driftwood, trough-shaped, 16 inches (40 cm) long. It had fallen from a hemlock tree and weathered for years before I found it and planted it with this finely textured moss, and with a hardship-dwarfed, 8- or 9-year-old tree of the same kind (*Tsuga mertensiana*) that provided the silvery trough. All the ingredients, including an extra handful of the local soil (in addition to the life-supportive clods dug up with the moss plants), were gathered within a few feet of each other on a mountainside.

And these ingredients made up just about the best mossy garden that I ever put together in a natural container, I would say regretfully, now that it has been stolen. I kept this composition on display for two summers in an assemblage of container plants that friends and I arranged each spring from 1984 to 1994, on a terrace outside a hospital's paraplegic ward, for the good of a friend in residence there, for other patients and their visitors, and for ourselves. Of all the nearly 100 container displays (mainly annuals, flowering shrubbery, and vegetables) on the terrace, this one attracted the most comment and, evidently, covetousness in someone who came by.

Ah well, the incident seems worth relating in that it brings into focus the fatal charm of horticulture's most purloinable plants. In order to attain status as a most purloinable plant (MPP) the live thing must not be too large to be sneaked out of the garden, and it must bear a certain mystique. The MPP seems to me to concentrate the attractiveness of all ornamental plants in one handy package, in the same way that all the world's avarice is distilled and pressed into a bar of gold—at the moment of thieving, anyway. The gold left unguarded will disappear. So will the MPP. Yet at times the magnetic quality of the MPP may be simply in its smallness. Smallness equal cuteness in plants, just as it does in puppies; cuteness equals covetousness and leads to purloinability, in plants at least. Sweet little alpines kept in special houses within botanical gardens are so eminently purloinable that they often require protection behind a mesh of steel. And small cactus plants—mute and mysterious gnomes that they are—make devilishly attractive targets. Keepers of another public garden far grander than the one my friends and I maintained have told me that the MPPs in their collection are small cacti planted beside paths. Never mind the plants' prickly armature, they are impossible to keep. Most purloinable plants— add to the list any mosses nicely displayed in a container.

Dicranoweisia. There are two species of *Dicranoweisia*, both of them moss mice, or moss biscuits if you would rather not entertain the notion of rodents. In any case, the two are mosses that usually form small colonies, rounded and domed. They are plants with two vastly differing weather faces: verdantly, vividly alive after a rain; in dry weather, mummies of themselves, ashen, shriveled, and brittle. *Dicranoweisia cirrata* is a western North American (Alaska to Arizona), European, and Australian plant that sometimes grows on rocks, or on roof tiles and thatch (in Britain). But its main perch is on wood such as that of logs, tree bark, roof shingles, fence posts, and even the totems of the Haida people (Plate 32). This species is one of the great camp followers among mosses.

A virtually identical twin, *Dicranoweisia crispula* (under a microscope the leaves of this moss show up flat along their margins, while those of the other species reveal recurved margins), is more of a wilderness inhabitant, clinging to rocks and logs, sometimes at low elevation but more usually in mountains. It ranges throughout the northern hemisphere.

Dicranoweisia cirrata, the camp follower and clinger on wood, has, against its natural inclination, been made into a ground cover in at least one experiment (as outlined in Chapter 7, Moss Carpets). Other values or uses of this plant include inspiration (one goes out in a rain, or afterward, finds the moss, and feels better for seeing a thing so joyfully green) and domestication as a garden pet. Just bring it home on the material whereupon it grows. It is easily tamed and is sometimes long-lived into the bargain.

Around 1980, moss gardener Marian Ritter brought home plants of *Dicranoweisia cirrata* attached to small fragments of a fallen cedar (*Thuja plicata*). Ever since, the moss has lived contentedly on its cedar staging, displayed beneath a pine tree beside the gardener's front walk. Over the years the upkeep of the display has amounted to nothing more than picking off any pine needles that rain and wind fail to brush away. The reward is in mounds of an Erin emerald at any time with rain.

Dicranum. One of the stars of moss gardening is *Dicranum flagellare*, a special green, bright and glowing at all times. Rain or drought, the color stays the same. In fact, when the plant is dry it takes on an even more interesting appearance than when moist. The narrow leaves, which in a rain have a combed appearance, neatly straight and smoothed down rather flat, become wavy (Plate 76). And then this moss suggests a shag rug, or curly lambskin unaccountably green.

The plant has one more nifty trick. It propagates itself chiefly by a special kind of fragmentation, not by the breakup of the whole plant but by detachment of tiny shuttlecocks of leaves tucked around the stem ends. Winds, and the feet of animals, knock them loose to form new plants. The hand of a person who strokes this moss (a likely action, for the pelt of the plant makes it seem almost a furry and pettable creature of some kind) becomes one more agent of its increase. Stroking the plant is also the best means I know of telling it apart from other, similar dicranums. No other that I've ever found or read about gives up little leaf tufts when you touch.

This species moves easily into the garden and lends itself to cultivation in the open ground or in containers, in full sun or in shade up to three-fourths of the day (but remember: any moss collected in a shady setting is stressed if it is brought to a sunnier place).

In the wilderness, *Dicranum flagellare* grows on fallen, decaying trees and on stumps, or on the ground in deep, peaty humus, or sometimes in scant soil on outcrops. The plant ranges across North America, in the southern provinces of Canada and the northern United States, but in the eastern part of the continent this moss travels south along the Appalachians

Plate 76. *Dicranum flagellare* in time of drought. Whatever the weather, this moss stays green.

to Tennessee and Arkansas. Across the Atlantic it grows in southeastern England and from place to place in Europe at low elevation (it is more a subalpine plant in North America).

North America is home to additional dozens of *Dicranum* species, some of which are similar to *D. flagellare*, except for its perhaps singular means of perpetuating itself. Then, too, the leaves of most of the other species crinkle in time of drought. Any of these other plants is a first-rate garden prospect.

Dicranum scoparium rates special mention for its being a moss of occasional natural occurrence in wooded lots (what luck!) that are converted into shady gardens. The specific name, *scoparium*, calls this plant broomlike, for its stiff, sickle-shaped needle leaves, about ⅝ inch (16 mm) long, of pale green or goldish color. Branches dressed with these leaves form a broad, deep mat, bold and sturdy in aspect. Use it as a ground cover beneath shrubbery, or in association with tall ferns. *Dicranum scoparium* grows in woods all around the northern hemisphere. A nearly alike, if not identical, plant is found in New Zealand.

Drepanocladus. *Drepanocladus uncinatus* (synonym, *Samionia uncinata*) is one of a number of similar, trans-American and European *Drepanocladus* mosses, all vigorous mat-forming plants, falcate of leaf. Some of the others grow in marshes or on damp soils, but this one is a plant of upland woods and even of sunny ground that bakes dry in summer. *Drepanocladus uncinatus* (Plate 77) is among the best of mosses for landscape gardening, fairly easy to establish from transplanted sods, and eye-catching in the garden landscape, as much a presence with its plump, trailing stems of long, recurved leaves as any miniature creeping shrub. It comes through winter best when covered with snow all season long, or where sheltered in deep shade. Those other, thirsty *Drepanocladus* species are just as valuable and easy as this one when they are grown in the wet places they love.

Entodon. The seven North American mosses of the genus *Entodon* range mainly east of the Mississippi. They grow as thick mats, deeply green or paler, or of a shiny goldish green. Leaves are of scale-form, held closely against the branches; upright spore cases are of cylindrical shape, sug-

Plate 77. *Drepanocladus uncinatus* (synonym, *Samionia uncinata*) in shady woods.

gesting Asian eggplants reduced to minuteness. In Nature, these mosses are clothiers of earth, boulders, and tree trunks. The terrestrial kinds are easy and worthy as garden ground covers.

Eurhynchium. A genus of woodland mosses, the eurhynchiums form thread-like or feather-like mats on leaf mold, moist logs, and the trunks of trees upward from the ground a few feet. *Eurhynchium oreganum* (synonym, *Stokesiella oregana*) is a Far Westerner, ranging from California to Alaska, and it is a fine-feathered friend for the gardener. It is in fact the only kind of elegantly plumy moss that I have ever been able to grow in the

Plate 78. *Eurhynchium oreganum* atop a stump in a half-sunny woodland garden.

open ground. The main stems of the mat are like slender quills, and these are aligned with numerous broad, leafy branchlets, pinnae-like, in fairly even rows on two sides of the quill. The entire pinion-frond is flattened in form (like a feather) and is held somewhat pressed down against the ground. The green of these leaf-feathers varies from yellowish (Plate 78) to ivy-dark, the color deepening in response to a richness of shade and humidity. The change toward a deeper green is typical of most kinds of moss that grow in shade as well as in sun. Typical as well is an alteration in the form of growth. Most sun–shade mosses, with this Oregon namesake moss certainly among them, grow taller and fluffier in shade.

Don't give up on this plant if it is brought home seemingly only to turn pale and desperate in appearance. *Eurhynchium oreganum* may need as much as 2 years to adjust to garden conditions. Give it the lushest shade that you can provide. I know of no foliage plant more deserving of a few feet in the front row of a woodland planting.

Eurhynchium praelongum (synonym, *Stokesiella praelonga*) inhabits western America and most of Europe. Over this far-flung range the plant has evolved into various subspecies and forms. They are mostly thread-like mosses, small mats made up of filiform runners, almost like green spider web for fineness but undisciplined and disorderly in their interweave. The webbing is airily open when the plant grows in shade, low and dense in part sun. The color of the plant varies as well, from mid-green in shade to a soft yellow-green in a sunnier place. This is a species that often volunteers in gardens, but if it does not it is worth planting as one of the daintier fabrics in a patchwork quilt of mosses.

Funaria. *Funaria hygrometrica* (Plate 79) is cosmopolitan, well known as an interloper in the pots of greenhouse or windowsill plants, and as a first-comer in ground bared by fire. It is a low-grower, forming patches of minute, tufty branches dressed with needle leaves. In fruit, *Funaria* becomes showy. The autumn and winter spore cases are big for the plant, pear-shaped, copious, orange-colored when ripe. This "weed" moss makes a worthy pot plant on its own and offers considerable compensation in being there when the plant one buys and brings home in a pot shared by the moss happens to die. I have tried making windowsill gardens out of *Funaria* together with rocks in small pots but have found it impossible to transplant. I'll try again, with spores.

Plate 79. *Funaria hygrometrica,* an interloper in greenhouses all over the world.

Grimmia. Grimmia pulvinata (Plate 80, at top of the photograph) has hair-tipped leaves that give this moss a resemblance to silver fox fur. Of the many species in the genus, this may be the most engaging. It grows on rocks throughout much of the world and is easy to accommodate in a garden. Take it home on its native mineral, place it high and dry in a hot, sunny place, and never wake it up with water when it is sleeping. The same garden technique is applicable to other, greener grimmias that are less foxy-silky in their leaves, and less readily identifiable.

Hygrohypnum. The hygrohypnums are mat-forming mosses native to the northern hemisphere's cool forests, alpine zones, and boreal latitudes. They frequent, most often, the saturated ground along the margins of streams, and moist rocks or logs in the vicinity. The numerous species (13 in Canada and the United States) are in many cases so alike that they challenge the specialist working with a microscope.

Hygrohypnum luridum (Plates 44, 81) is one of the more widely distributed species in the genus. The plant is in fact a world-circler, as much at home along fast-running streams in Tibet as in Tennessee. Its North American range extends coast to coast. *Hygrohypnum luridum* grows as a dense

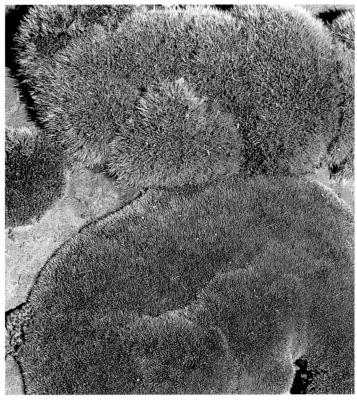

Plate 80. *Grimmia* mosses are of two types (both of which grow here on a slab of stone): those with pronounced hair points on the leaves, and those without. The hairy one here is *G. pulvinata*; the other, ? Of the scores of *Grimmia* species, most are difficult to tell apart.

Plate 81. *Hygrohypnum luridum,* magnified. Something like a mane, as propounded in the text. But to the naked eye, the plant resembles some sort of fabric.

interweave of mainly horizontal branches, cushiony on soil, compressed when growing on stone. Under magnification, a topside view of the plant, with its pattern of recurved leaves along the branches, reminds me of looking down at a horse's neck while astride the horse. The leaves are arranged like a rough mane. They grow from the top of the branch, where they part left and right, lie flat, and then curve down around either side of the branch. But farther down, they curve inward toward the branch's underside, lose their equine character, and become like the talons of a raptor. *Hygrohypnum luridum*, and others of its genus, are growable in a shady mossery that is naturally moist or watered unsparingly.

Hylocomium. Feather moss or fern moss, *Hylocomium splendens* (Plate 82) covers the forest floor with a loose and airy sweep of pinnate, almost downy-appearing fronds, wispily rooted in leaf mold, lightly attached to fallen twigs. Found around the northern world in cool woods, it is a plant as splendid as its Latin name suggests but not at all easy to transplant. There is no use even trying with this species unless one intends to keep it in a terrarium (where it will stay fresh a while even if it does not grow), or unless one provides a richly bosky place for it in the open, as beneath a grove of tall, shady conifers. In collecting *Hylocomium* for open-ground gardening, dig a sizable sod about 16 inches (40 cm) across, take it up with all the leaf mold and lumpy debris that will cling to it, and close it up in a big plastic bag to keep it moist until you get it home. Plant *Hylocomium* in leaf mold or peat moss.

The doubts and recommendations above apply as well to many other woodland mosses uneasy to coax into a garden life, notable among them such ferny foliages as *Ctenidium*, *Ptilidium*, and *Thuidium*, some of the very mosses one would most want to grow. These *can* be acclimated, however, with skill, and with the luck of having just the right conditions at home.

Hypnum. Repeat almost everything said above about *Hygrohypnum*. The two genera, *Hygrohypnum* and *Hypnum*, in the case of many of their species, are look-alikes and behave-alikes. The hypnums, too, make up a sizable group of mat-forming mosses, flat of branch, often flatter against their substrata than are the hygrohypnums. Many of the hypnums, too, are talon-leaved. Hypnums sometimes grow alongside water, but their more usual habitats are upland ground, rocks, and dead wood. Those that grow on stones or tree stumps in sun are tolerant of seasonal drought. As a rule the

Plate 82. Feather moss (*Hylocomium splendens*), with the moss *Hookeria lucens* at lower right.

hypnums are easy to peel off and transplant. They are valuable in container gardening, as scarfing on garden stones, and as ground covers over a small area.

Hypnum cupressiforme seems to me the leader of the pack. It is abundant in its worldly range, which includes the southern hemisphere. *Hypnum cupressiforme* is a highly variable moss, with forms substantial or wispy of branch. *Hypnum cupressiforme* var. *filiforme* hangs from bark or boulders in thread-like fringes. More typical is a rock-inhabiting form of the species, which so closely resembles *Hygrohypnum luridum*, as shown close up in Plate 81, that I decided not to use a perfectly good close-up that I had taken of the *Hypnum*. The two plants were indistinguishable in their photographs, and showing them both would have been duplicative. I hasten to say that I definitely had pictures of both kinds of moss, collected 7000 miles (11,000 km) apart in Canada and in New Zealand.

Isotachis. See Liverworts—Leafy Kinds.

Isothecium. *Isothecium stoloniferum* (called by others *I. myosuroides*) is a moss of several guises, to be found throughout much of the North American West. Its growth forms are so different one from another as to seem not to belong to the same species. The differences in color and in growth are typical of mosses that inhabit both sun and shade. As discussed earlier on under *Eurhynchium*, such plants are greener and looser in the latter environment. One of the *I. stoloniferum* forms is a petrophyte partial to rocks in partly sunny places. It is a moss of sharp beauty, crisp and natty, as if a shrub juniper reduced to tininess. This type of *I. stoloniferum* spreads slowly over sloping rock faces. Give this moss its customary part sun, perhaps placing it (attached to its native stone) amid a bed of other miniatures, and then watch over them all as carefully as you would guppies or puppies. Other growth forms of the *Isothecium* festoon tree branches and vertical rocks in shady woods. Where it grows as a branch-beard (Plate 83), *I. stoloniferum* dangles in streamers as long as 3 feet (90 cm); the more generous the rainfall and humidity, the longer the growth. Masses of this moss muffle sound in the forest and take on goblin shapes. It may be grown in a woodland garden that is richly shady, summer and winter. Or try it in a terrarium.

Lepidozia. See Liverworts—Leafy Kinds.

Plate 83. Wraiths of the moss *Isothecium stoloniferum* (also called *I. myosuroides*) in
deep woods.

Leptobryum. A citizen of the world in all hemispheres, *Leptobryum pyri-forme* is a moss fine and closely barbered in appearance, suggesting mole fur unexpectedly green, a plant eagerly opportunistic in its seeking and discovering niches and soils in which to grow. It follows ground fires and heals the scorched earth with its bryophytic fur. Likewise, it fur-coats fallow ground at the edges of paths and in garden beds that have not been dug for a year or so; it coats moist concrete walls and fills crevices in partly shaded sidewalks. *Leptobryum pyriforme* is the major pavement moss in many communities.

The plant is identifiable at a glance when it is carrying its springtime spore cases. These are pear-shaped, a feature commemorated in the species' name. Other characteristics include minute leaves, hair-like in their narrowness, wavy when moist and crinkly when dry. Collected sods of this moss go on living for years when they are pieced together as a ground cover in a container garden, as I have always done with the plant. I would guess that *Leptobryum pyriforme* will also lend itself readily to the pepper method of planting. When dry, it is a moss that crumbles easily, and a liberal sprinkling of the dry bits over the bare soil in a container garden, or beneath a bonsai, should result in quick greenery. For detailed directions, see Chapter 11, Bonsai Mosses.

Letharia. The lichen *Letharia vulpina* is a bright citron-yellow, string-branched species of foliose classification. It abounds on the bark of living conifers and on silvery dead wood in the interior mountains of western North America, and in those of continental Europe. It is a plant that does not readily adjust to garden life in coastal regions. In the Intermountain country of the West, however, it is as easy as cheat grass (*Bromus tectorum*) to bring home and establish in the garden, and a whole lot more desirable. Let me make a visually educated guess that *many* Intermountain gardens display this plant, for I have seen it in several. The display is often of the lichen on the wood where it has grown from a spore. Among all the species of lichens and bryophytes that attach themselves to wood, there is nothing quite like the special vibrancy of *L. vulpina* for galvanizing a handsomely dead old branch into new life.

The garden health of this lichen depends in large measure on its being positioned well above the ground, out of the way of harmful ground moisture. This need has been taken care of superbly in Ohme Gardens in Wenatchee, Washington, where much of the display of *Letharia* is of plants that

Plate 84. The lichen *Letharia vulpina* "planted" in the chinks of a log wall at Ohme Gardens, Wenatchee, Washington.

have been detached from snags and used as ornamental caulking (Plate 84) in a log-walled garden shelter open to the elements on one side. Some of these *Letharia* plants have been in place since the early 1960s; others, so I am told by Gordon Ohme, are replacements for specimens that visitors to this public garden slip into pocket or purse. Here is a lichen that has turned out to be a most purloinable plant (that horticultural status of the damnably, doomingly attractive discussed above, under *Dicranella*).

Leucobryum. Closely similar species of *Leucobryum* (white moss) grow in the four hemispheres of the globe. These mosses form dense, firm hummocks. In dry weather, you can drum on them resoundingly with your knuckles, so tightly packed are their branches. The colonies of *Leucobryum* send out flat extensions from the edges of the central hump and when many such individuals meet edge to edge on a stretch of ground, the highs and lows of them all produce a wavy surface convincingly like a cloud field (Plate 15) or an expanse of ocean. It is a plant that jingles the imagination. Children respond to it creatively, as in this scene that I chanced upon long ago and enjoy recalling to mind's eye once in a while: With hearty sailor-and-captain cries, two small boys in North Carolina ply a gulf of *Leucobryum* with toy boats made of scraps of wood.

Flat portions of white moss are easy to establish in a garden when set out as a mat, or a plant may be crumbled and the bits sown. Hemispheres of *Leucobryum* often break loose in a windstorm, or they are dislodged by an animal's hoofs, or the toes of a child, and then they make great kick or throw toys ("moss balls" to junior warriors), harmless even when lobbed toward somebody's head. Potted up, such domes of *Leucobryum* make engaging toys for grownups as well. Summer-dry and drum-hard, they may be brought indoors for a few days' duty as décor.

The various species of white moss are studies in subtlety of coloration. Typically these plants are of a greenish-bluish-whitish pallor when dry, deepening to the lightest of green after a rain. In eastern North America, *Leucobryum albidum* and *L. glaucum* grow in part shade within woodlands, or in open areas at the margins of bogs. In Britain, the same *L. glaucum* grows characteristically in the leaf mold of mature beeches. *Leucobryum neilgherrense* is an essential presence in certain of the historic gardens of Japan. *Leucobryum candidum* of New Zealand and of tropical islands in the Pacific is a forest-dweller, a plant that lights one's way along wooded trails with an almost phosphorescent brightness. In leaf form and hummocky habit all these plants appear, to the naked eye at least, identical. The thing about *Leucobryum* is that, wherever one encounters it in the world, meeting it is like bumping into an old friend.

Leucolepis. *Leucolepis acanthoneuron* (Plate 85; synonym, *L. menziesii*) is a moss of Pacific range, from Alaska to California, with a disjoined territory in Idaho. *Leucolepis* grows as a grove of treelets rather like those of *Climacium* (tree moss, Plate 74), but the first-named plant is soft in appearance, and soft as a kitten to the touch, while *Climacium* appears harsh and bristling of leaf and is just so when met with one's fingertips.

Leucolepis, as a young colony, forms a neat clump. The plant in Plate 85 is a youngster 3 years old, 7 inches (18 cm) across, 2½ inches (6 cm) high. With an age of several years more, it will extend into a small-scale ground cover about the size of a scatter rug. This colony has rooted firmly deep in fertile sand toward the edge of a seasonably dry creek bed, in part shade. During high water, the stream covers the moss, and deposits, in be-

Plate 85. *Leucolepis acanthoneuron* (synonym, *L. menziesii*) at streamside, growing in fine, fertile sand brought to it by high water. Alder "cones" at lower left are ½ inch (13 mm) long.

tween its treelet stems, fresh, silty sand, in an annual renewal of fertility remindful of life along the Nile (until recent years). *Leucolepis* also grows on shady rock surfaces deep with leaf mold, and in boggy ground, where it tolerates full sun. This species transplants with ease into a humusy shade garden. It is a first-rater among those mosses whose spread is not large, not small, but moderate.

Lichens. The genera *Acarospora*, *Buellia*, *Caloplaca*, *Cetraria*, *Cladonia*, *Letharia*, *Parmelia*, *Peligera*, *Ramalina*, *Rhizocarpon*, *Stereocaulon*, *Umbilicaria*, and *Xanthoria* appear alphabetically in this chapter. Chapter 10, In Containers, under Companion Plants, offers notes on *Usnea* lichens. Chapter 6, Camp Followers, under The Lively Roof, contains additional information on *Parmelia*. There are about 15,000 species of lichens in this world of ours. The above kinds are good ones with which to start a career of lichen gardening.

Liverworts—Leafy Kinds. These are moss-like plants of numerous genera of the order Jungermanniales that are often worldwide in range. Plants are either carpet-forming or clump-forming in habit and, as a rule, minute of leaf. Widespread over the globe, and extensive on the surfaces they cover, the leafy liverworts add up to enough breathing greenery to earn a place among earth's more effective oxygenators. Many inhabit forests as green garb on logs, tree bark, moist rocks, and duffy ground. At a glance this forest greenery might be taken for a true moss, or mosses, of dense, fine growth. But a close look reveals leaf differences, seaweed affiliations, as described in Chapter 2, Definitions.

If the true mosses are a difficult prospect for a greenhorn (such as myself) who delves into the literature in search of a plant name, then the Jungermanniales are next to impossible, as reticent as Rumpelstiltskin. He, you may recall, was that odd little fellow in the folk tale whose quirk it was to conceal his identity. And so, with him in mind, I end up calling all those unknowns that I meet in the woods Rumpel (for short).

But I have not drawn a total blank with the Jungermanniales. Plate 3 shows one that I have at least half-identified, a member of the genus *Porella*. I found it growing in the subdued light of hemlock (*Tsuga*) woods, side by side (as you see) with two other leafy liverworts of lesser spread. When I leaned closely over the *Porella*, the better to study it with a loupe, I noticed that the plant gave off an aroma that I can only call startling in that it nearly matched the sea scent of live mussels on a rock exposed by low tide.

Have I mentioned before, how many of the mosses, liverworts, and lichens are scented plants? With exhalations noticeable only at inches? Many are rather grass-like in scent, others scented quite like mammals of one kind or another, which I will not attempt to name, except in the case of a horsey *Cetraria*, as noted above, under that genus.

I should say that many a scented cryptogam can be allergenic and cause attacks of asthma, but only if a susceptible person sniffs closely at the plant or handles it and then brings hand close to face. These potent scents possibly protect the cryptogams against the appetites of molluscs, arthropods, and higher animals, signaling that the plants are unpalatable. Or, a plant perfectly good to eat may be sending out a false signal. In any case, the scented moss, liverwort, or other primitive miniature, lying there so vulnerably close to a world of exploring noses and jaws, is left alone by almost all herbivores.

The pungent *Porella* represents only one of the many genera of Jungermanniales that offer garden possibilities. Some of the others are *Cephalozia*, *Lepidozia*, *Lophocolea*, *Lophozia*, *Nardia*, and *Plagiochila*. Quite a pile-up of syllables, that, of names I have never carried in mind, nor recommend carrying; but mark the first in that line since it comes up again in a moment.

Any Rumpel that grows as a substantial mat is a likely subject for the garden. Any that is found in forest shade can be transported to the garden on its native wood or stone, or if growing on the forest floor, can be lifted as a sod and used as a patch plant in a moist and shady crazy quilt made up of many kinds of bryophytes. The liverwort might also be brought home as a small fragment, to be displayed as a pot plant. High humidity is a life need of many kinds that grow in moist shade, or on wet soil in sun as, for example, New Zealand's amazing "red moss," *Isotachis lyallii* (Plate 86). Certain sun-inhabiting kinds—those that are drought tolerant, dense of leaf, and pressed tightly against their substrate—are entirely worth a try as ground covers in bonsai gardening. Experimentation is called for with these plants, which so far remain among the least gardened of miniature cryptogams.

Yet even now there is a noteworthy garden performance in progress, a public performance at that, by the leafy liverwort species, *Cephalozia bicuspidata*. The plant is distinctive and readily identifiable, for once among the Jungermanniales, for its tooth-shaped leaf with two very long, prong-like lobes that suggest a bicuspid's roots. This global traveler has shown up in

Plate 86. "Red moss" (*Isotachis lyallii*), actually a leafy liverwort, on a wet cliff in New Zealand's Fiordland. Like so many of the world's more spectacular bryophytes, the plant is not easy in cultivation. It needs cool nights, dripping or rivuletting water, and sunshine. (photographer, Mo Yee)

the Peat House at Edinburgh's Royal Botanic Garden, where it has green-carpeted the staging of peat blocks and forms a fine foil for such sizable flowering plants as *Dimorphanthera kempteriana* of New Guinea (fountaining branches, shiny elliptical leaves, pink urn-form flowers). The tiny liverwort helps create grand pictures there (Plate 87).

Liverworts—Thallose Kinds. These plants, primarily of the order Marchantiales, are known variously as pad-form liverworts, thallose liverworts, or thallose hepatics. Many bryologists favor the latter term, disowning or disusing the time-honored English title, liverwort, in referring to hepatics of this or of the leafy kind as well. Some of the pad-form species are expansive growers, with individuals spreading to as much as a foot (30 cm) across or, when in company with others of their kind, joining up and covering as much of the supportive habitat as is allowed by any taller, competing plants. The strongest of the pad-formers are capable of hold-

Plate 87. The leafy liverwort *Cephalozia bicuspidata,* be-greening peat blocks in the Peat House of the Royal Botanic Garden, Edinburgh. The overarching shrub is the New Guinean *Dimorphanthera kempteriana.*

ing their places for many years in wilderness or in a garden not too disciplined. In such easier gardens they sometimes appear voluntarily in fallow ground or on a moist wall. Flatness is their style. Their thin pads lie as flat as flounders; certain species are ruffled along the thallus edges, like the fins of a flounder in motion.

Of all the many thallose liverworts, the classic species in the classic genus is *Marchantia polymorpha*, a plant of global range. The genus *Marchantia* contains numerous species, but none, as far as I have seen, startlingly different from *polymorpha*. This plant is as much at home in natural places (stream margins, soil scorched by fire, wet rocks, coastal heaths, inland moors) as it is in the human encampment (along damp pathways, in rain gutters, on greenhouse benches, in pots with more proper plants). The sly arrival of *Marchantia* (by spore or gemma) in a container where a sanctioned plant grows may be harmless if the plant is tall enough. But if the plant is a low-grower and is left to be overgrown by the smothering pads of the hepatic, the result can be quickly detrimental, and even total death in time. *Marchantia*, to most gardeners who have met it, is an execrable thing.

Yet it has admirers, perhaps even a buyer or two. Listen to this: A nursery in the Netherlands, "specialists in strange plants," according to Michael Fletcher in his *Moss Grower's Handbook*, has offered *Marchantia* for sale "at a high price." And why not? When examined without prejudice, *Marchantia*, one of the strangest plants the world ever grew, may yet be seen to possess a certain beauty of no ordinary kind. It is a plant that exemplifies Bacon's dictum, "There is no excellent beauty that hath not some strangeness in the proportion." It is also a plant that, when viewed biliously, may be seen as plain ugly.

Turn to Plate 2, if you will, for a clear view of a female *Marchantia polymorpha*, distinguishable by stalked appendages shaped like starfish, wherein spores incubate. Males carry analogous structures, also atop stalks, not starfish but shallowly lobed disks. *Marchantia* also reproduces asexually by means of gemmae, tiny eggs in cups that erupt from the pads, eggs that encapsulate the parent plant—genes, tissue, and will. Fletcher describes these nests of eggs as "elegant." Another writer, whom I introduce shortly, sees them as "warts." I myself find both views entirely apt.

Marchantia and other sizable thallose hepatics of such commonly encountered genera as *Conocephalum* (Plate 14) and *Lunularia*, and also of certain of the smaller kinds that hide away in woodlands, rock clefts, or furrowed bark, can be grown in containers, each for its intriguing self. Some kinds, of course, are more willing to accept domestication than others. As a general technique applicable to many of the thallose liverworts, pry up an entire young plant together with a piece of its substrate. If the liverwort is a terrestrial, nestle it in a pot nearly filled with airy, humusy potting soil. If the liverwort grows on stone or bark, bring it home attached to this material and bed it in gravel or crushed crockery within a container. *Marchantia* and other especially hearty members of the thallose clan will also grow from detached lobes pressed upon potting soil. Keep any sort of newly planted pad-former moist, and shade it for the first few weeks or until it perks up and starts growing. Then give it as much sun or shade as that in which you found it growing.

These plants crave moist air as well as a moist substrate. While a few are drought tolerant, most others will give up when subjected to a single day of complete dryness. Terrarium culture or a shaded location in a greenhouse suits many kinds. If you would use them in container gardens together with companion plants, choose companions that are at least nearly a foot (30 cm) tall; tallish bromeliads, aroids, or ferns will be safe with the most roisterous of the hepatics; ferns will provide an especially complementary foliage.

And when any of the pad-formers invites itself into the garden as a path plant, it is a thing to be trodden upon respectfully:

Step Lightly on Your Liverwort

No exquisite blossom to delight you in the Spring
But a quiet mediocrity this raspy bryophyta brings.
Why is the corrugated interloper, so supine,
Puckered green and brown, much maligned?
Languishing dejected, unique and bizarre,
This raspy liverwort—sometimes black as tar.
This austere scabrous plant, survivor extraordinaire
Growing for its own sake, requiring no care
On sodden barren ground—requiring only air.
Insects do not relish it, slugs just slip away.
So step lightly on your liverwort. Let it stay.
Every garden needs liverwort to remind the human race
Someday you'll be wrinkled with warts upon your face.

by Janet Logg

Lophocolea. See Liverworts—Leafy Kinds.

Lophozia. See Liverworts—Leafy Kinds.

Lunularia. See Liverworts—Thallose Kinds.

Lycopodium. Lycopodiums bear the common name club moss but are no more moss than a swallowtail butterfly is avian. The "club" in their name pertains to their spore-bearing structure, an upright, club-like cone, while the nominal "moss" refers to the fine, furry habit of some kinds. The living members of the genus are contemporary representatives of the ancient, awesome order of lycopods, plants that reached their evolutionary zenith in the Carboniferous bogs. They stood there as tall as today's larch trees and ranked among the largest and most abundant plants on earth. The descendants of those monster lycopods are small and unprepossessing, except when one remembers their august pedigree. The approximately 400 species of *Lycopodium* remaining on the planet are almost all tropical or subtropical. But a few lycopodiums dwell in temperate, alpine, or arctic regions, where they have evolved into low, creeping, stem-rooting plants that imitate the ways, and somewhat the appearance, of mosses. Portraits of some of the best-known among these come next in line, following a discussion of their peculiar status as a garden legend.

Or so I perceive them, as plants that thrive in far greater abundance in garden literature than in gardens. In a half century of garden touring, my total sightings of hardy species of club moss, in gardens other than my own, add up to rare specimens of *Lycopodium clavatum*, and none of any other kind. Surely I have missed a few, but I suppose not so very many. In considerable part, the legendary *Lycopodium* must owe its origin to the works of Liberty Hyde Bailey and of his daughter Ethel Zoe Bailey, specifically, to L.H.B's *Standard Cyclopedia of Horticulture*, first published in 1900, revised and republished in 1928, and to the more recent series of hortuses ascribed to the Bailey Hortorium, Cornell University, digests that have largely followed the *Cyclopedia*'s original listing of lycopodiums. L.H.B's stated premise for including plants in the books was that all the species listed were soundly established in North America's home gardens at the time of publication. His *Cyclopedia* includes six species of hardy *Lycopodium* (*annotinum, clavatum, complanatum, lucidulum, obscurum,* and *selago*) along with three tropical lycopodiums as being garden fixtures by the year 1928. However, the *Cyclopedia*'s article on club mosses was written not by

Bailey but by a specialist in cryptogamic plants, Lucien Marcus Underwood.

Now, in the garden writing of Underwood's time, the late nineteenth century and the early twentieth, it was a fairly common practice to recommend plants known only in the wild or on herbarium sheets. Such recommendations were often made without the caveat that the plant might not yet have been brought into cultivation. Plants were then coming in from far places so copiously, in such a rush, that it seemed safe to list as gardenable, if not already gardened, any unknown kind that possessed the likely good looks even as a pressed specimen. Just possibly, L. H. Bailey, the chief of that prodigious project, the *Cyclopedia*, was undermined a bit by Underwood and perhaps by other contributors who may not have precisely followed his resolution to put in only bona fide, garden-tamed plants.

Therein, it would seem to me, lie the beginnings of a pleasant pipe dream, propagated ever since in horticultural writing, of lycopodiums romping merrily in residential gardens. Certain more recent authors have clearly cribbed from works published under the Baileys' names. Near duplication of the wording in those source books gives the tracking writers away. Not that these gleaners are guilty of anything much; they are in fact good guys, just like me. We all do it. Every one of us whose job it is to recommend and describe plants for the garden is a student of the Baileys and of other progenitors, a borrower of at least a binomial or two, and of a bit of accompanying data. At the very least. I would even go as far as to say that any garden writing more than about 10 percent new, rather than newly raked over, amounts to landmark literature.

In his article on *Lycopodium* for the *Cyclopedia*, L. M. Underwood, an original in writing of the genus, allows that "the hardy species are not always easy to get started." True, so true. His saying so suggests that he himself, or somebody he knew, was at least trying if not succeeding at all remarkably. A low rate of success in starting the plants carries on to this day.

Transplanting hardy lycopodiums from the forests, glades, and montane barrens where they grow is uneasy but can be done (instructions below, at *Lycopodium clavatum*). Starting these plants from cuttings rather than from collected clumps is also an uneasy business but can be accomplished regularly with at least one kind, or so we are told by a supplier of terrarium plants located in Maine. The company's catalog notes that *L. lucidulum* is "the only [native] Club Moss that readily roots and adapts very well under glass." Hmm. I gather that the supplier sends out lengths of branch that are rootless or at best sketchily rooted, as is usual with the branches of a running club moss such as this. I infer further that *L. lucidulum* is unusual, unique in the experience of the supplier, in its willingness to root down and grow on from branch cuttings kept under glass.

The Baileys' hortuses go out on a limb by stating that lycopodiums, categorically, are "propagated by cuttings." Questions arise. But propagation under glass (in a greenhouse, cold frame, or terrarium) would be the way to do it, all right, when and if it is doable. I am inclined to disbelieve the easement given in the hortuses and to accept the word of the terrarium supplier, who also sells other lycopodiums and would have every reason to tout them if they were easy-doers, that propagation from cuttings just will not work with most kinds.

Another commercial grower of cryptogamic plants, Judith I. Jones, a crackerjack at this work, tells me that none of the hardy lycopodiums of ropy, runabout habit is any more growable from cuttings than a pine tree is from twigs. It can be done, but with a tiny rate of strike and certainly not in commercial quantity. However, Judith Jones finds the clumpy, shrublet species (such as *Lycopodium alpinum* and *L. selago*) to be tractable in the fullest horticultural sense in that, yes, they will grow from branch cuttings. If the hardy lycopodiums are a garden legend, they are also a garden hope.

Lycopodium alpinum (Plate 88) and its sister species (or subspecies) *L. sitchense* are very similar little branchy bushlings with scale leaves; they stand, at most, ½ foot (15 cm) tall. You may be able to tell them apart by their branches, usually flattened in *alpinum*, usually rounded in *sitchense*, but these differences are inconsistent. *Lycopodium alpinum* is a world-circler in the far north, and a ranger in the New World down to Québec in the east and to mountainous parts of the Pacific Northwest. *Lycopodium sitchense* is native to eastern Asia and to western North America, southward to much of the same alpine and subalpine Pacific Northwest as that occupied by its near relative. The two plants grow on sunny slopes and in open, half-shady conifer forests. In places where these species meet they baffle the botanist more than ordinarily by their occasional hybridizing.

If you would bring either of these club mosses into your garden, please do bone up on my cautionary notes (at *Lycopodium clavatum*, below), which apply to all hardy lycopodiums. Then, grow either *alpinum* or *sitchense*, and any other *Lycopodium* that I discuss, in a container or in open ground, in sandy, humusy, mildly acidic soil of such kind that cassiopes and gen-

Plate 88. Left to right: *Lycopodium alpinum* in a garden with planted mosses and *Sedum spathulifolium.*

tians would also enjoy (the media recommended in Chapter 10, In Containers, under The Soil, serve nicely). Lycopodiums ask for moist ground, rapid drainage, and considerable humidity. A shaded location may be necessary to help conserve moisture.

Now that I think of it, everything I recommend here in the way of soil, moisture, drainage, and tempering shade is just as wholesome for about 10,000 other not-too-easy alpines of all kinds, that either love the sun or tolerate it well in their wilderness homes but are subject to frying in the sun of a lowland garden.

Lycopodium clavatum (running pine, Plate 5) grows around the world, a magnificent primitive universally admired, notoriously difficult to transplant. Few gardeners (outside of Japan, where *clavatum* has long been cultivated) have ever succeeded but only because the plant is usually found growing in rotting wood or on stone, from which it comes away bare-rooted. If the roots are bared even momentarily, the plant will probably die (quite possibly the problem may not be exposure to air but the loss of some vitally assistant organism in the substrate—I am guessing here). If you can find *L. clavatum* or any other species in this "difficult" genus, growing in soil, and can lift the plant with a goodly clod of earth, you have almost surely won. Lycopodiums moved with their roots in soil are often so amenable that they will grow heartily and will flower (or, more exactly, cone) in their first year, and onward.

Lycopodium complanatum (ground cedar, Plate 4) is a boreal circumpolar plant, ranging southward in the United States to mountainside woods. The species is basically a forest plant but is also a frequent pioneer on sunny mountain slopes. It forms trailing stems and, at intervals, upright branches to a foot (30 cm) tall or a little more that are flattened and much divided like those of a cedar tree (*Thuja*). Ground cedar is all a shining green. "A good plant" this, to bestow upon it a favorite compliment and recommendation given to deserving plants by knowing British gardeners. Those three seemingly simple words, as spoken and written in British horticulture, have extended meaning: that the plant is distinctive, comely in its features and growth, not overly common, and all in all, distinguished. "A good plant" is a term of discovery, a milder Eureka!, which fits here.

Lycopodium lucidulum of eastern North America has been called, in print, shining club moss. This has the clunky sound of a paper name, not the ring of true folk terminology. It would be difficult to imagine such folk as Prudence and Zeke using it conversationally while on their annual foray into the woods to gather Christmas greens (a traditional use of eastern American lycopodiums and also of one that grows in the Philippine Cordillera). *Lycopodium lucidulum* grows principally in open woodland, where its branches spread out flat and lengthy and then swing upward to nearly a foot (30 cm) tall (they are less flattened and shorter in hot sun). Along their entire run the branches are dressed with needles that suggest those of hemlock but out-gloss them. A good plant, as is the one that comes next.

Lycopodium obscurum (ground pine) is an inhabitant of woods and of half-sunny woods' margins in Asia and North America (and there, southbound to the Pacific Northwest, Indiana, and the Appalachians). It is a plant with subterranean stems that shoot along beneath leaf mold. From these stems arise needly, pine-like treelets, less than a foot (30 cm) tall, studded with tiny cones.

Lycopodium selago inhabits Europe, Asia, Pacific North America south to Oregon and the Montana Rockies, and eastern North America down to North Carolina in the Appalachians. The plant grows on mossy cliffs and talus slides; along the edges of sunny streams in the mountains, sometimes intermingled with *Sphagnum* moss; and in dense woods. In sunny locations, this short-stoloned club moss presses its needle leaves tightly against bushy, upright branches, which altogether gives the plant the appearance of one of the needled cassiopes, 2–10 inches (5–25 cm) tall, depending on poorness or richness of soil, and on the expansive influence of shade, or on the repressiveness of strong sun. In sheltering woods *L. selago* grows rangily upward and holds its needles widely outward from its branches. This woodland phase of *selago* bears close resemblance to *L. lucidulum*. *Lycopodium selago* craves humidity, especially in a sunny place. If you can grow cassiopes (or gentians or houstonias) in sun, you can probably also grow *selago* there and enjoy its distinctive solar growth form.

Marchantia. See Liverworts—Thallose Kinds.

Mnium. There are several western American mniums; others are eastern in the New World or are transatlantic. These moss species all appear rather like translucent little sea lettuces, some with leaves elliptical and pointed, others quite narrow and toothed of leaf; one other has heart-shaped (punctate) leaves. When dry, these plants crinkle up, only slightly in some kinds, strongly in others. None, in my experience at least, is easy-coming when transplanted; they tend to go into a funk for a year or two afterward. Even so, clumps of *Mnium*, brought home from woodland, will slowly take hold in a garden that provides them with leafy soil, dappled shade, and shelter from drying wind. In favored gardens within the natural range of the plant, *Mnium*, arriving as spores, may form a carpet, especially where soil is left undug for several years. A certain member of the genus, *M. hornum* (Plate 89), native to eastern North America and Europe, is particularly apt to volunteer. In Britain, this is a plant of importance in several of the famous landscape gardens in the public domain; coming into the garden party as a gate-crasher, it adds a welcomely natural and native note of green to the magnificent artifice of layouts of plant species brought from around the world. To be precise, it adds *two* notes of green, one of a light hue in spring, a darker shade by summertime.

Nardia. See Liverworts—Leafy Kinds.

Neckera. *Neckera complanata* (Europe and eastern North America), *N. pennata* (North America, with nearly identical twin or triplet siblings in Europe, Africa, and Japan), and others in the genus are sylvan mosses that

Plate 89. A small portion of a mat of *Mnium hornum*, with beginning invasions of *Polytrichum juniperinum* (at right) and *Atrichum undulatum* (the single wavy rosette at lower left). This confrontation is going on in a mossery described in Chapter 7, Moss Carpets, under Method Three.

adhere to stones, tree trunks, and branches. Their green leaves are tiny and complanate in arrangement, that is, flattened against the surface on which the plant grows. *Neckera complanata* and *N. pennata* are reasonably easy to establish in a deeply shaded garden. Even more amenable is *N. crispa*, a terrestrial species native to Europe, of a wonderful silvery green color when it grows in all the shade and humidity it craves (yellowish where not completely at home).

Parmelia. A large group of papery lichens, *Parmelia* is global in distribution. Many of the species grow in lowlands, especially near seacoasts; others inhabit mountain heights. The media on which the various species fix themselves include rocks, bark, dry wood, stained-glass windows in Gothic cathedrals (they are trouble there), asphalt, and almost any other firm material left alone and out in the weather for at least a few years. An old boot or bottle, stone or branch, charmed into life by *Parmelia* lichens, may make a fascinating garden display. Brought home on their footholds, parmelias must be placed where they receive as much sun and breeziness as in the place they were found. For that matter, lichens of almost any kind are exacting on these points.

Parmelia conspersa is a world-circler, abundant where it grows. "If you glance at a rock covered with a papery lichen and say that it is *Parmelia conspersa*, you will be right at least 50 percent of the time!" says John Bland, lichenologist, speaking of his experience as a trekker on eastern American trails. The plant forms rounds of grayish lichen lace, flat against sunny mineral surfaces. At the perimeter of the lichen, the current year's growth extends in little, irregular frond-like lobes of lighter color than the older, interior portion of the plant. In some plants (Plate 8), the gray of these outward-bound extensions contains the slightest hint of violet. In others, the gray lobes carry greenish or yellowish tints. Sooner or later any of the plants develop fruit cups (apothecia) of mocha or chestnut brown.

This is a lichen worth leisurely examination for the richness it reveals, and worth cultivating for the riches it brings, that certain, singular sensation of wealth that no monetary stash can convey, none other than the good feeling that comes of growing a good plant well. As with any rock-inhabiting lichen (or moss) that the gardener takes home, half the display is in the rock itself. So, the more attractive that half, the more attractive the plant. If the rock is considered in terms of background architecture, its value shows up as exactly that of a splendid old brick or stone wall which enhances the shrubbery or perennials arranged against it.

Hello, hello!, I said to the plant when I found *Parmelia conspersa* growing on a not inhumanly big boulder of porphyry-hued jasper for sale on an outdoor table at a rock-hound shop. Riches for a paltry sum. The purplish rock makes a fine color contrast with the ashy lichen. Several inches across, the rounds of *Parmelia* on the rock have remained healthy in garden conditions for 6 or 7 years at this juncture and continue to expand across the rock face at a growth rate of about ¼ inch (6 mm) annually. The plant on its stone goes well with cacti and other succulents on the sunny railing, or sometimes on the garden table, where I place them for the summer. During winter the lichen stays outdoors, while the tender succulents are brought inside.

Peligera. Foliose lichens, peligeras are native around the world. They crop up from the ground or in an established carpet of moss, poking forth in shapes fan-like or rounded and ear-like, metallically greenish or bluish in tone. *Peligera*, in the midst of garden moss, forms an attractive added note *if* one can look on it with ease. (It will not take over totally. And tearing it out would entail the loss of a lot of moss along with the lichen.)

Philonotis. The melodiously named *Philonotis fontana* belongs to a moss genus containing a number of other species limited in range and of modest garden value. They all like damp rocks and moist soils. *Philonotis fontana* itself rounds the northern hemisphere, is ubiquitously abundant, and is one of the more rewarding mosses for small-scale gardening. Its New World range covers the continent south of permanent snow and north of Florida. It is a seeker of seeps, mires, and slow streams, where it grows as an emergent, that is, as a plant that stands about half-submerged in shallow water. But elsewhere it stands fully emerged on wet ground. In either setting, *P. fontana* is a great drinker. A ¼ cup (70 ml) of water can be squeezed from a mere handful of its branches.

This moss makes squishy cushions and quilts, formed of tightly packed, upright stems, dense with tiny leaves that are shingled in arrangement, suggesting a shaggy-scaled saurian of some kind. The plant's color varies, seasonally and regionally. North American representatives of the species are usually clear-green in springtime, darkening to olive-green by late summer, while European *Philonotis fontana* typically matures a bluish green.

Philonotis fontana sometimes arrives spore-borne or duck-delivered in water gardens, where it is usually an improvement on the landscaping. I have seen the plant volunteering as a ground cover on a gardener-made islet in a lily pond, intermingling with the shafts of a horticultural form of tule (*Scirpus lacustris* 'Zebrina' or *Schoenoplectus lacustris* 'Zebrina'), an ensemble of a beauty rare and strange. The location was sunny. Another volunteer colony of *fontana* grows along the margin of a pond in a fern garden under shade cloth (66 percent shady).

A planting of *Philonotis fontana* that I set out in a shady bed of open, fast-draining soil, kept constantly moist by irrigation, carries on in easy health. And I have found this moss to be easy as a pot plant, or perhaps I could say, as a moss-mollusc (Plate 54), in a seashell container garden where the *Philonotis* replaces the snail. I cannot claim the sanction of "good taste" for this little gardening adventure of mine. The container probably outshines the thing contained, and that is not so good in container gardening. But just maybe this is my best and boldest opus as a moss gardener, an effort that pushes the rules and gets them out of a rut. The moss-mollusc is watered as often as is needed to keep it saturated. The cup of the deep, 10-inch- (25-cm-) long shell really should have been drilled to form a drainage hole at the bottom, but I have been reluctant to mar its perfection by doing so. Instead, I tip the shell now and then while flooding the moss with a stream of water, an action that washes away harmful salts that build up by evaporation. The garden's other simple needs include an application of acidic fertilizer in solution three times a year, spring, summer, and fall, and a place outdoors in sunshine. Before winter I "shell" the moss with a knife blade and plant it in the ground to prevent breakage of the container by frost.

Plagiochila. See Liverworts—Leafy Kinds.

Plagiothecium. A maker of woodland carpets, *Plagiothecium* is a genus of mosses generally with complanate (flattened) leaves and branches, and with a determined belief in manifest destiny. Where one of their kind takes a liking to a woods, it will take over the floor space as well as any object close to the floor. The *Plagiothecium* overwhelms most other bryophytes in its progress over earth, logs, low rocks, and scattered bones but does not hinder ferns or flowering plants that stand taller. In its domain, the deeply carpeting *Plagiothecium* sponges up sounds, quieting the forest, intensifying its sanctum sanctorum ambiance.

Transplanted from woodland to a shady garden (into the best of devil's-food-cake-like beds of soil, springy with humus), *Plagiothecium* proves to be willing, but slow, to acclimate. With this moss, as with a transplant of any sort, a remove from rich shade in wilderness to the reduced humidity of the average shady garden is a blow to the plant's native vigor. To help the new planting adjust, water it well during dry weather. (Forgive me if I sound like a nagging, niggling grandpappy about such basic tenets of moss gardening that I have so often repeated.)

Half a dozen species of the genus *Plagiothecium* are found in Europe (including Britain), and half a dozen in North America's wooded regions. In several cases, the same plants are native to both continents. Two similar intercontinental species with promising garden futures are *P. denticulatum*, a bright, shiny green, and *P. undulatum*, pale green and glossy when moist, whitish and dull when dry. Other distinguishing features include *undulatum*'s wavy leaves and wrinkled spore cases (in dry condition) compared with *denticulatum*'s smooth leaves and smooth spore cases. The New World range of *denticulatum* extends over the forested regions of the East,

West, and South while *undulatum* covers the Far West from Alaska to California and includes Idaho in its territory. The two mosses may be found in the same region but their zealous territoriality usually keeps each in its own woodland.

Plate 90 shows *Plagiothecium undulatum* together with an animal co-habitant of deep woods, the sight of which critter may be a shock to the gardener not properly introduced. Gardener, this is no lowlife, garden-variety slug. This is the celebrated banana slug of Pacific Northwest forests, an animal that grows nearly as big as the eponymous fruit. Naturalists in the Northwest greatly admire the tawny mollusc, which stays in the woods

Plate 90. *Plagiothecium undulatum,* with the beloved (by many) banana slug of Pacific Northwest woods.

and never (better make that very rarely) ventures into gardens of town, suburb, or country. In this, it is quite unlike the dastardly black slug of garden havoc, originally European, accidentally imported.

See also, in this chapter, the moss *Pseudotaxiphyllum elegans*. It used to be a *Plagiothecium* and, certain technicalities aside, is still very like one.

Pohlia. Several species of the moss genus *Pohlia* range widely in North America and in much of the rest of the world. Pohlias are low, fine mat plants, easily cultivated if not allowed to become too hot and dry. Some are shade plants; others that grow naturally in sun are better for being in part shade in the garden rather than in the full blast of summer. Tidy little pets in an alpine collection, they are also usable as bonsai covers.

Pohlia annotina and certain others carry gemmae (or bulbils) at the bases of their elliptical leaves. *Pohlia annotina* may grow as a self-sown carpet of at least several years' duration in undisturbed garden ground. But often a stronger moss, such as a *Polytrichum*, also self-sown, finally forces it out and takes its place.

Pohlia cruda and *P. wahlenbergii* (two pohlias without gemmae) grow near sea level and up to above timberline in mountainous regions. In the lowlands they are curtailed, inconspicuous growers. But in the mountains they are profligate, forming great stretches of moss cover, a kind of fine, smooth, green plush. When moist, the first-named plant is a light green while the other is a bluish green; both species turn whitish when dry.

Surprisingly, these montane mosses, bibulously exuberant, topers of the cold water of melting snow, will accept transplantation down into the snowless environment of a city or country garden. Give them lots of water. Or maybe do not grow them but enjoy them as subjects of visual and tactile gardening only, as friends and I often do, in taking a picnic up into the mountains and spreading it out on one or another of these pohlias, party to our party.

Polytrichum. Pronounced as Polly Trickum, I love that shady lady of a name. The plants enlisted under it also have an English name that you may prefer: hairy cap mosses. They cover much of the world. The "hairy caps" of these plants serve as chapeaus for their spore capsules, which are produced abundantly during spring and early summer. Jiggle the capsules when they are ripe and they will release a cloud of luminously bright, yellow spores with a greenish tinge. Recommended entertainment.

Unlike many mosses, in which male and female organs are present in the same individual, *Polytrichum* plants are entirely separate as to sex. Females carry egg-bearing structures and support the spore-bearing sporophyte that develops following fertilization. Males bear flower-like rosettes formed of stiff bracts, glassy-clear or brownish in color. Plate 1 shows these structures.

Males and females appear to be identical in their leafy green stems. Either sex grows as a patch or, when undisturbed for many years, as a lawn of as much as a ¼-acre (0.1-hectare) extent. The unit of the plant is a tuft of fir-like needles arranged around a wiry, upright stem. In aggregate the stems of needles are like an even-topped forest seen from miles high. When dry the needles close up against their stem, and the colony of wizened stems waits out the drought looking deathly, but the plants are patiently safe for weeks or months.

In a garden the plants will acclimate to constant watering and will stay green as long as moisture is present. Polytrichums are easily transplanted, easily kept healthy when their simple needs are met: sun, half shade, or even four-fifths shade; any acidic soil, clayey, loamy, sandy, or gravelly. But, as cautioned on another page, when transplanted from a fertile place, *Polytrichum* does not take kindly to poorer ground.

The three polytrichums discussed below range throughout much of the world. The larger species are unsurpassed among mosses as cover plants for sunny ground; the smaller has charm as a cover for a few feet or inches of soil, either in the open or in a container. A number of other *Polytrichum* species grow in North America and on other continents, plants that closely resemble one or another of these three and are as handsome in gardens.

The likenesses do not stop there. A whole other group of mosses, the pogonatums, are dead-ringers for the polytrichums. The best way I know to tell them apart is by their differing spore capsules, once the hairy caps have dropped off. *Polytrichum* capsules have ridges; those of *Pogonatum* are smoothly rounded cylinders. Pogonatums make first-rate garden mosses, with uses like those of their better-known cousins.

Polytrichum commune (Plate 48) is king of the genus, with P. *juniperinum* as its consort, and P. *piliferum* as their junior-size heir apparent. *Polytrichum commune* reigns by the power of often being the biggest, and simply by being there. This is the *Polytrichum* most often present as a planting or natural occurrence in the gardens of Japan and the rest of the world. But the queen species, *P. juniperinum*, as well, is frequently in residence in the world's gardens.

To the naked eye, *Polytrichum commune* and *P. juniperinum* are really much alike, differing mainly in their potential height. In wet, rich soil, the king species is capable of stretching upward to half a yard (46 cm) tall, compared to the queen's 6 inches (15 cm) or so in like conditions. Either species inhabits soils wet, moist, or dry; and in the more arid places either plant is reduced to a height of 2 inches (5 cm), or one, or even less. The surest way to tell them apart is in a close examination of the leaves. Those of *P. juniperinum* have smooth margins, while those of *P. commune* are saw-edged. But these features are visible only under at least 10 power magnification. Never mind. Either plant is a marvel for the moss gardener.

Polytrichum juniperinum is a name that seems a misnomer. I have never been able to see in this plant anything of juniper, a scale-leaved conifer; but of needle conifers, easily enough with a willing eye. Curiously, in spite of the premier position in gardens that is held by its close relative *P. commune*, *P. juniperinum* ranks first among polytrichums in the world at large. Indeed, it is the putative champion among cosmopolitan mosses of all kinds. Certainly none has a more worldly range: throughout the entire globe except for polar ice and most tropical lands.

Polytrichum piliferum, when growing as a lowlander, stands as tall 2½ inches (6 cm); as a mountaineer it grows more and more compact with elevation and increasing severity of habitat, down to ½ inch (13 mm). This minor species is easily told from other polytrichums by its hair-tipped needles. They give the plant an attractive whitishness especially noticeable when it is dry.

Porella. See Liverworts—Leafy Kinds.

Pseudotaxiphyllum. *Pseudotaxiphyllum elegans* (synonyms, *Isopterygium elegans*, *Plagiothecium elegans*) is a moss natively European and North American (in wooded regions) that grows as a flattened pelt, a mere ¼ inch (6 mm) thick on partly sunny ground, somewhat looser in shade. The pelt is made up of tiny, spear-point leaves in two ranks along slim, brief branches, most all of which are neatly agreeable in heading southward, sunward, as they grow. Silvery green when dry, the plant turns greener with moisture. The world's best garden employment of this plant is perhaps in the Nitobe Memorial Garden at the University of British Columbia, where it volunteered and now covers many yards of ground (Plate 91).

Plate 91. *Pseudotaxiphyllum elegans* (synonyms, *Isopterygium elegans, Plagiothecium elegans*), dry and of a silvery green, beside a pea-gravel path in the Nitobe Memorial Garden, University of British Columbia. In part sun, this moss is perhaps the most compressed of all those that are useful as garden ground covers. At Nitobe it is lower to the ground than the particles of gravel, which, true to name, average the size of peas.

Racomitrium. Several of the world-circling members of the moss genus *Racomitrium* are rock-dwellers, attractive, and fairly amenable to a garden life; several more grow as mats on soil as well as on rocks, are easily domesticated and of major importance in moss gardening.

Racomitrium aciculare, a dark green species, covers boulders that rise from streams or rest on stream banks, and here it withstands—probably enjoys—being submerged during a season of high water. Brought home to the garden on its rock and placed in or beside a garden stream, it may never realize that it has been captured and will go right on growing as a happy wild thing. Brought home to a garden where there is no stream *R. aciculare* will need plentiful watering except in summer, when it should receive only rainfall, however scanty.

Racomitrium heterostichum (Plate 5) is another dark green rock moss, superficially quite like the last-named plant. This one grows in tufts and patches on acidic stones on sunny hillsides and mountains throughout western North America, and in Europe. In eastern North America it is a frequent inhabitant of tree trunks, logs, and fence posts as well as rocks. Brought into cultivation on its native stone or wood, *R. heterostichum* will usually acclimate without difficulty, but irrigation is risky. While there may be no harm in watering this moss if it drains and dries out quickly, too much wetness will cause damping off.

I have a little moss-on-a-rock garden (Plate 22) that features *Racomitrium heterostichum* in a planting by Nature on an egg-shaped clay stone only 6 inches (15 cm) long. Despite its smallness this garden amply demonstrates the lifestyle of moss as a petrophyte. By careful count 24 separate *Racomitrium* plants cling to this rock (as do innumerable *Buellia* lichens, dark gray splotches studded with black dots). Twenty-three of the racomitriums are of the species *R. heterostichum*; the remaining plant is of yet another of the rock-clingers in this genus, *R. fasciculare*, yellow-green, located near the summit of the stone. Some of the moss plants measure as little as ⅛ inch (3 mm) across, but all are at least a decade old, judging from their growth during the 4 years I have kept watch: there has been mighty little of it. Each moss plant occupies a pock in the stone that holds moisture and collects nutritious dust in amount just enough to sustain life. So, with rock mosses, a lean life and plenty of exercise (in withstanding winds) promotes tough resilience and longevity. I resist any mention of an obvious parallel.

Racomitrium lanuginosum and its allied species, *R. canescens* and *R. varium*, are tide-like in growth, slowly, inexorably creeping over the ground and up over rocks. All three of these mosses show sharply differing dry-weather and wet-weather faces. When dry, they turn grayish (or even whitish in the case of *R. lanuginosum*). With rain, they instantly fluff up and change to a chartreuse (Plate 92).

Racomitrium lanuginosum and *R. canescens* are worldly in range. In North America, the first-named plant grows southward to the Pacific Northwest and to New England; the second-named, down to California, Colorado, Michigan, and New York. In Europe (including Britain) these two are typically mosses of subalpine and alpine elevations, inhabiting marshes, dry ground, and hot rocks; wherever they grow, they are often the dominant ground covers or rock covers. In some other regions, such as the Pacific

Plate 92. *Racomitrium lanuginosum* after a rain. In dry weather it turns gray and woolly-appearing.

Northwest, these same two species inhabit elevations high and low, down to sea level. *Racomitrium varium,* a Pacific Northwest endemic, grows as a terrestrial at various elevations and also favors rotting logs in open woods.

Any of the three species appears fabric-like in its flat growth and its knobby, densely matted branches. When any one of them is peeled off the soil, rocks, or logs where it grows, it comes away as easily and as pliably as wool off a sheep, especially when the moss is taken up in moist condition. These racomitriums often cover acres or even miles of ground and in such vastness will not mind being collected in quantity somewhat greater than would be seemly in less mossy places.

I have found them to be among the most accommodating of mosses, settling into the garden as soon as planted; growing forth and covering ground at a satisfying rate, not too slow, not immoderately; and repelling many small weeds. They perform best when grown in an open, breezy location, on sloping ground, or on rocks. In spite of the fact that marshland is a part of their habitat (in Europe, anyway), their garden response to irrigation is uncertain. It is safer not to water, especially in hot, droughty weather, which can result in their popping off—blackening suddenly.

Ramalina. A large, international genus of foliose lichens, *Ramalina* is often found dangling from tree trunks and twigs, in clusters of raggedy, noodle-like strips, colored a dull yellow in the case of many species. Ramalinas frequently fall from trees during windstorms, and afterward, lying there as haplessly as beached sea life, they are often bagged by those of us who fossick in the woods for terrarium furnishings. Therein, they make fine display plants while they last, but their life span in captivity is often no more than a few months.

Rhizocarpon. *Rhizocarpon geographicum* (one of a number of closely similar rhizocarpons) bears a species' and a common name, map lichen, both of which names romanticize the special quality of this lichen's (and of related lichens') black-margined masses on a matrix stone. They suggest land masses in cartography. *Rhizocarpon geographicum* grows around the world on hard, acidic rocks, mainly in mountainous regions.

This plant is one of the most appressed and slowest of crustose lichens, a rock painting of dot pattern (when it is not being a map), a work in pointillism, of faintly green-tinged yellow dots on a black ground, a pattern interesting to the naked eye and wondrous when viewed under magnification.

I grow map lichen—more accurately, it grows itself—on chunks of quartz brought home from high mountains and kept on a sunny garden railing, but occasionally carried indoors for a few days just to improve acquaintance with the plant (Plate 7). Actually, I find the cultivation of map lichen to be as much a gardening of mineral as of vegetation. This form of life seems a flowering of the rock to which it clings, a florescence of infinitesimal progress in response to the ages rather than the seasons. For nearly a decade I have been watching my map lichens bloom, an exercise that requires the watcher to come back annually, or not much sooner, in order to observe any change whatsoever. The lichens on the quartz have expanded a mere grass stem's breadth or two during the years I have kept watch. Since the individual patches average nearly an inch (2.5 cm) across, their age, taken from the observed rate of growth, easily spans several decades and may be closer to the century mark.

Look to this infinitely calm plant for a supply of calmness when needed. Of all the world's worth of lichens and of other primitive miniatures, plants known for their special ability to soothe, this one is especially efficacious. It sits there ensconced on its rock, like a swami in the Himalayas, body and soul fastened on eternity, a seer worthy of empathy. One fixes one's gaze and mind on the map lichen, and it works as a chart for smooth sailing.

Rhytidiadelphus. Three species in the moss genus *Rhytidiadelphus*, *R. loreus*, *R. squarrosus*, and *R. triquetrus*, range all around the northern hemisphere, down to southern Appalachia in the New World. The three are sturdy ground covers, fairly fast-growing. Easily transplanted, they make durable, light green fabric in a patchwork quilt of mosses laid out in a cool, leaf-moldy, mostly shady place. But one of the three, *R. squarrosus*, performs well in hot sun, in poor soil, and in the midst of competing grass. I am being a bit facetious, for this one is none other than that most infamous taker-over of grass, the moss that more than any other has given the whole clan of Bryophyta a bad name with lawn devotees. It is a plant identifiable at a glance and a touch: it is made up of stiff stems dressed somewhat sparsely with narrow leaves that curve back and around almost far enough to form circles; color, light green when shaded, tannish in sun and drought.

If you have made up your mind that you do not want to harbor lawn mosses of this or of any other kind, they may be killed out with the use of products concocted for the purpose and sold in garden stores. These chemical killers turn the moss into black blotches, a sight much less presentable than the living moss. The blotches remain for up to half a year, or until the lawn fills in—if it ever does (ruined places may need to be raked clear and then reseeded) or until the moss returns from spores. They don't tell you all that on the product label. Tolerance in dealing with lawn mosses may have more to be said for it than have toxins.

In some lawns, *Rhytidiadelphus squarrosus*, that archenemy, forms a ground cover just as valuable and sightly as any grass, as for example in a half-century-old lawn in a boulevard median, of which Plate 93 shows a small patch. Typical of many park lawns around the world, and of about a million easy-does-it home lawns as well, this one consists of a serviceable mixture of grasses and international lawn weeds growing in full sun. The lawn is mowed regularly (blades must be set at least 2 inches (5 cm) high to keep the moss from being torn up) but never fertilized or weeded. In places *R. squarrosus* grows as grass-free patches as much as a yard (90 cm) across, nicely clothing the ground. In other places grass and the other flowering plants predominate. If there were some chemical that would kill the competitors without harming the moss, the latter would make a perfectly good lawn on its own, one that would require no mowing.

Of the other two related mosses, *Rhytidiadelphus loreus* is a forest plant with recurved leaves, softly green and translucent in shade. The leaf stems glow with a dilute reddishness, as if lighted by an interior energy source.

Plate 93. *Rhytidiadelphus squarrosus,* living the life of Riley in a grass lawn intermixed with allowed weeds.

Attractive and easy to establish and maintain, this species is one of the several most rewarding of all the ground-covering mosses (but it will overgrow smaller kinds). Nearly equal in value is the third member of the *Rhytidiadelphus* trio, *R. triquetrus,* a denizen of open woods and pastures, a pale green carpet with stocky branches and triangular leaves that curve slightly.

Selaginella. The world's 700 species of *Selaginella* mainly inhabit tropical and subtropical lands. But a few selaginellas are temperate, far northern or high alpine in habitat. The several selaginellas that have evolved in cold, harsh regions have compressed their bodies earthward and reduced their leaf size to little slivers, until they have become so close and small that they quite resemble some of the more cautious mosses. But most of the selaginellas, being more equatorial in origin, stand taller and leafier. Some of these resemble the more fern-like of mosses; others are even too much like ferns, in their ample and frondy leaves, to have any logical place in this book on mosses and their miniature imitators.

    Selaginella involvens is a Japanese plant, occasionally displayed in bonsai and *saikei* exhibits in the United States, and may be available commercially somewhere in the country. Or, perhaps the plants on view have been imported. How to describe the species? The nearest thing to it in appearance is a cycad. Imagine a cycad with its stout trunk and umbrella cap of hard fronds reduced to a few inches. But the selaginella's fronds are more intricate, more lacy than the pinion-like leaves of the cycad.

Selaginella involvens is old in Japanese cultivation. Fanciers there have selected several dozen foliar forms, some variegated, some twisted of leaf, few as desirable as the unadorned wilding, except of course to the extremist collector. In certain communities in Japan, nursery families specialize in fancy forms of this plant. The growers live in houses raised off the ground, providing storage space beneath. Here the selaginellas are wintered in completely dry condition since the fancy forms are sensitive to winter wet. The wild plant, however, is hardy in winter snow and rain, or so I have found it to be in the Seattle area.

Selaginella kraussiana, an African native, is yet more mossy than ferny in appearance. In any tabulation of the nurseries that offer it, and of the gardens that grow it, this species would probably rate as the most important of the selaginellas. Growable as a container plant indoors or out, it is also a mat-maker of fairly fast spread when grown in shady ground outdoors. The plant will survive light frost. In the ocean-moderated climate of North America's Pacific Coast, it is capable of prospering as a ground cover in sheltered gardens as far north as the U.S. Department of Agriculture hardiness zone 7 extends. On North Island, New Zealand, Mediterranean in climate, *S. kraussiana* has gone feral (coastal California take heed) in forest preserves within the bailiwick of the city of Auckland, and in wooded gardens. Where the plant prospers it prospers well enough to cover all available shady ground. This may not be at all bad in a garden, may in fact be good—a beautiful ground cover at no cost of coin, time, or energy, a perfectly nice weed *except* where one wants to grow anything else that is much less than a foot (30 cm) high. The *Selaginella* would flow right over the competition. But tall woodland plants are safe in its presence; they are probably even benefited. And the *Selaginella* is easily kept back by raking it off the ground.

Selaginella kraussiana, a seeming moss-fern, stands a few inches tall, with tender, easily torn fronds that in outline resemble the foliage of cypress (*Cupressus*), or of certain cypress-needled mosses. The branches of the *Selaginella* root down skimpily as they grow onward.

Nurseries sell *Selaginella kraussiana* in a number of color forms, among them a rich green (the pretty pest in New Zealand, and a generous ground cover in certain Pacific Northwest gardens), a variegated form (seldom seen, probably due to instability), and a chartreuse form (*S. kraussiana* 'Aurea', Plate 94, exactly like the typical plant in the cut of its leaves). The latter is widely available at plant shops, where it is sold as a houseplant (often under peppier made-up names). I have not seen 'Aurea' in any sizable open ground planting but would guess that it has at least much of the strength and determination to advance that is shown by the species' greener phase. Indoors or outdoors, any form of *S. kraussiana* needs moisture, dotes on humidness, will tolerate only brief sunlight, and is most at home in full shade, but in the brightest of light within shade.

Selaginella lepidophylla, resurrection plant, is abundant in parts of the desert Southwest of the United States. During summer and autumn drought the plant curls up into a dry brown ball seemingly as defunct as the husk of a sun-dried armadillo. With winter and spring rain it unfurls as a richly green and ferny bushlet. Resurrection plant is collected commercially and sold in roadside souvenir shops as an object of presto change-o amusement. The vendor will, as a rule, offer dry plants and usually will have one

Plate 94. *Selaginella kraussiana* 'Aurea', usually grown as a houseplant, potentially a woodland garden ground cover.

demonstration plant sitting in a saucer of water, green and lively for all appearance, but actually in distress. The plant dies when it is unnaturally awakened too often or for too long a time. Open-ground cultivation is suitable only in a desert. Elsewhere, grow this species as a pot plant, wintered dry and cold (as the Japanese do with *S. involvens*) and summered out in the sun and rain, but never watered except perhaps as a rare treat for the child mind.

Selaginella sanguinolenta 'Compressa' (Plate 6) is a non-moss that considerably resembles the true moss *Hypnum cupressiforme*, seeming to be an enlargement of it. Out of sight are the selaginella's bright red underground stem portions that have inspired the specific name *sanguinolenta* (meaning, bloody). The plant pictured is 10 inches (25 cm) in diameter, at about 10 years of age, and thus belongs to horticulture's slow-growth gemmery. The taller companion plant in the same container is *S. caulescens*, a hardy fern-like member of the genus (several other ferny selaginellas are well-known greenhouse plants). The other, rather *Cassiope*-like green mound in view is *S. remotifolia* 'Compacta'.

All three selaginellas are Japanese in origin and were sent to me in the 1960s by Dr. Tsuneshige Rokujo of Tokyo. Through this introduction these plants have likely become available, to some slight extent, in the North American nursery trade (more about this immediately below). The three specimens in Plate 6 are kept outdoors year-around in the frostproof stoneware pots seen in the picture, in a sheltered, mostly shaded spot within the garden of Steve Doonan and Phil Pearson, Issaquah, Washington.

Selaginella sibirica grows as a mat made up of many furry paws, of a grizzly green. This species is one other of the Japanese selaginellas sent to me long ago by that keenest of amateur plant swappers, Dr. Rokujo, who has exchanged rarities, as I know, with gardeners all over the world. For years I, as a mail-order nurseryman, offered the selaginellas I received from him. Knowing the acquisitive eagerness characteristic of the trade when it comes to marketable new plants, I expect that other nurseries specializing in alpines and bonsai garnishments will have snapped up these still-novel selaginellas and saved them from commercial extinction in North America.

If it turns out that you can't find *Selaginella sibirica*, however, you may have readier access to its near relative, *S. densa*, similar in appearance, abundant and widespread on the high plains of North America's West. It may even be available at a nursery or two. As container plants, *S. densa* and *S. sibirica* are equally handsome. Their cones are an added attraction in early summer but later become shriveled and unsightly. Dead-heading neatens the plant.

I have *Selaginella sibirica* as an 8-year-old, 1-foot- (30-cm-) long plant tumbling over soil and rocks in a bonsai pot. Gray *Cladonia* lichens have come voluntarily to fill bare places. During summer the *Selaginella* enjoys being kept watered but is content in being allowed to go dry. In autumn I place the container garden on a shelf under broad eaves at the sunny south side of the house. There it stays crisp-dry until spring, when it is again set out under the open sky for the summer.

Selaginella sibirica is also growable in the open ground but is wintered there less certainly (at least in the soft and rainy winter of my Pacific Northwest home) than when kept dry. The same goes for *S. densa*. As open-ground plants these two are safer where winter provides protective snow the whole season.

Selaginella wallacei inhabits cliff crevices and ledges, where at an age of decades the plant spreads to perhaps 2 feet (60 cm) across. This native of North America's Pacific Coast makes an easygoing citizen in an alpine garden or in a container. Grow it in half shade.

Sphagnum. *Sphagnum* mosses, in life, advance with an oozy ease over the bog surfaces and wet soils of the world. This populous group of plants numbers about 30 species in the British Isles alone, some 50 in North America, and many more about the world. *Sphagnum* moss, long dead and layered down by time, and then excavated, is that marvelous stuff of many uses, from the flavoring of Scotch whisky to the amending of the soil in a million gardens. But it is the live plant that most excites moss gardeners, to whom the *Sphagnum* species are among the most popular bryophytes. The greatest attraction of these plants may be coloration.

The many sphagnums, for example, those in Plates 95–97, offer the gardener a range of colors in addition to greens, and unexpected in mosses. Greens there are in abundance, greens darker and lighter, up to a whitishness with only a tinge of verdancy. Then there are *Sphagnum* mosses in rose-red, dark wine, tangerine, ochre, fawn, and more. Actually, all these more colorful plants are green in their interior branches unreached by the sun. Colors other than green result from the effect of sunlight on the outer parts of *Sphagnum* plants receptive to transformation. Some individuals of a species are changeable, others are not. In those that are, sun suppresses

Plate 95. *Sphagnum capillifolium*, a wine-dark member of a many-colored genus of mosses, with richly green *Polytrichum commune*.

Plate 96. *Sphagnum imbricatum*, orange, lemon, and lime, in its various rosettes.

Plate 97. *Sphagnum palustre*, straw-colored during dry summer weather (prolonged rain turns it green). This approximately 20-year-old plant has formed a cushion 5 feet (1.5 meters) across, 2½ feet (75 cm) thick; at the edge of a garden pond. Superlatively happy here in mud at shoreline, the *Sphagnum* has the strength to hoist itself up over good-size boulders. Companion plants: *Hosta* and *Andromeda polifolia* (at upper right), a shrublet that likes nothing better than to root and romp through live *Sphagnum*.

the basic greenness and brings out the other colors. Reversely, a colorful plant, moved into shade by a moss gardener, usually turns a woodsy green.

In form the *Sphagnum* mosses are much alike. They are mat plants, the topmost, live part of which consists of rosettes (technically, capitula) of densely packed branches facing skyward. The mat builds upon itself, accumulating an underneath branch depth of several inches or feet, browning and dying closely below the surface, decaying lower down. The deep, underneath portion of the plant wicks up water to its living surface.

Ideal places in which to grow *Sphagnum* mosses are along the sunny margins of springs, garden bogs, and ponds. Yet many of the species, even some of those collected from wetlands, will acclimate to life in a moist, shady bed suited as well to other mosses, ferns, and forest plants. (The only disappointment is in the sphagnum's loss of color.) The *Sphagnum* species will also grow in a terrarium kept out of hot sun or, better yet, in a deep flowerpot filled nearly to the top with the sphagnum's long under-growth or with commercial peat moss. The live portion of the *Sphagnum*, attached to the brown stems (now packed in the pot) should be set in even-ly, the numerous living rosettes kept flat across their communal surface and straight up. Place the be-mossed pot in sun or part shade, and keep it saturated by watering as often as necessary, probably once a day in hot, dry weather. Better that the pot has a drainage hole, which will help pre-vent the stagnating of water. But in the dog days of summer it may be nec-essary to keep the pot in a bowl or deep saucer, and when watering, to fill both that and the pot.

Sphagnum moss dislikes heavily chlorinated water but may endure it (as we do) and show no readily apparent ill effects. Alkaline or calciferous water, however, acts as a quick killer. Distilled water is perfectly safe, rain-water usually so, spring water or brook water yes or no, depending on local minerals and purity.

In a region of freezing winter, pot-grown sphagnums (an improper word, that; kindly allow it in place of the correct but hideous plural, sphagna) can be brought through the season safely by taking them out of their con-tainers and planting them in the open ground in a sheltered, shady place. In my own trials, those that I have wintered outdoors in shade have greeted spring unharmed, while those in sunny, exposed places have expired. Other moss gardeners winter sphagnums in terraria or in uncovered con-tainers kept in greenhouses or alpine houses.

It may be that many gardeners who grow *Sphagnum* really do not take a moss gardener's pleasure in it but have merely an incidental interest in this moss as the rooting medium of choice in the culture of insectivorous plants. *Dionaea, Drosera, Sarracenia*, and other devourers of arthropod pro-tein revel in the steady moistness of live *Sphagnum* about their roots, and in its steady humidification of their foliage. *Sphagnum*, growing in a green-house or in a terrarium with such alimentary plants, may remain healthy, good-looking, and serviceable up to about 3 years. Eventually it grows lank and then must be replaced (but retained about the roots of any compan-ion plants).

Stereocaulon. A sizable genus of fruticose lichens, *Stereocaulon* is world-wide in distribution. These lichens grow on rocks or on barren mineral soil, where they are first-comers, even preceding such pioneers as the *Poly-*

trichum mosses. Stereocaulons make little cushions of themselves, or little shrubs or trees, typically of a silvery gray color and often with branches that divide and redivide into a material as fine and spriggy as Brussels lace. The stereocaulons transplant readily when dug with a clump of their native earth, or when brought home secure on their native rock. Many of them (I hazard to say, having had good luck with several) will make model citizens in container gardens, where they will live long and grow not too slowly, with just enough motility to give reassurance that one is taking care of something alive and responsive. Some other lichens leave one with doubts about that.

Stereocaulon paschale is an abundant cosmopolite of the northern hemisphere, found on the stilled surface of poor soil in the more northerly of the United States, in Canada, northern Europe, and elsewhere. Portrayed in Plate 9 are three plants of *S. paschale* that were dug years earlier and at once planted on a shard of crockery-like pahoehoe lava. (A small pot, or a saucer drilled with a hole for drainage, would have served just as well.) I had brought home, with these lichens, a small extra quantity of the soil in which they had been growing, enough of it to fix them on the stone. Atop this soil, to hold it in place, I planted a cover of *Pohlia* moss. The lichens grow and expand about ¼ inch (6 mm) annually and at the time of writing measure 2½–3½ inches (6–9 cm) across. They are never watered; watering proved fatal in an earlier attempt of mine at growing this plant.

Thuidium. One of those rare bryophytes with well-founded folk names, *Thuidium delicatulum* (feather moss or fern moss) is found in forests throughout North America. Europe has a similar species, *T. tamariscinum*. These are large, frondy mosses that somewhat resemble the more fern-like of the selaginellas. They are part of the sadness of moss gardening, the fact that the splendidly lacy ones are so generally ungrowable. Humidity, humidity, humidity is what they crave, the condition of deep woods.

Tortula. A genus of small-leaved, tufting or cushioning mosses, the tortulas are characteristically hairy by way of having leaves that terminate in a long, translucent hair point. These plants, when dry and shriveled, take on a frosted whitishness of surface, the hair points having become closer together and more noticeable. Many of the tortulas cling to rocks and the bark of tree trunks and are easily brought into cultivation as container plants on a bit of this or that home-base material. One of the species, *T.*

muralis (Plate 34), is a major camp follower, inhabiting concrete walls and the mortar of brickwork around the world, as well as calcareous rocks in wilderness or in gardens.

Umbilicaria. *Umbilicaria*, rock-tripe, is a genus of foliose lichens of global distribution. The Latin name derives from the plants' method of attachment to their native rocks: by means of a bit of a cord at the base of the leaf. The unlovely English name commemorates the netted pattern on the underside of the leaves, a little like that of honeycomb tripe. The umbilicarias bear another resemblance, no more nor less strained than that of likening these plants to stomach lining, to dry rose petals, crinkled and dulled to a brown, black, or gray. They are more attractive than I, or other fanciers, make them seem to be. The fall of rain on the plant expands its shriveled petals, turning *Umbilicaria* into a stone-flower of sorts. Kept on a sunny garden table or railing, the stone and its flower may carry on their unhasty coexistence for years, the flower unfolding with rain, closing in time of drought. In dry weather the plant should be left alone, unwatered, unawakened. In cool, moist weather, it can be soused with an acidifying fertilizer, if one is feeling especially caring at the moment.

Xanthoria. *Xanthoria* is a genus of foliose lichens that adhere closely to their matrices and seem more crustose than leafy. That is about enough of science with its nuts and bolts of plant mechanism. It takes poetry to bring plants to life in language, and even to convey, in the case of those lichens that grow on stone, some sense of their almost geological patience:

> Sharing the stillness of the unimpassioned rock, they share also its endurance . . . Far above among the mountains, the silver lichen spots rest, starlike, on the stone; and the gathering orange stain upon the edge of yonder peak reflects the sunset of a thousand years.

The quotation forms the finale of a prose poem by John Ruskin on the transcendent existence of mosses and lichens. Clues of color and habitat indicate that the gathering orange stain is none other than *Xanthoria* while the silver lichen spots are almost certainly *Parmelia*. In cultivation, the xanthorias offer a relative immortality that, to borrow a bluff phrase favored by vendors of tweeds in Scotland, "will see you out." The following paragraph offers a case in point.

Xanthoria elegans (Plate 66) inhabits mountaintops and rooftops in Britain. In North America it is an inhabitant of cliffs and boulders throughout the West of Canada and the United States, while in the East it ranges down to the northeastern states at various elevations and travels even farther southward on the higher stones of the Appalachian chain. In color the species varies from mellowy yellows, through hues of orange, to scarlet, the latter being particularly inviting to the hunter-gatherer of the gardenable. For example, consider a garden friend of mine, the late Marvin Black, an arborist by profession and a home gardener with a love for all plants, from trees to the tiniest. My friend brought a sample of scarlet *X. elegans* home from a mountain, on a baguette of basalt upon which it had been born perhaps a couple of centuries earlier. He kept the stone and plant on his mantelpiece for more than three decades. Occasionally, during rainy weather, he would place the lichened rock outside for a wash up and a drink up. In all those years the rich red of the lichen never faded. I can't say that it grew. It may have, but I neglected to make the periodic measurements necessary to find out, and it is too late now. I wonder whatever became of that lichen on that slender length of stone? Could be that one of Marvin's closer cronies grabbed it up and carries on with it as a kind of torch in the horticultural Olympics? Rock lichens are really like an undying flame.

Xanthoria parietina, colored a rich orange-yellow, grows widely and abundantly in the British Isles and inhabits eastern North America as well. The plant fastens onto outcropping stones, especially those that are nitrogen-enriched by perching birds, onto stone walls, tree bark, and roofs of mineral material (Plate 30), whereupon it glows as warmly as, say, a compliment on one's cryptogamic gardening such as, "You've done some fascinating things with lichens and mosses." Such will come.

Now at the last, in the nature of a benison, let me say again what I have had to say before: Even if you cannot find any of these plants to work with, it matters not at all. Whatever miniature cryptogams you do find will offer garden possibilities when you think small.

CHAPTER FIFTEEN

Potential Nursery Plants

Late in life I have come on fern.
Now lichens are due to have their turn.

from "Leaves Compared with Flowers," by Robert Frost

ND NOT only with the New England ruralist, with gardeners as well.
Lately, even the lichens, lowly of lowlies among cryptogams, have
gained admirers enough to have become salable in nurseries, albeit in a
small way (but an increasing one). In their tenuous appearance in the
trade, lichens join mosses and other moss-like spore-bearers, plants that
have long been grown and sold—never in quantities large enough, nor at
sources numerous enough, to spoil their value as items of the connoisseur's quest. Nor does it seem likely that the commercial status of any of
the lesser cryptogams will ever heat up to anything like the degree of a fad
such as the late twentieth century bedazzlement with ornamental grasses.
Happily. For garden fads go before a fall that is just as pratting as the crash
of any other kind of ephemeral fashion. What we may expect instead in
the garden future of the mosses, the lichens, and the others, is a measured
arise with no falling back. There will always be about these plants sufficient obscurity to help keep them fresh. So I believe.

Sales of mosses and moss allies for garden planting go back to old China
and Japan. As mentioned in Chapter 7, Moss Carpets, mosses were grown
commercially in China before the Second World War, probably by a num-

ber of nurseries. At least one grower is remembered, a nurseryman elderly in the 1930s, who had likely been in business since the nineteenth century. Of the 75 kinds of mosses that he offered a number were used as underplanting for *p'en-tsai* (bonsai-like dwarfed trees, an art form ancient in his country as is indicated by Chinese tomb paintings of A.D. 560, depicting *p'en-tsai*, or trees very like, in pots).

One might suppose that all such fragile old artistry had perished under the layered lunacies of twentieth century wars, topped off by the Cultural Revolution. Not so, far from it, as I have learned in a conversation with Robert G. Hearst, a member of a group of bonsai enthusiasts from the continental United States, Puerto Rico, Mexico, and New Zealand, who in August 1994 visited China expressly for the purpose of studying the country's bonsai techniques and bustling bonsai production. (Contemporary Chinese call their miniaturized trees *penjing*, the older name *p'en-tsai* apparently having gone out of fashion, but the Japanese term bonsai, known the world over, seems readily applicable in that the Chinese trees are now being trained in styles indistinguishable from those of Japan.) Mr. Hearst estimates that the country has in production a million and a half bonsai, both for fanciers within the country and for export. He found that while the Cultural Revolution was indeed death on bonsai in some cities, the art survived in others. Nowadays, the government encourages a bonsai industry as a moneymaker.

The Chinese moss the soil at the base of their bonsai trees. With tree production at a million and a half and rising, the country will require for its bonsai—if my rough calculations are not far off—an amount of moss equaling in measure a good 60 baseball fields, bleacher to bleacher. That is just enough for the initial mossing, in an industry that is going to use up vast quantities of moss in future. China plans on sustained production of bonsai, with new trees being started year after year to keep up stocks. The production-line manufacture of millions of bonsai will probably require nursery production of moss on a large scale for the first time anywhere. But both collected and volunteer moss may supply part of the need. And now that I think of it, 60-plus baseball fields' worth of moss is a figure that will be way off if the Chinese will be exporting a lot of pre-bonsai, bare-root. But in any case the country is likely to become the biggest moss gardener ever.

In Japan, that other horticultural ancient, a number of mosses, several selaginellas, and even a *Lycopodium* (the cosmopolitan *L. clavatum*), continue to be grown or collected commercially, just as some of these plants have been since time forgotten, for use as ground covers, in bonsai gardening, and in container landscaping (*saikei*). Meanwhile, in North America, plants of these same groups, and lichens as well, are sold in numbers totaling a few thousands yearly as terrarium furnishing. On rare occasions in the United States and Canada, the making of a Japanese-style garden calls for *Polytrichum* moss in quantity. That, at present, is about the extent of North America's trade in mosses and others among the lesser cryptogams for garden planting. In commercial measure, it is a mom-and-pop enterprise, with all inherent fusty charm.

May the trade remain just so small and cozy. Within such a frame there is still room for the establishment of a dozen or two little nurseries specializing in these little plants. An eighth-acre (0.05-hectare) spread would be vast enough, and one to five devotees staff enough, for such a place. It is a prerequisite that these people be a bit fervent, in a quasireligious sense, about the plants in which they specialize, slightly obsessed, as specialty nursery folk always are, evangelists catering to eager acolytes. Unlike some other evangelicals, the interests of those who run specialty nurseries are seldom focused on the kitty. In this type of plant business most practitioners consider the earning of one's daily crust a pesky distraction from their true vocation: caring for, and communing with, a special group of plants. A love for plants presides, and many a commercial dud is carried lovingly along with more salable items. The real profit is in discovering that the plant cultivates the person just as much as the person cultivates the plant.

All that is a matter of nostalgia with me, a retired specialty nurseryman. Now that I have eulogized the more spiritual aspects of the profession, the rest of this is about coaxing a living from it, however pestiferous the consideration. My experience in the business has provided me, perhaps, with a certain amount of insight into the nursery future of mosses and the other lesser cryptogams. I have an inkling that the earlier decades of the twenty-first century will bring on these plants as regular nursery fare, propagated rather than collected, and supplied to a steady clientele. Even now I see a ready market, almost totally ignored, for at least a few thousand flats of carpeting mosses, and for additional thousands of pot-grown mosses and various other primitives. Such plants will prove to be, to use a hustler's phrase, nice little earners.

My predictions are based in part on my own sales records. I ran a mail-order nursery in which the specialties were ground covers and miniature plants, flowering or spore-bearing. Among the latter, my stock included saxatile ferns, equisetums, hardy selaginellas, and a single true moss, *Polytrichum piliferum*. At the time I didn't know its identity. I listed the plant in a section of my catalog headlined "Tiny Plants for Container Landscaping" and described it (accurately) as a dwarf relative of the hairy cap moss so often employed in Japanese gardens. The moss proved to be a brisk seller, as did all the primitives that I cataloged.

Had I known then even half as much as I know now about the means of growing mosses and such, and of the ways of using them in the garden, I am sure that I could have developed a market for any number of the more stalwart, more readily propagated plants for use in open-ground gardening, and could have found additional sales for some of the slower, smaller mosses and others as pot plants. In short order, too. The project would have been intellectually—and financially—nourishing. It would have been a discoverer's route. I wish I had taken it. I did not. Others will. For those entrepreneurs, I have some plant names to name.

Mosses that are generally easy to propagate by division, that will probably be easy to grow in nursery flats, and that are certainly recommendable for their relative ease and sturdy permanence as ground covers, include *Amblystegium, Calliergonella, Dicranum, Drepanocladus uncinatus* (synonym, *Samionia uncinata*), *Eurhynchium, Homalothecium, Pogonatum, Polytrichum, Pseudotaxiphyllum* (or *Isopterygium* or *Plagiothecium*), *Racomitrium canescens, Racomitrium lanuginosum, Rhytidiadelphus loreus*, and a host of others native to this or that vicinity, perhaps including your own— plants whose garden values frankly I know nothing about.

Mosses that will make attractive, salable pot plants add up to too many, by thousands, to enumerate. Most of the species in this book are worth a try, and so, I dare say, are most of those in any other book. Where I have called some moss ungrowable or barely tractable, I hope I have not hexed the plant unjustly. Let us say that you will tame the "difficult" species with an ease that I have never managed.

Out of the supernumerary thousands, I single just one moss as being representative of the magnetic attractiveness of mosses in general when neatly grown as pot plants: *Leucobryum*, particularly when it forms domed growth in the pot. A plant I had was fetching enough to have brought home one of my most treasurable experiences as a moss gardener. I had placed the dry, dormant *Leucobryum* indoors for duty as a centerpiece and conversation piece, on a coffee table in a room where we were to have a party. One after another the guests, none of whom happened to be a dedicated gardener, walked over to the plant to meet it, by touch as well as by sight. One after another, they stroked the moss dome delicately with fingertips, an act that was an education for the strokers, a tolerable trauma for the moss, and a vision of rare delight for me. My one small regret was that *Leucobryum*, when dry, is really not a very strokeable moss. Its domed growth is as hard as a week-old biscuit. But even so, the child-wonder never left the eyes of those who petted the plant. And there were, of course, questions: What's its name? Where does it grow? Answering extensively, I gave them my *Leucobryum* story in the North Carolina setting, the one I have given my reader in Chapter 14, Portraits.

I cannot recall ever having enraptured an audience so with a household spider plant (*Chlorophytum*), *Sansevieria*, or African violet (*Saintpaulia*). Certain instincts of mine, those same instincts that have turned me into one of the world's more scarred and seasoned veterans among impulse buyers of plants, tell me that what we have in *any* nicely potted moss is a see-buy commodity.

Aside from moss, other miniature cryptogams that are amenable to pot culture, and likely to be nice little earners, include selaginellas (easy-natured in containers), lycopodiums (not so easy), and certain lichens that, as pot plants, maintain a fresh, improving appearance year after year. Among such lichens are some of the shrub-form cladonias (for example, the one in Plate 72), *Letharia* (Plate 84), *Rhizocarpon* (Plate 7), some of the stereocaulons (as in Plate 9), and others, surely, whose accommodativeness remains to be discovered.

Lichens, as promised at the beginning of this chapter, have begun to be offered as nursery plants, but not in pots, not that I have seen anywhere, rather in artworks and on craft works sold in nurseries. The only true art utilizing lichens that I have seen so far is in several wreaths masterfully constructed and modestly priced at $45.00, in which several kinds of lichens on twigs had been woven into a harmony of lichen colors as sonorous, if you will allow the chiming of aural and ocular senses, as those of a grouse. I was enchanted, and gazed and gazed at those wreaths (trying to decide whether to buy, or to attempt to absorb all that they had to convey to me in one long look) until some friends with whom I was shopping pleaded with me to come on. Elsewhere, I have seen other lichened wreaths, but with added plastic holly leaves and berries, which ruined them for me and narrowed, to a single season, any appeal they might have had for other shoppers.

Craft works with lichens include wood-butcher birdhouses of rustic design. These are around by the thousands. I find them to be corny-cute, yet not altogether honest as merchandise. Or, as I prefer to suppose, they are probably not sold crookedly but ignorantly: Almost always the lichens (*Letharia, Usnea,* and others) have been glued on the wood, in which circumstance the plants can neither live nor even keep their life colors very long. As I have learned. I have tried gluing lichens of these same kinds onto wood and stone, with no success at all. Apparently the lichens take up a vital part of their sustenance through their "stem," and the ability of the plant to transfer the elements it needs is cut off when the plant is detached from the thing on which it grows.

Lichens that grow *naturally* on old farmyard lumber that is salvaged and born again as, perhaps, a garden bench, have a better chance, a very good chance, of years' more life when the bench is placed in the same degree of sun in which the plants have always grown. I have seen several such lichen-befurred benches in nurseries. I admired one of these pieces of garden furniture well enough to consider buying. But the price, $985.00 for a two-seater, dissuaded me. I think I will make my own lichened bench out of new, bare lumber, since I have no access to old, lichened boards. I will use lumber untreated with any copper compound (poisonous to lichens) and place my bench in the sun, where I will brush it frequently with a solution of acidic fertilizer. Nearby, I will station pot-grown lichens of kinds that delight in silvery dry wood. These will certainly sense the opportunity in the situation, when their time comes to disburse spores. Eight or ten years, or even more, must roll by, I would suppose, before the bare wood becomes richly lichened. However, the waiting will keep me futuristic, and young. Just maybe I will realize this daydream of mine.

Lichened wood has been combined with mosses in the works of craftspeople who sell at fairs. They make smallish, approximately 16- by 10- by 5-inch- (40- by 25- by 13-cm-) high boxes out of old lumber shaggy with the lichens *Parmelia* and *Usnea.* Within the boxes the crafters place leaf mold, or some other growth medium, and press upon it four or five different kinds of moss in a freeform tapis vert. Prices of $30.00 to $45.00 per box bring in a decent profit for a day's hawking at the fair. I am all admiration, as long as the plants in combination are of kinds that require the selfsame exposure. But I wonder if a handsomely crafted box planted with mosses really needs lichens on it in order to be salable? I think not.

Anyway, those are a few of the successful experiments by sellers of cryptogamic miniatures. If you are thinking of going into this lesser field of nursery work, here are a few random tips from an old-time seller-cum-customer: Offer a broader range of plants than the primitive miniatures alone. Small plants sell much better if they are placed on tables or racks closely in the customers' view. If you will be selling by mail, and relying on a sparsely illustrated catalog (as I did), it will pay to be something of a song-and-dance artist in words. Give the people pizzazz. And advertise. Small ads work almost as well, for a specialty nursery, as would sizable and costly ones, since customers will be looking for you with keener eyes than are ever peeled for petunias and other commonplace fare.

Further Reading

MAIN libraries in major cities offer heavyweight taxonomic treatises on such minor cryptogams as mosses, liverworts, and lichens, works addressed to the advanced student but in some cases penetrable even by the greenest of amateurs. There is a short if crude way into any taxonomic book that is especially well illustrated, that is, with drawings of whole plants of the various species, rather than of mere fragments of this or that organ. When such a reference is available, then the hopeful greenhorn has only to carry a small specimen of an unidentified plant into the library and compare it with pictures in the book until an exact match turns up, and with it a name for the nameless (a 12-power loupe, or one of at least 10 power, taken along, will be of help). Sometimes this system works, sometimes it doesn't, since certain species are so closely alike they can only be told apart by microscopic examination. A more orthodox search for a plant's name and fame is by the use of the "key" almost certainly provided by the great book one consults, a written key to plant identification, decipherable by students with at least some training in bryology or lichenology and a whole lot of patience. But pictures are vital to the beginner.

Three books have proved especially helpful to me, an eternal novice, in my long search for identification pictures of mosses and other primitive miniatures that I have found in garden use, or have planted personally, three books that are purchasable at no staggering cost. Two of these are British and European in the plant territory they cover; one is North

American. Because so many of the genera, and even the species, of miniature cryptogamic plants that are found on one continent are also found on the other, these three books support each other as sources of plant identification.

Naturally, I, a gardener located in North America and not in Europe, would rather use easy books on my subject plants that are also based in the New World. No luck though. In North America we lack a literature that Britain and some other countries possess in strength: regional guide books on the bryophytes and lichens, illustrated with color photographs or watercolors of at least a majority of the regional species; books totable enough and casual enough to take along on the wilderness trail. Until now the New World has perhaps remained culturally too new for such books. But we North Americans are rapidly coming of age and sageness in our appreciation of all the life forms, large and small, in our wilderness home (allow me a voice in both Canada and the United States, since I garden in both countries). Our increasing appreciation of wilderness, probably inspired by the plainly visible fact that we are losing it with awful precipitousness, brings us up to a time of readiness for handbooks on, for example, meeting the mosses; so does our constantly finer pursuit of gardening ready us for these least of ornamentals, which represent a kind of ultimate refinement in horticulture.

While we await the publication of more companionable books in North America, the three that I as a moss and lichen gardener recommend as being of help in identifying these plants we work with are *Collins Guide to the Ferns, Mosses and Lichens of Britain and Northern and Central Europe*; *How to Know the Mosses and Liverworts*; and *Grasses, Ferns, Mosses and Lichens of Great Britain and Ireland*. These are described below with some other recommendable books:

Collins Guide to the Ferns, Mosses and Lichens of Britain and Northern and Central Europe. By Hans Martin Johns. Originally in German, the English translation dates from 1983. Collins Books, London.

"Over 750 species described," "655 colour photographs," the book tells us on its 5- by 8½-inch (13- by 22-cm) cover. The pictures—mainly of mosses, liverworts, and lichens—are good and sharp identification photographs, six or seven to a page. They are accompanied by equally clear plant descriptions. The book includes densely scientific discussions of plant anatomy and life processes for those readers who enjoy the deep plunge.

The Forest Carpet: New Zealand's Little-Noticed Forest Plants—Mosses, Lichens, Liverworts, Hornworts, Fork-Ferns, and Lycopods. By Bill and Nancy Malcolm. 1989. Craig Potton Publishing, Nelson, New Zealand. Distributed in North America by Timber Press, Portland, Oregon.

In the 1960s Bill Malcolm pursued a career in American universities as a researcher and teacher of physiological ecology. Then in 1971 the Malcolms, their three daughters included, emigrated from the United States to take up life in New Zealand. The couple bought a farm in hill country near Nelson and for 10 years raised cattle, planted trees, and made pottery.

More recently the Malcolms have studied and photographed the mosses, lichens, liverworts, and other members of the cryptogamic weave that makes up the forest carpet in their adopted land. What they have to show, and to say, about these plants in their book is, however, less regional than universal in scope. The work deals with anatomical features and life processes shared by entire classes of the smaller spore-bearers wherever they grow. Since they grow just about everywhere, the Malcolms' book will prove to be topical to mosserians in all lands.

This volume might sound like a botanical tough nut but is decidedly not so. It is in fact botany made palatable to those of us who usually hate scientific vegetables. The text is conversational. The pictures are a visual feast. There are more than 150 close-up color photographs and photomicrographs printed grandly, mostly full page (approximately 8 by 11 inches, 20 by 28 cm) or half page. Typically, these pictures show the leafy tips of moss tufts, or edgewise parts of liverwort or lichen pads, or individual organs. Stranger than strange, many of the life forms portrayed appear to come from an unexplored planet, which in a sense they do. The cosmic metaphor extends to pictures of the pocky surfaces of certain pad-form cryptogams, considerably like moony terrains.

The Malcolms' camera work adds up to an album of fine art photography, of photographs that have more than one life. There are pictures of patterned arrangements of cells that resemble textiles, pictures of the abstract expressionist productions that crustose lichens patiently make of themselves. Several of the photographs are works of composition and lighting related to Edward Weston's black and white visualizations of bell peppers as sculpture. Other pictures show kinship to Georgia O'Keefe's scandalously intimate flower paintings. There are trips here for the voyeur as well as the voyager. Or if you prefer, you can reject all the fancying and see these pictures as plainly as O'Keefe claimed that she saw her paintings: "Nonsense! They're just pictures of flowers."

Lengthy captions or short essays, averaging several hundred words, accompany each photograph. In addition to discussions of anatomy and life functions, there are muse-worthy asides about the roles of certain miniature spore plants in the global drama of life, for example,

> The explosion and near melt-down of the Russian Chernobyl reactor in mid-1986 dumped so much strontium-90 and caesium-137 on Lapland that the *Cladina* there [a lichen popularly called reindeer moss] has become dangerously radioactive. The *Cladina* doesn't mind, though—like most lichens, it accumulates and readily tolerates staggering levels of radioactive isotopes (radionuclides). Trouble is, by eating the Cladina the reindeer then pick up the radionuclides second-hand, and by now they're carrying around such a heavy 'body-burden' that the Lapp reindeer farmers are facing financial ruin—they can't sell the reindeer meat in their traditional European markets because it's too 'hot,' . . .

I take it that what we have in this book is an explanation of physiological ecology, and a course in Professor Malcolm's specialty.

Forests of Lilliput: The Realm of the Mosses and Lichens. By John Bland. 1971. Prentice Hall, Englewood Cliffs, New Jersey.

The author devoted 20 years to the compilation of this book, scholarly time invested in gathering a remarkable collection of oddments about the practical and superstitious values of the title plants. An absorbing read for those of us who would know how human beings have related to these lowly (but powerful) plants throughout history.

There are, additionally, chapters (in the language of the laity as much as can be) on the anatomy of bryophytes and lichens, on miniature gardening with these plants, and on their identification. In all, 210 pages, 50 black and white photographs, and 13 line drawings (dotted lines) limned by Stanley Wyatt with veil-like lightness and humor as evanescent as the smile of Tenniel's Cheshire cat. You will really have to see these since words fall short.

Grasses, Ferns, Mosses and Lichens of Great Britain and Ireland. By Roger Phillips, but something of a committee project in which the section on mosses was edited by Alan Eddy; on lichens, by J. R. Laundon; on grasses and on ferns, by two other authorities. 1980. Pan Books, London.

This is a picture book in which more than 300 of the color photographs are of mosses and lichens. Some pictures have been printed full page (7 by 10 inches, 18 by 25 cm); others, three, five, or six to a page but amply large, considering that they are of tiny plants close up. Many plants were photographed in the wild and the results, at best, are worth framing and hanging on a wall. Phillips' book seems to me extraordinary for its dozens of pictures taken by the author—the work of other photographers appears as well—which capture not only the identifying features of the plant, and something of its habitat, but also that most elusive quality in plant illustration, the life force unique to the species. Here it comes forth from the page with a pow and, like Popeye, announces, "I am what I am."

How to Know the Mosses and Liverworts. By Henry S. Conard. 1956. Revised by Paul L. Redfearn, Jr. 1979. Wm. C. Brown Company, Publishers, Dubuque, Iowa.

How to know the mosses and liverworts of North America, that is, by studying them with a compound microscope in conjunction with this book. Its hundreds of line drawings are primarily of single leaves, of other isolated organs, or of clusters of cells. Plant genera, however, if not species, are usually illustrated by so-helpful drawings of the entire plant. Also of assistance is this book's listing of the natural range of each species, province by province, state by state. Conard and Redfearn's volume becomes triply useful when consulted side by side with the *Collins Guide* and Roger Phillips's book described above, both of which are lavishly illustrated.

Moss Grower's Handbook: An Illustrated Beginner's Guide to Finding, Naming and Growing over 100 Common British Species. By Michael Fletcher. 1991. Seventy Press, Berkshire, England.

Well, in terms of exploratory garden writing, he has beaten me to the North Pole. This, I believe, is the first book ever written on the subject of moss growing, in English at least. I don't know what there might be in Japanese.

As a grower of mosses and liverworts, the author is a purist. He truly grows what he grows, starting out with tiny tufts of each species rather than with the generous wads of each that I am more inclined to collect. His book is imbued with the contemporary British sense of conservation as a national religion. My American excuse for being a more profligate gatherer-grower is that his England and its mosses are far more finite than the march of mossy woods in my own country—which attitude I recognize as an antique of a kind that led to the extinction of the passenger pigeon, whose flocks are said to have darkened the sky. We are all conservationists now, of deepening conviction. Or had better be.

Anyway, Michael Fletcher plants collected bits of bryophytes in pots. Terrestrial species are, in many cases, provided with scant soil in pots mostly filled with peat. Certain of the petrophytes are pressed in between broken pieces of roof slate that have been wedged into the pot. And he has devised other exacting ways of growing other exacting species. Most of his cultures (his word) are kept in a greenhouse devoted to bryophytes.

In his book, Michael Fletcher seems totally a grower and not at all a landscaper with the plants he grows. So, there is little overlap in what he has to say, and in what I have had to offer. As a grower he knows a lot that I do not. Everything that I have not told you about the growing of mosses, in test tubes, for example, is in this book of his. I would have told you if I had known.

Index of Mosses
and Other Bryophytes

pages with illustrations in *italics*